ADOBE® INDESIGN® CS4

CLASSROOM IN A BOOK®

The official training workbook from Adobe Systems

www.adobepress.com

Adobe

Adobe InDesign CS4 Classroom in a Book

Adobe Press books are published by Peachpit, a division of Pearson Education located in Berkeley, California. For the latest on Adobe Press books, go to www.adobepress.com. To report errors, please send a note to errata@peachpit.com. For information on getting permission for reprints and excerpts, contact permissions@peachpit.com.

Writers: John Cruise and Kelly Kordes Anton
Project Editor: Susan Rimerman
Production Editor: Lisa Brazieal
Development/Copyeditor: Judy Walthers von Alten
Technical Editors: Gabriel Powell and Cathy Palmer
Proofreader: Liz Welch
Compositor: Jan Martí
Indexer: Karin Arrigoni
Media Producer: Eric Geoffroy
Cover design: Eddie Yuen
Interior design: Mimi Heft

Printed and bound in the United States of America
ISBN-13: 978-0-321-57380-3
ISBN-10: 0-321-57380-3

9 8 7 6 5 4 3 2 1

WHAT'S ON THE DISC

Here is an overview of the contents of the Classroom in a Book disc

Lesson files ... and so much more

The *Adobe InDesign CS4 Classroom in a Book* disc includes the lesson files that you'll need to complete the exercises in this book, as well as other content to help you learn more about Adobe InDesign CS4 and use it with greater efficiency and ease. The diagram below represents the contents of the disc, which should help you locate the files you need.

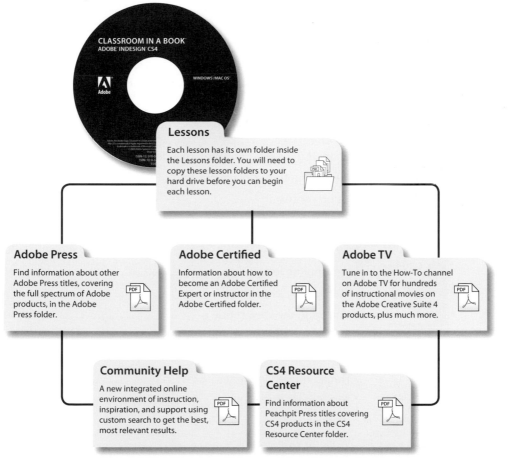

Lessons

Each lesson has its own folder inside the Lessons folder. You will need to copy these lesson folders to your hard drive before you can begin each lesson.

Adobe Press

Find information about other Adobe Press titles, covering the full spectrum of Adobe products, in the Adobe Press folder.

Adobe Certified

Information about how to become an Adobe Certified Expert or instructor in the Adobe Certified folder.

Adobe TV

Tune in to the How-To channel on Adobe TV for hundreds of instructional movies on the Adobe Creative Suite 4 products, plus much more.

Community Help

A new integrated online environment of instruction, inspiration, and support using custom search to get the best, most relevant results.

CS4 Resource Center

Find information about Peachpit Press titles covering CS4 products in the CS4 Resource Center folder.

CONTENTS

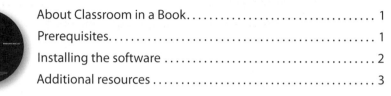

6   WORKING WITH TYPOGRAPHY

7   WORKING WITH COLOR

8 WORKING WITH STYLES

9 IMPORTING AND MODIFYING GRAPHICS

10 CREATING TABLES

11 WORKING WITH TRANSPARENCY

12 WORKING WITH LONG DOCUMENTS

13 OUTPUT AND EXPORTING

14 CREATING RICH INTERACTIVE DOCUMENTS

GETTING STARTED

Welcome to Adobe® InDesign® CS4, a powerful design and production application that offers precision, control, and seamless integration with other Adobe professional graphics software. Using InDesign, you can produce professional-quality, full-color documents on high-volume color printing presses, or print to a wide range of output devices and formats, including desktop printers and high-resolution imaging devices. You can also create dynamic documents that can be exported as Adobe Flash® files with buttons, hyperlinks, and page transitions, or as Portable Document Format (PDF) files with bookmarks, hyperlinks, buttons, movies, and sound clips, and you can convert your documents for use on the Internet by exporting layouts to XHTML or XML.

Writers, artists, designers, and publishers can communicate to a broader audience than ever before and through an unprecedented variety of media. InDesign supports this with its seamless integration with other Creative Suite 4 components.

About Classroom in a Book

Adobe InDesign CS4 Classroom in a Book® is part of the official training series for Adobe graphics and publishing software from Adobe Systems, Inc.

The lessons are designed so that you can learn at your own pace. If you're new to Adobe InDesign CS4, you'll master the fundamentals and learn to put the software to work for you. If you've already been using Adobe InDesign CS4, you'll find that Classroom in a Book teaches many advanced features, including tips and techniques for using the latest version of InDesign.

Each lesson provides step-by-step instructions for creating a specific project. You can follow the book from start to finish, or do only the lessons that meet your interests and needs. Each lesson concludes with a review section summarizing what you've covered.

Prerequisites

Before beginning to use *Adobe InDesign CS4 Classroom in a Book*, you should have a working knowledge of your computer and its operating system. Make sure that you know how to use the mouse and standard menus and commands, and also how to open, save, and close files. If you need to review these techniques, see the printed or online documentation included with your operating system.

Installing the software

Before you begin using *Adobe InDesign CS4 Classroom in a Book*, make sure that your system is set up correctly and that you've installed the proper software and hardware.

The Adobe InDesign CS4 software is not included on the Classroom in a Book CD; you must purchase the software separately. For complete instructions on installing the software, see the Adobe InDesign CS4 Read Me on the application DVD or on the web at www.adobe.com/support.

Installing the Classroom in a Book fonts

The Classroom in a Book lesson files use fonts that come with Adobe InDesign CS4. Some of the fonts can be found on the product DVD, and some will be installed with InDesign for your convenience. These fonts are installed in the following locations:

- Windows: [startup drive]\Windows\Fonts\
- Mac OS: [startup drive]/Library/Fonts/

For more information about fonts and installation, see the Adobe InDesign CS4 Read Me included with your product.

Copying the Classroom in a Book files

The *Adobe InDesign CS4 Classroom in a Book* CD includes folders containing all the electronic files for the lessons in the book. Each lesson has its own folder; you must copy the folders to your hard disk to complete the lessons. To save room on your disk, you can install only the folder necessary for each lesson as you need it, and remove it when you're done.

To install the Classroom in a Book lesson files, follow these steps:

1 Insert the *Adobe InDesign CS4 Classroom in a Book* CD into your CD-ROM drive.

2 Create a folder on your hard drive and name it **InDesignCIB**.

3 Do one of the following:
   - Copy the Lessons folder into the InDesignCIB folder.
   - Copy only the single lesson folder you need into the InDesignCIB folder.

Saving and restoring the InDesign Defaults file

The InDesign Defaults file stores program preferences and default settings, such as tool settings and the default unit of measurement. To ensure that the preferences and default settings of your Adobe InDesign CS4 program match those used in this book, you should move the current InDesign Defaults file to a different location before you begin working on the lessons. When you have finished the book, you can return the saved InDesign Defaults file to its original folder, which restores the preferences and default settings used before you started working on the lessons.

To save the current InDesign Defaults file, follow these steps:

1 Quit Adobe InDesign CS4.

2 Locate the InDesign Defaults file.

- In Windows, the InDesign Defaults file is located in the Documents and Settings\Username\Application Data\Adobe\InDesign\Version 6.0\en_US folder.

- In Mac OS, the InDesign Defaults file is located in /Users/your user name/ Library/Preferences/Adobe InDesign/Version 6.0/en_US.

3 Drag the InDesign Defaults file to another folder on your hard drive.

When you launch Adobe InDesign CS4 after moving the InDesign Defaults file to another folder, a new InDesign Defaults file is automatically created and all preferences and defaults are reset to their original factory settings.

To restore the saved InDesign Defaults file after completing the lessons, follow these steps:

1 Quit Adobe InDesign CS4.

2 Locate your saved InDesign Defaults file, drag it back into its original folder, and replace the current InDesign Defaults file.

▶ **Note:** In Windows, if the Application Data folder is hidden, choose Folder Options from the Tools menu, click the View tab, and then select Show Hidden Files and Folders. Click OK to close the Folder Options dialog box and save any changes.

Additional resources

Adobe InDesign CS4 Classroom in a Book is not meant to replace documentation that comes with the program or to be a comprehensive reference for every feature in InDesign CS4. Only the commands and options used in the lessons are explained in this book. For comprehensive information about program features, refer to any of these resources:

- Adobe InDesign CS4 Community Help, which you can view by choosing Help > InDesign Help. Community Help is an integrated online environment of instruction, inspiration, and support. It includes custom search of expert-selected, relevant content on and off Adobe.com. Community Help combines content from Adobe Help, Support, Design Center, Developer Connection, and Forums—along with great online community content so that users can easily find the best and most up-to-date resources. Access tutorials, technical support, online product help, videos, articles, tips and techniques, blogs, examples, and much more.

- Adobe InDesign CS4 Support Center, where you can find and browse support and learning content on Adobe.com. Visit www.adobe.com/support/indesign/.

- Adobe TV, where you will find programming on Adobe products, including a channel for graphic designers and a How To channel that contains hundreds of movies on InDesign CS4 and other products across the Adobe Creative Suite 4 lineup. Visit http://tv.adobe.com/.

Also check out these useful links:

- The InDesign CS4 product home page at www.adobe.com/products/indesign/.

- InDesign user forums at www.adobe.com/support/forums/ for peer-to-peer discussions of Adobe products.

- InDesign Exchange at www.adobe.com/cfusion/exchange/ for extensions, functions, code, and more.

- InDesign plug-ins at www.adobe.com/products/plugins/indesign/.

Adobe certification

The Adobe Certified program is designed to help Adobe customers and trainers improve and promote their product-proficiency skills. There are four levels of certification:

- Adobe Certified Associate (ACA)

- Adobe Certified Expert (ACE)

- Adobe Certified Instructor (ACI)

- Adobe Authorized Training Center (AATC)

The Adobe Certified Associate (ACA) credential certifies that individuals have the entry-level skills to plan, design, build, and maintain effective communications using different forms of digital media.

The Adobe Certified Expert program is a way for expert users to upgrade their credentials. You can use Adobe certification as a catalyst for getting a raise, finding a job, or promoting your expertise.

If you are an ACE-level instructor, the Adobe Certified Instructor program takes your skills to the next level and gives you access to a wide range of Adobe resources.

Adobe Authorized Training Centers offer instructor-led courses and training on Adobe products, employing only Adobe Certified Instructors. A directory of AATCs is available at http://partners.adobe.com.

For information on the Adobe Certified program, visit www.adobe.com/support/certification/main.html.

Checking for updates

Adobe periodically provides updates to software. You can easily obtain these updates through Adobe Updater, as long as you have an active Internet connection.

1 In InDesign, choose Help > Updates. The Adobe Updater automatically checks for updates available for your Adobe software.

2 In the Adobe Updater dialog box, select the updates you want to install, and then click Download And Install Updates to install them.

Note: To set your preferences for future updates, click Preferences. Select how often you want Adobe Updater to check for updates, for which applications, and whether to download them automatically. Click OK to accept the new settings.

1 INTRODUCING THE WORKSPACE

In this lesson, you'll learn how to do the following:

- Work with tools.
- Use the Application bar and Control panel.
- Manage document windows.
- Work with panels.
- Save your own customized workspace.
- Change the magnification of the document.
- Navigate through a document.
- Use context menus.

 This lesson will take approximately 45 minutes.

The intuitive InDesign CS4 interface makes it easy to create compelling print and interactive pages like this. It is important to understand the InDesign work area to make the most of its powerful layout and design capabilities. The work area consists of the Application bar, Control panel, document window, the menus, pasteboard, Tools panel, and other panels.

Getting started

In this lesson, you'll practice using the work area and navigating through a few pages of *Check Magazine,* a print and online publication. This is the final version of the document—you won't be changing or adding text or graphics, only using it to explore the InDesign CS4 work area.

● **Note:** If you have not already copied the resource files for this lesson onto your hard disk from the Adobe InDesign CS4 Classroom in a Book CD, do so now. See "Copying the Classroom in a Book files" on page 2.

1   To ensure that the preferences and default settings of your Adobe InDesign CS4 program match those used in this lesson, move the InDesign Defaults file to a different folder following the procedure in "Saving and restoring the InDesign Defaults file" on page 2.

2   Start Adobe InDesign CS4. To ensure that the panels and menu commands match those used in this lesson, choose Window > Workspace > [Advanced], and then choose Window > Workspace > Reset Advanced.

3   Choose File > Open, and open the 01_Start.indd file in the Lesson_01 folder, located inside the Lessons folder within the InDesignCIB folder on your hard disk. Scroll down to see page 2 of the document.

4   Choose File > Save As, rename the file **01_Magazine.indd**, and save it in the Lesson_01 folder.

Looking at the workspace

▶ **Tip:** If you are familiar with InDesign CS3, you can see what is new to CS4 by choosing Window > Workspace > What's New. Click each menu to see new commands highlighted. To return to a standard workspace, choose an option from Window > Workspace.

The InDesign work area encompasses everything you see when you first open or create a document:

*   Application bar (new to InDesign CS4)

*   Tools panel

*   Control panel, other panels, and menus

*   Document window

*   Pasteboard and pages

You can customize and save the work area to suit your work style. For example, you can choose to display only the panels you frequently use, minimize and rearrange panel groups, resize windows, add more document windows, and so on.

The configuration of the work area is referred to as the workspace. You can choose among default, special-purpose configurations (Typography, Printing and Proofing, and so on) and save your own workspaces.

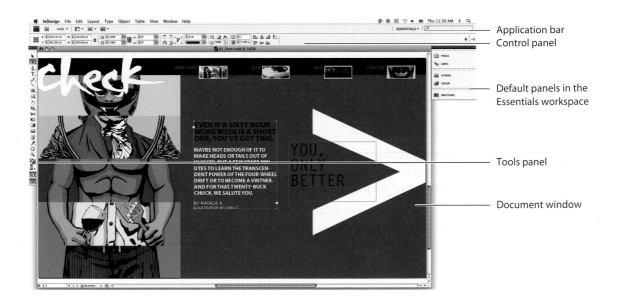

Application bar
Control panel

Default panels in the Essentials workspace

Tools panel

Document window

About the Tools panel

The Tools panel contains tools for selecting objects, working with type, and drawing as well as controls for applying and changing color fills, strokes, and gradients. By default, the Tools panel is docked (essentially, glued) to the upper-left corner of the work area. In this exercise, you will undock the Tools panel, change it to horizontal, and experiment with selecting tools.

1   Locate the Tools panel. Scroll to the left to see the Tools panel against the pasteboard rather than the document.

2   To undock the Tools panel and make it float it in the workspace, drag the panel by its gray title bar to pull it into the pasteboard.

> **Tip:** To undock the Tools panel, you can drag either the title bar or the gray dotted bar just below the title bar.

When the Tools panel is floating, it can be a two-column vertical panel, a single-column vertical panel, or a single-column horizontal row.

3   With the Tools panel floating, click the double arrow (▶▶) at the top of the Tools panel. The Tools panel becomes one horizontal row.

As you work through the lessons in this book, you'll learn about each tool's specific function. Here you'll familiarize yourself with the Tools panel and some of the tools.

▶ **Tip:** You can select a tool by either clicking the tool in the Tools panel or by pressing the tool's keyboard shortcut. Because the default keyboard shortcuts work only when you do not have a text insertion point, you can also add other key commands to select tools, even when you are editing text. To do this, use the Edit > Keyboard Shortcuts command. For more information, search for Keyboard Shortcuts in InDesign Help.

4 Position the pointer over the Selection tool (▸) in the Tools panel. Notice that the tool's name and shortcut are displayed in a tool tip.

5 Click the Direct Selection tool (▸) and hold down the mouse button to display a pop-up menu of tools. Select the Position tool (⊕) and notice how it replaces the Direct Selection tool.

Some tools in the Tools panel display a small black triangle in the lower-right corner to indicate the tool has additional related, but hidden tools. To select a hidden tool, click and hold down the mouse button to display the menu; then select the tool that you want.

6 Click the Position tool again, hold down the mouse button to display the menu, and choose the Direct Selection tool. This is the default tool that displays.

7 Point at each tool in the Tools panel to see its name and shortcut. For tools with a small black triangle, click the tool and hold down the mouse button to see its pop-up menu of additional tools.

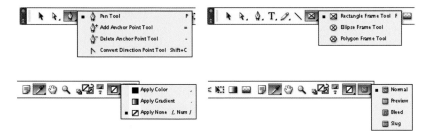

8 Click the double-arrow (⇥) in the Tools panel to turn it into a two-column vertical panel. Click the double-arrow again to return to the default Tools panel.

9 To dock the Tools panel again, drag the gray dotted line at the top of the Tools panel to the far left of the screen. Release the Tools panel to fit it neatly into the side of the workspace.

10 Choose View > Fit Page In Window to reposition the page in the center of the document window, if it isn't already centered.

Reviewing the Application bar

Across the top of the default work area is the Application bar, which lets you launch Adobe Bridge CS4; change the magnification of the document; show and hide layout aids such as rulers and guides; change the screen mode among options such as Normal and Preview mode; and control how document windows display. At the far right, you can select a workspace and search Adobe help resources.

- To get familiar with the controls in the Application bar, point at each to display its tool tip.

- To show and hide the Application bar in Mac OS, choose Window > Application Bar. You cannot hide the Application bar in Windows.

▶ **Tip:** When you hide the Application bar, the view scale controls display in the lower-left corner of the document window.

Reviewing the Control panel

The Control panel (Window > Control) offers quick access to options and commands related to the current page item or objects you select. By default, the Control panel is docked just below the Application bar; however, you can dock it below the document window, convert it to a floating panel, or hide it altogether.

1 Scroll to center the first page in the document window.

2 With the Selection tool (✹), click the text "Fashion + Lifestyle" on page one. Notice the information in the Control panel. It reflects the position, size, and other attributes of the selected object.

3 In the Control panel, click the X and Y arrows to see how to reposition a selected frame.

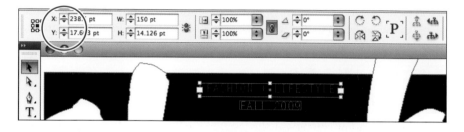

4 Using the Type tool (T), select the text "Fall 2009." Notice that the information in the Control panel has changed. The options and commands that now appear allow you to control text formatting.

5 In the upper-left corner of the Control panel, click the "A" button to display character formatting controls. Choose a different option from the Type Style menu to reformat the selected text.

The Control panel can also be moved if you don't like it docked at the top of the document window.

6 On the Control panel, drag the vertical bar at the left into the document window. Release the mouse button to make the panel float.

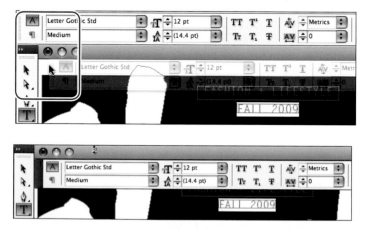

The Control panel can be docked either at the top of the workspace or at the bottom.

7 To dock the Control panel again, drag the vertical bar on the left side back to the top of the window, just beneath the Application bar. A blue line appears, indicating where the panel is going to be docked when you release the mouse button.

Reviewing the document window

The document window contains all the pages in the document. Each page or spread is surrounded by its own pasteboard, which can store objects for the document as you create a layout. Objects on the pasteboard do not print. The pasteboard also provides additional space along the edges of the document for extending objects past the page edge, which is called a bleed. Bleeds are used when an object must print to the edge of a page. Controls for switching pages in the document are in the lower left of the document window.

1 To see the full size of the pasteboard for the pages in this document, choose View > Entire Pasteboard.

2 If necessary, click the Maximize button to enlarge the document window.

- In Windows, the Maximize button is the middle box in the upper-right corner of the window.

- In Mac OS, the Maximize button is the green button in the upper-left corner of the window.

● **Note:** On Mac OS, the Application bar, document windows, and panels can be grouped into a single unit called the Application frame. This mimics working in a Windows application. To activate the Application frame, choose Window > Application Frame.

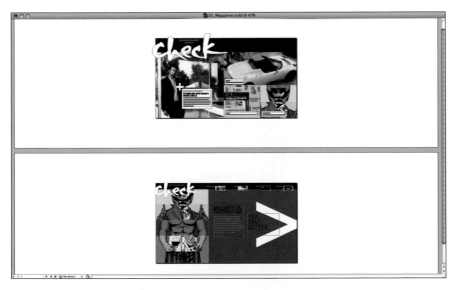

3 Choose View > Fit Page In Window to restore the view.

Now you'll move to another page.

▶ **Tip:** Use the pasteboard as an extension of the work area. You can import multiple placed images or text files and keep them on the pasteboard until you are ready to use them.

4 In the lower left of the document window, click the arrow next to the Page Number box.

5 From the menu of document and master pages that appears, choose 2.

6 Click the arrow to the left of the Page Number Box to switch back to page 1.

Working with multiple document windows

You can have more than one document window open at a time. Here, you'll create a second window so that as you work, you can see two different views of the same document simultaneously.

1 Choose Window > Arrange > New Window.

A new window titled 01_Magazine.indd:2 opens. The original window is now titled 01_Magazine.indd.

▶ **Tip:** The Application bar provides quick access to options for managing windows. Click the Arrange Documents button to see all the options.

2 In Mac OS, choose Window > Arrange > Tile to display the windows side by side.

3 Select the Zoom tool (🔍) in the Tools panel.

4 In the window at the left, draw a marquee around the white box containing the headline "Operative Words" to zoom in on the artwork.

Notice that the window at the right stays at the same magnification. This configuration lets you see how any changes you make in the white box affect the rest of the layout.

5 Choose Window > Arrange > Consolidate All Windows. This creates a tab for each window.

6 Click the tabs in the upper-left corner (below the Control panel) to control which document window displays.

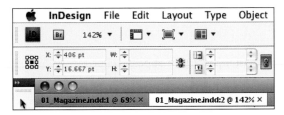

7 Close the 01_Magazine.indd:2 window by clicking the Close Window button (the X) on the tab. The original document window remains open.

8 In Mac OS, resize and reposition the remaining window by clicking the Maximize button at the top of the document window.

Working with panels

Panels provide quick access to commonly used tools and features. By default, panels are docked at the right side of the screen (except the aforementioned Tools panel and Control panel). The default panels differ depending on the selected workspace, and each workspace remembers its panel configuration. You can reorganize panels in various ways. Here you'll experiment with hiding, closing, and opening the default panels in the Advanced workspace.

Expanding and collapsing panels

In this exercise, you will expand and collapse a panel, hide the panel names, and expand all the panels in the dock.

1 In the default dock to the right of the document window, click the Pages panel icon to expand the Pages panel.

● **Note:** A dock is a collection of panels that are "glued" together.

This technique is handy if you want to open a panel, use it briefly, and then close it.

You can choose from several techniques to collapse a panel.

2 When you've finished using the Pages panel, click the double arrows to the right of the panel names or click the Pages panel icon again to collapse the panel.

Tip: To find a hidden panel, choose the panel name from the Window menu. If the panel name has a check mark, it is already open and in front of any other panels in its panel group. If you choose a checked panel name from the Window menu, the panel closes.

Now you'll open a panel that isn't showing in this workspace, by choosing it from the menu bar.

3 Choose Window > Info to open the Info panel.

4 To add the Info panel to the dock, drag it by its title bar below the Character Styles panel; release the mouse button when the blue line appears.

You can drag the Info panel icon up or down within the dock to reposition it. Next, you'll hide the panel names to display only icons. Then, you will expand all the panels in the dock.

5 Drag the left edge of the panel dock to the right until the names are hidden.

Click the Expand Panels button to collapse and expand the panels.

Drag the left edge of the panel dock to collapse the panels into icons.

6 To expand all the panels in the dock, click the double arrow in the upper-right corner of the dock.

If you click the double arrow again, the panels collapse back to icons without names.

Rearranging and customizing panels

In this exercise, you will drag a single panel out of the dock to create a free-floating panel. Then, you will drag another panel into that panel to create a custom panel group. You will also ungroup the panels, stack them, and collapse them to icons.

1 With the dock expanded, drag the tab of the Paragraph Styles panel, to remove the panel from the dock.

● **Note:** To see the panels better, scroll to the right to display the pasteboard behind the panels rather than the document page.

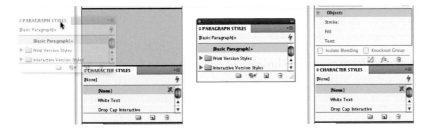

A detached panel is called a floating panel.

2 To add the Character Styles panel to the floating Paragraph Styles panel, drag its tab into the blank area of the Paragraph Styles panel title bar. Release the mouse button when the blue line appears along the perimeter of the Paragraph Styles panel.

This action creates a panel group; you can drag any panel into a group. Grouping the Character Styles and Paragraph Styles panels can be helpful if you are editing text and don't need the other panels to be expanded.

3 To ungroup the panels, drag one of the panel tabs out of the panel group.

You can also stack floating panels in a vertical arrangement. You'll try that now.

4 Drag the tab of the Paragraph Styles panel to the bottom of the Character Styles panel. Release the panel when a blue line appears.

The panels are now stacked rather than grouped. Stacked panels attach vertically to each other. You can move the panels as a unit by dragging the topmost title bar.

Next, you'll experiment with resizing the stacked panels.

5 Drag the lower-right corner of each panel to resize them. Click either the double arrow in the upper-right corner or just the title bar across the top, to collapse the stacked panels to icons.

6 Click either the double arrow or the title bar again to expand the panels.

7 Regroup the panels by dragging the tab of the Paragraph Styles panel up next to the Character Styles panel tab. Minimize the panel group by clicking the gray area next to a panel's tab. Click the area again to expand the panels.

8 Leave the panels this way for a later exercise.

Using panel menus

Most panels have additional panel-specific options. To access these options, you click the panel menu button to display a menu with additional commands and options for the selected panel.

In this exercise, you will change the display of the Swatches panel.

1 Drag the Swatches panel out of the dock at the right to create a free-floating panel.

2 In the upper right of the Swatches panel, click the panel menu button (⬛) to display the panel menu.

You can use the Swatches panel menu to create new color swatches, load swatches from another document, and more.

3 Choose Large Swatch from the Swatches panel menu.

4 Leave the Swatches panel as is for the next exercise.

Customizing the workspace

A workspace is a configuration of panels and menus. InDesign features a variety of default workspaces for special purposes, such as Books, Printing and Proofing, and Typography. You cannot modify the default workspaces, but you can save your own. In this exercise, you will save the customizations performed in the previous exercises.

1 Choose Window > Workspace > New Workspace.

2 In the New Workspace dialog box, type **Swatches and Styles** in the Name box. If necessary, select Panel Locations and Menu Customization. Click OK.

▶ **Tip:** You can control which commands appear in the InDesign menus by choosing Edit > Menus. You can save the menu customization with your custom workspace.

3 Choose Window > Workspace to see that your custom workspace is selected. Choose each of the other workspaces to see the different default configurations. Click the menus in addition to looking at the panels; workspace-specific features are highlighted.

4 Choose Window > Workspace > [Advanced] to return to the Advanced workspace.

● **Note:** If you want to delete the custom workspace, choose Window > Workspace > Delete Workspace. Select Swatches and Styles from the Name menu and click Delete.

5 Choose Window > Workspace > Reset Advanced to return to the default configuration.

Changing the magnification of a document

Controls in InDesign let you view documents at any level between 5% and 4000%. When a document is open, the current magnification percentage is displayed in the Zoom Level box in the Application bar (above the Control panel) and next to the filename in the document's tab or title bar. If you close the Application bar, the zoom controls appear in the lower-left corner of the document window.

Using the view commands and magnification menu

You can easily enlarge or reduce the view of a document by doing any of the following:

• Choose a percentage from the Zoom Level menu in the Application bar to enlarge or reduce the display by any preset increment.

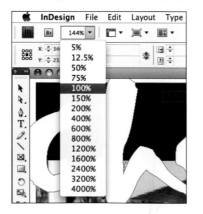

- Type a percentage in the Zoom Level box by placing an insertion point in the box, typing the desired viewing percent, and then pressing the Return or Enter key.

- Choose View > Zoom In to enlarge the display by one preset increment.

- Choose View > Zoom Out to reduce the display by one preset increment.

- Choose View > Fit Page In Window to display the targeted page in the window.

- Choose View > Fit Spread In Window to display the targeted spread in the window.

- Choose View > Actual Size to display the document at 100%. (Depending on the dimensions of your document and your screen resolution, you may or may not see the entire document onscreen.)

Using the Zoom tool

In addition to the view commands, you can use the Zoom tool to magnify and reduce the view of a document. In this exercise, you will experiment with the Zoom tool.

1 Scroll to page 1. If necessary, choose View > Fit Page In Window to position the page in the center of the window.

2 Select the Zoom tool (🔍) in the Tools panel and position it over the yellow car at right. Notice that a plus sign appears in the center of the Zoom tool.

3 Click once. The view changes to the next preset magnification, centered on the point where you clicked. Now you'll reduce the view.

4 Position the Zoom tool over the car and hold down the Alt (Windows) or Option (Mac OS) key. A minus sign appears in the center of the Zoom tool.

5 With the Alt or Option key still depressed, click once over the car; the view is reduced.

You can also use the Zoom tool to drag a marquee around a portion of a document to magnify a specific area.

6 With the Zoom tool still selected, hold down the mouse button and drag a marquee around the car, and then release the mouse button.

The percentage by which the area is magnified depends on the size of the marquee: the smaller the marquee, the larger the degree of magnification.

Tip: You can also change the magnification using key commands. Use Ctrl+= (Windows) or Command+= (Mac OS) to increase the magnification, and Ctrl+- (Windows) or Command+- (Mac OS) to decrease the magnification.

7 In the Tools panel, double-click the Zoom tool to switch to a 100% view.

Because the Zoom tool is used frequently during the editing process to enlarge and reduce the view of your document, you can temporarily select it from the keyboard at any time without deselecting any other tool you may be using. You'll do that now.

8 Click the Selection tool (↖) in the Tools panel and position it in the document window.

9 Hold down Ctrl+spacebar (Windows) or Command+spacebar (Mac OS) so that the Selection tool icon becomes the Zoom tool icon, and then click the car to magnify the view. When you release the keys, the pointer returns to the Selection tool.

Note: Mac OS X may override this keyboard shortcut and open the Spotlight window. You can disable system shortcuts in your Mac's System Preferences.

10 Hold down Ctrl+Alt+spacebar (Windows) or Command+Option+spacebar (Mac OS) and click to zoom out.

11 Choose View > Fit Page In Window to center the page.

Navigating through a document

There are several different ways to navigate through an InDesign document, including using the Pages panel, the Hand tool, the Go To Page dialog box, and controls in the document window.

Turning pages

You can turn pages using the Pages panel, the page buttons at the bottom of the document window, the scroll bars, or a variety of other commands. The Pages panel provides page icons for all of the pages in your document. Double-clicking any page icon or page number in the panel brings that page or spread into view. In this exercise, you will experiment with turning pages.

Tip: To turn pages, you can also use commands in the Layout menu: First Page, Previous Page, Next Page, Last Page, Next Spread, and Previous Spread.

1 Click the Pages panel icon to expand the Pages panel.

2 Double-click the page 2 icon to center the second page in the document window.

3 Double-click the B-Master icon above the page icons to display it in the document window. Click the Pages panel icon to collapse the Pages panel.

4 To return to the first page of the document, use the menu in the lower left of the document window. Click the down arrow and choose 1.

Now you'll use the page buttons at the bottom of the document window to change pages.

5 Click the Next Page button (the right-facing arrow) next to the Page Number box to switch to the second page.

▶ **Tip:** In addition to the Next Page and Previous Page buttons next to the Page Number box, you can use Last Page and First Page buttons.

6 Click the Previous Page button (left-facing arrow) next to the Page Number Box to switch back to the first page.

7 Choose Layout > Go to Page.

8 In the Page box, type **2.** Click OK.

▶ **Tip:** You will use Go To Page command enough that it is worth remembering the keyboard command: Ctrl+J (Windows) or Command+J (Mac OS).

Go to Page

Page: ⬍2   OK

Cancel

9 Using the vertical scroll bar, go back to page 1.

Using the Hand tool

The Hand tool in the Tools panel lets you "push" the pages of a document around until you find exactly what you want to view. In this exercise, you will experiment with the Hand tool.

▶ **Tip:** When you're using the Selection tool, you can press the spacebar to temporarily access the Hand tool. When you're using the Type tool, press the Alt (Windows) or Option (Mac) key to use the Hand tool.

1   With page 1 centered in the document window, select the Hand tool (✋).

2   Click and drag in any direction to move the page around, and then drag upward in the document window to navigate down to page 2.

3   Click the Hand tool. Click the page, then hold the mouse button down to display a view rectangle. Drag the rectangle to view a different area of the page or a different page. Release the mouse button to display the page.

4   In the Tools panel, double-click the Hand tool to fit the spread in the window.

Using context menus

In addition to the menus at the top of your screen, you can use context menus to display commands relevant to the active tool or selection.

▶ **Tip:** You can display a context menu when the Type tool is selected and in text. The Type context menu lets you insert special characters, check spelling, and perform other text-related tasks.

1   Using the Selection tool (▸), click any object on the page (such as the frame containing the name of the magazine, "Check").

2   Right-click (Windows) or Control-click (Mac OS) the text frame. Note what options are available.

To display context menus, you position the pointer over a selected object or anywhere in the document window, and click with the right mouse button (Windows) or press Control and hold down the mouse button (Mac OS).

3 Select different types of objects on the page and display the context menus for them to see what commands are available.

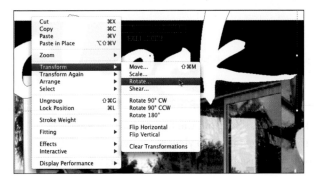

Exploring on your own

Now that you have explored the work area, try some of the following tasks using either the 01_Magazine.indd document or your own document.

1 Choose Window > Info to display the Info panel. Notice the information provided about the document when no objects are selected. Click to select individual objects and see how the Info panel changes as you select them.

2 Learn more about existing key commands and how you can change them by exploring the Keyboard Shortcuts dialog box (Edit > Keyboard Shortcuts).

3 Review the menu configurations and how you can edit them in the Menu Customization dialog box (Edit > Menus).

4 Try organizing your panels to meet your needs, and create your own workspace by choosing Window > Workspace > New Workspace.

Finding resources for using InDesign

For complete and up-to-date information about using InDesign panels, tools, and other application features, visit the Adobe Web site. Choose Help > InDesign Help. You'll be connected to the Adobe Community Help Web site, where you can search InDesign Help and support documents, as well as other Web sites relevant to InDesign users. You can narrow your search results to view only Adobe help and support documents, as well.

If you plan to work in InDesign when you're not connected to the Internet, download the most current PDF version of InDesign Help from www.adobe.com/go/documentation.

For additional resources, such as tips and techniques and the latest product information, check out the Adobe Community Help page at community.adobe.com/help/main.

● **Note:** If InDesign detects that you are not connected to the Internet when you start the application, choosing Help > InDesign Help opens the Help HTML pages installed with InDesign. For more up-to-date information, view the Help files online or download the current PDF for reference.

Review questions

1 Describe two ways to change the magnification of a document.

2 How do you select tools in InDesign?

3 Describe three ways to display a panel.

4 Describe how to create a panel group.

Review answers

1 You can choose commands from the View menu to zoom in or out of a document, or fit it to your screen. You can also use the Zoom tool in the Tools panel, and click or drag over a document to enlarge or reduce the view. In addition, you can use keyboard shortcuts to magnify or reduce the display. You can also use the Zoom Level box on the Application bar or document window.

2 To select a tool, you can either select the tool in the Tools panel or you can press the tool's keyboard shortcut. For example, you can press V to select the Selection tool from the keyboard. You select hidden tools by positioning the pointer over a tool in the Tools panel and holding down the mouse button. When the hidden tools appear, select the tool.

3 To make a panel appear, you can click its panel icon or the panel tab, or choose its name from the Window menu, for example, Window > Object & Layout > Align. You can also access type-specific panels from the Type menu.

4 Drag a panel's icon off the dock to create a free-floating panel. Drag the tab of any other panel into the title bar of the new, free-floating panel. A panel group can be moved and resized as one panel.

2 GETTING TO KNOW INDESIGN

Lesson Overview

In this quick tour, you'll get an overview of the key features of InDesign CS4 including:

- Using Adobe Bridge to access files
- Checking on potential production issues with the Preflight panel
- Viewing and navigating your document
- Creating, placing, and styling text
- Placing and manipulating graphics
- Targeting layers

 This lesson will take approximately 60 minutes.

Hecho en Mexico

Exploring Mexican Folk Art

One of the most exciting things about vacationing in Oaxaca is the large artist community that lives and works there. My wife Judith and I traveled there last May and came home with many more pieces for our collection than we had ever imagined. Judith is a collector by nature. Every square inch of our tiny Manhattan apartment is filled with a treasure from one of our trips. I wanted to experience more than just the exchange of money with a merchant—I wanted to meet the artists. Having grown up in a family of sculptors (my father took commissions for his work from around the world), I wanted to see how these people crafted their pieces, how they lived, and what their art meant to them. Judith was more interested in buying art, but she finally agreed to go with me to meet a folk artist I heard about named Henry Luis Ramos.

As Judith and I stepped into the adobe shop, a cheerful black-haired boy greeted us. "My father's expecting you," he said as he led us down a hall into a spacious room filled with hundreds of statues, clay pots, and tin artifacts that Ramos designed.

The brilliantly colored pieces captivated me. I couldn't stop investigating and touching them. I could see the influence of the Mayan culture and other native tribes. "My father did these," the boy said with a wide grin. In the center of the room, at a heavy

This interactive demonstration of Adobe InDesign CS4 provides an overview of key features.

Getting started

You'll start the tour by opening a partially completed document. You'll add the finishing touches to this six-page article on Mexican folk art, written for an imaginary travel magazine. In the process, you'll organize your work and try different techniques for creating a layout and adjusting its design.

● **Note:** If you have not already copied the resource files for this lesson onto your hard disk from the Adobe InDesign CS4 Classroom in a Book CD, do so now. See "Copying the Classroom in a Book files" on page 2.

1 To ensure that the preferences and default settings of your Adobe InDesign CS4 program match those used in this lesson, move the InDesign Defaults file to a different folder following the procedure in "Saving and restoring the InDesign Defaults file" on page 2.

2 When the Welcome Screen appears, close it.

3 Start Adobe InDesign CS4. To ensure that the panels and menu commands match those used in this lesson, choose Window > Workspace > [Advanced], and then choose Window > Workspace > Reset Advanced.

4 Click the Go To Bridge button (Br) in the Control panel. By default, the Control panel is docked to the top of the document window.

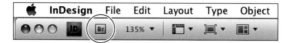

5 In the Folders panel in Adobe Bridge, locate and click the Lesson_02 folder, located inside the Lessons folder within the InDesignCIB folder on your hard drive.

6 In the Content panel, in the middle of the Adobe Bridge window, click the 02_End.indd file. The Metadata panel, on the right side of the Adobe Bridge window, displays information about the 02End.indd file.

By scrolling through the Metadata panel, you can view information about the document, including colors, fonts, version of InDesign used to create it, and more. You can scale the preview thumbnails in the Content panel by using the Thumbnail slider at the bottom of the Adobe Bridge window.

7 Double-click the 02_End.indd file in Adobe Bridge to open it. This is what the document will look like when you complete this lesson.

8 Scroll through the document to see all the pages. You can leave this file open to act as a guide or choose File > Close to close it.

Viewing the lesson document

Before you start working on the magazine layout, you'll look at the document you're about to format.

1 Adobe Bridge remains open until you exit it. Return to Adobe Bridge and double-click the 02_Start.indd file.

2 Choose File > Save As. Type the new name, **02_Tour.indd**, in the Save As dialog box. Leave the file type as an InDesign CS4 document, and click Save.

3 Click the Pages icon (⬚) in the dock at right to view the Pages panel.

4 Drag the Pages panel tab to the left, out of the panel group. You can now reposition the Pages panel as necessary.

▶ **Tip:** Feel free to move and rearrange panels in this lesson as needed. For information on managing panels, see Lesson 1, "Introducing the Work Area."

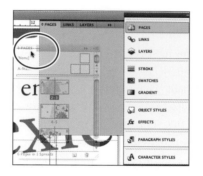

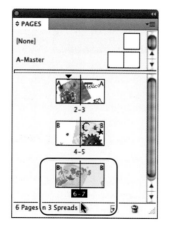

▶ Tip: To start a document on a left-facing page, select the first page in the Pages panel, and then choose Numbering & Section options from the panel menu. Enter **2** (or another even number) in the Start Page Numbering At box and click OK.

As you can see, the lesson document starts on a left-facing page—page 2. This is a common setup for a magazine article or other type of document. By default facing-page documents always start on a right-facing page.

5   In the Pages panel, double-click the numbers 6-7 below the page icons to view the last spread in the document. You may need to scroll to see these.

6   View each page in the document, by trying the following methods:

-    Double-click the numbers below the page icons to display the full spread in the document window.

-    Double-click an individual page icon to display only that page in the document window.

-    To center the spread in the window, double-click the Hand tool (✋) in the Tools panel.

Now that you've seen all three spreads, let's go back to page 3 and start working.

7   In the Pages panel, double-click the page 3 icon to view page 3.

Preflighting as you work

New to InDesign CS4, Live Preflight lets you monitor documents as you create them to prevent potential printing problems from occurring. In publishing, preflighting is the process of ensuring that a document is created properly for its intended output. For example, preflighting can ensure that a document has all the font and graphic files it needs and that no RGB graphics are used in a CMYK workflow. In the past, preflighting was considered a post-production process.

You can create or import production rules (called profiles) against which to check your documents.

1 Choose Window > Output > Preflight to open the Preflight panel. You can also click the Preflight button in the lower-left corner of the document window.

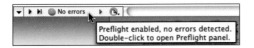

Using the [Basic] or default preflight profile, InDesign finds no errors, as indicated by the green Preflight icon in the lower-left corner of the Preflight panel.

2 Select B&W Job (embedded) from the Profile menu.

3 In the Error column, click the arrow next to COLOR. Then, click the arrow next to Cyan, Magenta, or Yellow Plate.

Since the profile specifies black-and-white output, 33 errors related to color plates are reported.

> **Tip:** If InDesign detects any preflighting issues as you work—for example, if text is overset or you import an RGB graphic—the error is reported in the lower-left corner of the document window. To continually check your work, you can leave the Preflight panel open.

4 Select [Basic] from the Profile menu again.

5 Click the Preflight panel's close button.

6 Choose File > Save to save your work so far.

Changing the View mode

Now you'll see what happens when you change the View mode of the document window using the Mode buttons at the bottom of the Tools panel.

1 Click and hold down the Mode button (▣) at the bottom of the Tools panel and choose Preview. Preview mode displays artwork in a standard window, hiding nonprinting elements such as guides, grids, and frame edges.

2 Now choose Bleed (▣) from the Mode menu to preview the document with its predefined bleed area that extends beyond the page boundaries.

3 Select Slug (▣) from the Mode menu to preview the document with the predefined slug area.

The slug area is an area outside of the page and the bleed area that can contain information, such as printer instructions or job sign-off information.

4 Finally, select Normal (▣) from the Mode menu to return to Normal view.

Viewing guides

In this document, the guides are hidden. You'll turn on the guides to see your layout grid and make it easy to snap objects into place. The guides do not print and do not limit the print area. Guides are for your reference only and can be helpful when aligning objects and text on a page.

1 If necessary, in the Pages panel, double-click the page 3 icon to view page 3.

2 Choose View > Grids & Guides > Show Guides.

Adding text

With InDesign CS4, text is always contained by a frame or flows along a path. You can either add text to a frame that has already been created, or you can create the frame while you import text.

You're ready to start working on the magazine layout and its copy. First, you'll add a secondary headline to page 3. To add text, you can use InDesign CS4 or import text created in separate word-processing programs.

1 Select the Type tool (T). Align the pointer with the vertical guide that runs through the "x" in "Mexico" and the horizontal guide under the word.

2 Drag to create a text frame for a headline as shown.

When creating a frame with the Type tool, InDesign CS4 places the insertion point in the frame. If the text frame is not aligned exactly to the guides, use the Selection tool (▶) to click the corners of the box and enlarge or reduce them as necessary. Then, select the Type tool and click inside the text frame.

3 Type **Exploring Mexican Folk Art** in the text frame.

4 With an insertion point still in the text, choose Edit > Select All.

5 In the Control panel, click the Character Formatting Controls icon (**A**) and do the following:

- From the Font Family menu, select Adobe Garamond Pro. (Adobe Garamond Pro is alphabetized on the list under *G*, not *A*.)

- Select Semibold from the Font Family submenu or from the Type Style menu below the Font Family menu.

- Select 18 pt from the Font Size menu to the right of the Font Family menu.

▶ **Tip:** You can select individual words and characters using the Type tool to format text, as you would with traditional word-processing software.

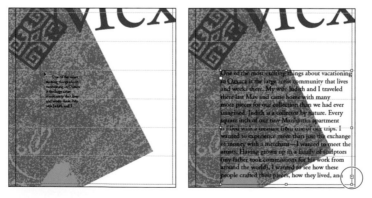

6 Choose File > Save to save your work.

Threading text in frames

Now that you've formatted the text, you'll add a travel article to the document. Because it's long, not all of the article will fit on the page. You'll thread the text so that it flows correctly throughout the document.

Placing and flowing text

You'll start by selecting an article describing the trip of travelers Judith and Clyde to Oaxaca that was saved as a Microsoft Word file. You'll place this file on page 3 and then thread the text throughout your document.

1 Make sure that no objects are selected by choosing Edit > Deselect All, and then choose File > Place. In the Place dialog box, make sure that Show Import Options is deselected.

2 Navigate to the Lesson_02 folder in the Lessons folder, and double-click the 02_Article.doc file.

The pointer changes to a loaded text icon (📄). With a loaded text icon, you have several choices. You can drag to create a new text frame, click inside an existing frame, or click to create a new text frame within a column. You'll add this text to a column in the lower half of page 3.

● **Note:** If the text frame is not placed properly in the left column, use the Selection tool to drag the frame handles to move the frame to the proper location.

3 Position the loaded text icon just below the fourth guide from the bottom margin and just to the right of the left margin, and click.

The text flows into a new frame in the lower half of the first column on page 3. When a text frame has more text than it can fit, the frame is said to have overset text. Overset text is indicated by a red plus sign (+) in the out port of the frame, which is the small square just above the lower-right corner of the frame. You can link overset text to another frame, create a new frame into which the overset text flows, or expand the size of the frame so that the text is no longer overset.

4 Select the Selection tool (↖), and click the out port in the selected frame. The pointer becomes a loaded text icon. Now you'll add a column of text to the lower half of the second column.

5 Position the loaded text icon immediately below the fourth guide from the bottom margin and just to the right of the second column guide (be sure not to click the previously created text frame above), and click. Text now fills the lower portion of the right column.

Hecho en Mexico

Exploring Mexican Folk Art

One of the most exciting things about vacationing in Oaxaca is the large artist community that lives and works there. My wife Judith and I traveled there last May and came home with many more pieces for our collection than we had ever imagined. Judith is a collector by nature. Every square inch of our tiny Manhattan apartment is filled with a treasure from one of our trips. I wanted to experience more than just the exchange of money with a merchant—I wanted to meet the artists. Having grown up in a family of sculptors (my father took commissions for his work from around the world), I wanted to see how these people crafted their pieces, how they lived, and

what their art meant to them. Judith was more interested in buying art, but she finally agreed to go with me to meet a folk artist I heard about named Henry Luis Ramos.

As Judith and I stepped into the adobe shop, a cheerful black-haired boy greeted us. "My father's expecting you," he said as he led us down a hall into a spacious room filled with hundreds of statues, clay pots, and tin artifacts that Ramos designed.

The brilliantly colored pieces captivated me. I couldn't stop investigating and touching them. I could see the influence of the Mayan culture and other native tribes. "My father did these," the boy

Issue 3

6 Choose File > Save.

Threading text

You'll continue to thread text to the next page, because the article is long. First you will click the out port and then link to a text frame—a technique called manual threading. You can also thread text using semi-automatic and automatic threading.

1 Using the Selection tool ( ), click the out port in the frame that is in the second column on page 3.

This prepares InDesign CS4 to flow the overset text from this text frame to another frame.

2 In the Pages panel, double-click the page 4 icon to center page 4 in the document window.

3 Hold down the Alt (Windows) or Option (Mac OS) key and click the loaded text icon in the upper-left corner of the first column.

The text flows into the left column. Since you held down the Alt or Option key, the pointer remains a loaded text icon, and you do not need to click in the out port before flowing text from this frame. This is called semi-automatic threading.

4 Position the loaded text icon in the upper-left corner of the second column on page 4, and click.

Now you'll flow the remaining text into the two columns at the bottom of page 7.

Tip: Whenever the pointer displays a loaded text icon, you can click any tool in the Tools panel to stop flowing text. No text is lost, and any overset text remains intact.

5 Click the out port in the text frame on the second column of page 4.

6 In the Pages panel, double-click the page 7 icon, centering page 7 in the document window.

7 Hold down the Alt (Windows) or Option (Mac OS) key, position the loaded text icon in the left column, just below the guide on page 7, and click. Release the Alt or Option key.

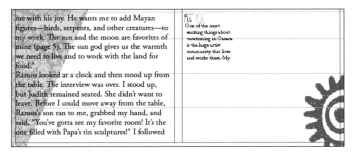

Depending on where you click to create the frame and the version of the fonts in use, text may fit exactly or be slightly overset. Either way, you will create a frame in the column at right to contain text as it reflows.

8 Position the loaded text icon in the second column below the guide, and click. Any remaining text from the story flows into the second column.

You have finished threading text frames in this document. A threaded set of frames is called a story.

9 Choose File > Save.

Fine-tuning the layout

Now you'll further polish the layout by adding a pull quote, modifying the text frame containing the pull quote, and adjusting graphics.

Adding a pull quote

To make the design on page 4 of your document stand out a bit more, you'll add a pull quote. Text from the article has already been copied and placed into a frame on the pasteboard, which is the area outside of the page. You will position this pull-quote text frame in the middle of page 4 and finish formatting it.

1 Choose View > Fit Page in Window.

2 In the lower-left corner of the document window, click and hold down the arrow to the right of the page number indicator. Select page 4 from the list of available pages.

If you cannot see the pull-quote text frame on the pasteboard to the left of page 4, drag the horizontal scroll bar to the left until the pull quote is visible.

3 Using the Selection tool (⭡), select the pull quote.

4 On the left side of the Control panel, click the center point in the reference point locator (⊞) and enter an X value of **4 in** and a Y value of **3 in**. Press Enter or Return. InDesign moves the selected object to the specified location.

5 Using the arrow keys on the keyboard, nudge the location of the frame. The bottom of the frame should pass through the middle of the red star. The pull quote should now be centered between the columns of text on page 4.

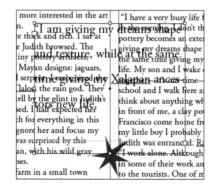

Wrapping text around an object

The text in the pull quote is difficult to read because the main story text does not wrap around the text frame, but instead overlaps it. You'll wrap the main story text around the edges of the pull-quote text frame, so that the text from the main story does not cover up the pull quote.

1 Make sure that the pull-quote frame is selected.

2 Choose Window > Text Wrap. In the Text Wrap panel, click the third button from the left side (▣). This causes text to wrap around the object's shape.

3 Type **.1389in** into one of the Offset fields and press Return.

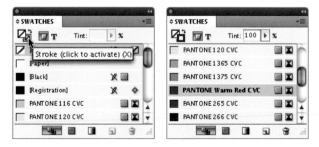

Within the top illustration:

> quickly, but she seemed
> more interested in the art
> that fill
> Ramos
> thick a
> the tabl
> Judith l
> was cov
> pottery
> which
> designs
> a two-h
> recogni
> symbol
> god. They were beautiful!
> I could tell by the glint in Judith's eye that she was

> "I am giving my dreams shape
> ...ure, while at the same
> ...ing my Xalapan ances-
> ...v life."

> maybe you k
> is so far away
> small town i
> of Pennsylva
> Bellefonte, v
> and I lived i
> old Victorian
> overlooks th
> put down a f
> holding and
> table.
> "I have a ve
> from daybre
> the evening.
> of it as work
> becomes an extension of my hand

> TEXT WRAP
> □ Invert
> 0.1389 in   0.1389 in
> 0.1389 in   0.1389 in
> Wrap Options:
> Wrap To: Both Right & Left Sides
> Contour Options:
> Type:
> □ Include Inside Edges

4 Close the Text Wrap panel. You can always access this panel and other panels from the Window menu as you need them.

5 Choose File > Save.

Adding a stroke to the frame

Now you'll change the color of the text frame so that the stroke, which appears as a border, matches the color of the red star. The Swatches panel lets you efficiently apply, edit, and update colors for all objects in a document.

This magazine article is intended for printing at a commercial press, so it uses CMYK process colors. The necessary colors have already been added to the Swatches panel.

1 Choose Window > Swatches.

2 With the text frame still selected, click the Stroke box (⊞) at the top of the Swatches panel.

Selecting the Stroke box causes the selected text frame's border to be affected by the color you select.

3 Select PANTONE Warm Red CVC. You may need to scroll down to see it.

> SWATCHES   SWATCHES
> Tint: %   Tint: 100   %
> Stroke (click to activate) (X)   PANTONE 120 CVC
> [Paper]   PANTONE 1365 CVC
> [Black]   PANTONE 1375 CVC
> [Registration]   PANTONE Warm Red CVC
> PANTONE 116 CVC   PANTONE 265 CVC
> PANTONE 120 CVC   PANTONE 266 CVC

4 To change the weight of the stroke, right-click (Windows) or Control-click (Mac OS) the frame, and select Stroke Weight > 0.5 pt from the context menu.

● **Note:** Once you wrap the text around the pull-quote frame, the main article text may be overset. If so, Live Preflight reports the error in the lower-left corner of the document window.

The context menus provide an easy way to change many attributes of a selected object, including the stroke weight.

5 Click the pasteboard to deselect all objects, and then close the Swatches panel.

6 Choose File > Save.

Changing the frame and text position

The text in the pull-quote frame is too close to the edge, making it unattractive and difficult to read. You'll now change the position of the text within the frame and change the style of the border.

1 Using the Selection tool (▶), click the pull-quote text frame to select it, and then choose Object > Text Frame Options.

2 In the Inset Spacing area, type **.075** in the Top box, and press Tab.

3 Make sure the Make All Settings The Same button (🔟) in the center is selected (unbroken), so that the same value is used for all four sides of the frame.

4 Choose Center from the Align menu, and click OK.

Text Frame Options dialog box

▶ **Tip:** You can use the Control panel to easily adjust other important attributes for objects on a page, such as size and position.

5 With the frame still selected, do the following in the Control panel:

- From the Stroke Type menu, choose Thick-Thin.

- From the Stroke Weight menu, choose 4 pt.

6 Choose File > Save.

Adjusting the size of a graphic

Next you will adjust the size of the crescent moon picture on page 5.

1 If necessary, scroll to view page 5.

2 Using the Selection tool ( ), click to select the picture of the blue crescent moon.

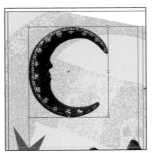

3 In the Control panel, choose 50% from the Scale Y Percentage menu.

Both the vertical and horizontal sizes adjust proportionally, because the Constrain Proportions For Scaling button ( ) to the right of the scaling percentages is selected. To adjust one value independent of the other, deselect this button.

▶ **Tip:** To avoid the possible loss of quality, bitmap graphics, such as those scanned or taken with a digital camera, should generally not be scaled disproportionately or beyond 120% of their original size. In this case, you reduced the size of the graphic proportionally, which generally has no adverse impact on its quality.

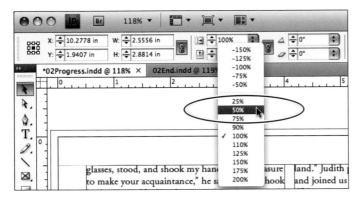

● **Note:** When the graphic is selected with the Selection tool, the field will continue to report 100%; select the graphic with the Direct Selection tool to see the scaled size.

4 Choose File > Save.

Working with styles

Now you'll try out styles to see how using them lets you quickly and consistently format text and objects and—more importantly—easily make global changes by simply editing the style. InDesign CS4 contains a variety of styles: paragraph, character, object, table, and cell styles.

• A paragraph style includes formatting attributes that apply to all text in a paragraph. You do not need to select text to apply a paragraph style, because it applies to all text in the paragraph where the pointer is located.

• A character style includes only character attributes, making it useful for formatting selected words and phrases in a paragraph.

- An object style lets you create and apply formatting to selected objects. Using an object style, you can set fill and stroke color, stroke and corner effects, transparency, drop shadows, feathering, text frame options, and even text wrap on a selected object.

- Table and cell styles let you control table and cell formatting.

Applying paragraph styles

You'll start by applying styles to the magazine article's text, and then move on to using object styles. To save time, the paragraph styles that you'll apply to the text have already been created. These styles will help you quickly format the body text in the article.

1   In the Pages panel, double-click the page 3 icon to center it in the document window.

2   Select the Type tool (T), and then click anywhere in the columns of text that you previously placed on this page.

3   Choose Edit > Select All to select the text in all the threaded frames containing the story.

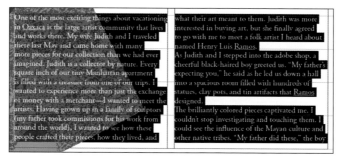

4   Choose Type > Paragraph Styles to display the Paragraph Styles panel.

▶ **Tip:** You can also apply styles in the Control panel, using either the Character Formatting or the Paragraph Formatting controls.

5   In the Paragraph Styles panel, click Body Text to format the entire story with the Body Text style.

6   Choose Edit > Deselect All to deselect the text.

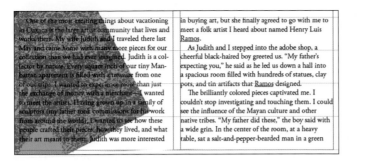

Now you'll apply a different paragraph style to the first paragraph of the story.

7 Using the Type tool, click anywhere in the first paragraph on page 3.

8 In the Paragraph Styles panel, select Body Text / Drop Cap. Paragraph styles can include a variety of text formatting options, including drop caps.

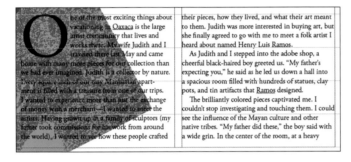

9 Choose File > Save.

Formatting text for the character style

To emphasize page references in the paragraphs of the magazine article, now you'll create and apply a character style. First, you'll use the Control panel to italicize the text and make it 1 point smaller. You'll then base the character style on this formatted text, allowing you to easily apply this same style to other text throughout the document. Text must be selected to apply a character style.

1 In the Pages panel, double-click the page 7 icon to center it in the document window. To make sure that you can read the text at the bottom of this page, press Ctrl + (Plus sign) (Windows) or Command + (Mac OS) to zoom in.

The text has three references to other pages: (page 7), (page 2), and (page 5). If necessary, use the scroll bars to display this portion of the document window.

2 Using the Type tool (T), select the (page 7) reference along with the period following it.

▶ **Tip:** Typesetters generally apply the same style to any punctuation following the styled word.

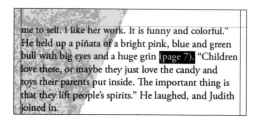

3   In the Character Formatting Controls area of the Control panel, select Italic from the Type Style menu.

4   Type **11** in the Font Size box. The page reference is now formatted.

5   Choose File > Save.

Creating and applying a character style

Now that you have formatted the text, you are ready to create a character style.

1   Make sure that the text you formatted is still selected, and choose Type > Character Styles to display the Character Styles panel.

2   Hold down the Alt (Windows) or Option (Mac OS) key and click the Create New Style button at the bottom of the Character Styles panel.

A new character style named Character Style 1 is created, as shown in the New Character Style dialog box. This new style includes the characteristics of the selected text, as indicated in the Style Settings area of the dialog box.

3   In the Style Name box, type **Italic** and click OK.

4 Using the Type tool (T), select the (page 7) reference and click Italic in the Character Styles panel to apply the style.

Even though you established the style using this text, you still need to apply the style. Applying a style tags the text so that it updates automatically when the character style attributes are changed.

5 Apply the character style Italic to the (page 2) reference in the same column, and to the (page 5) reference in the other column.

k in tin." He | ran to me g
favorite pieces | r
ols (page 2). | re
all in his room | n
with his joy. He

CHARACTER STYLES
[None]
[None]
Italic

Because you applied a character style instead of a paragraph style, the formatting affected only the selected text, not the entire paragraph.

6 Choose View > Fit Page in Window, and then close the Character Styles panel.

7 Choose File > Save.

Applying object styles

Use object styles to apply multiple formatting attributes to an object, including text and graphics frames. To save time, the object style that you'll apply to the pull quote on page 4 has already been created.

1 In the Pages panel, double-click the page 4 icon to center it in the document window.

2 Using the Selection tool (↖), click the pull quote to select its text frame.

3 Choose Window > Object Styles to display the Object Styles panel.

4 In the Object Styles panel, hold down the Alt (Windows) or Option (Mac OS) key and click Pull-Quote to format the selected object with the Pull-Quote object style.

● **Note:** Holding down the Alt or Option key when applying a style to an object or text clears any existing formatting.

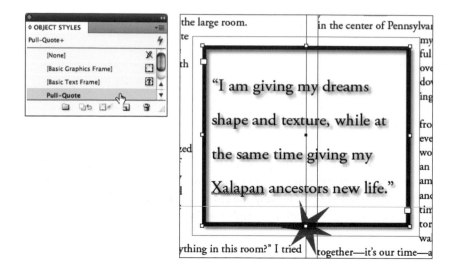

5 Choose File > Save.

Working with graphics

● **Note:** As you learn about the difference between frames and their content, you may want to make frame edges visible by selecting View > Show Frame edges.

To complete the magazine layout, you'll reposition some graphics at the same time you practice using the selection tools, try out layers, and crop an image. Graphics used in an InDesign CS4 document are placed inside frames. When working with placed graphics, you should become familiar with the three selection tools.

- The Selection tool ( ) is used for general layout tasks, such as positioning and moving objects on a page.

- The Direct Selection tool ( ) is used for tasks involving the content of a graphics frame, or drawing and editing paths; for example, to select frame contents or to move an anchor point on a path. The Direct Selection tool is also used for selecting objects within groups.

- The Position tool ( ), hidden under the Direct Selection tool, works in conjunction with the Selection tool to help control the placement of content within a frame, as well as to change the size of the frame. You can use this tool to move a graphic within its frame, or change the visible area of a graphic by adjusting its crop.

Positioning graphics within a frame

On the first spread, two of the frames need to be resized for their pictures, or the pictures within them repositioned.

1 Select page 2 in the page box in the lower-left corner of the document window to navigate to page 2. Press Ctrl+0 (zero) (Windows) or Command+0 (Mac OS) to fit the page in the window.

2 Using the Direct Selection tool (⟍), position your pointer over the picture of the red sun, which is only partially visible. Notice that the pointer changes to a hand, indicating that you can select and manipulate the content of the frame. Drag the picture to the right, making the entire sun visible. With the Direct Selection tool, you can reposition a graphic within its frame.

▶ **Tip:** The Fitting commands make it easy to fit graphics in frames and to fit frames to graphics. For example, choose Object > Fitting > Center Content to center a graphic within its frame.

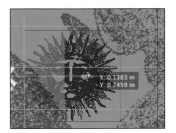

3 Using the Selection tool (▶), click the picture of the blue hand on the upper-left side of the page.

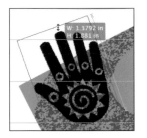

4 Drag the top-center handle upward to expand the size of the frame. By making the frame larger, more of its contents becomes visible.

▶ **Tip:** You can preview the picture as you move or resize the frame if you pause briefly after you first click the frame and then resize or move the frame.

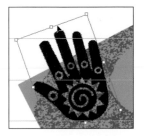

5 Choose File > Save.

Using the Position tool

The dynamic Position tool (⚒) lets you work with the content of a frame, whether it's a graphic or text. When you place the Position tool over a graphic, it changes to a hand icon (✋), indicating that you can manipulate the content within that frame. When you place the Position tool over a text frame, the pointer changes to an I-beam, indicating that you can add or edit text.

1 Select the Position tool by holding down the mouse button on the Direct Selection tool in the Tools panel. When the Position tool appears, select it.

2 Press Ctrl+J (Windows) or Command+J (Mac OS) and type **3** in the Go To Page dialog box, and then press Enter or Return. This keyboard shortcut takes you to page 3. Roll over the text "Exploring Mexican Folk." Notice that your pointer changes into the text I-beam.

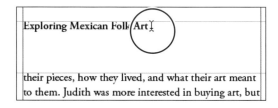

3 Triple-click the text to select it.

4 In the Character Formatting Controls area of the Control panel, drag to select the value in the Font Size box. Type **20** and press Enter or Return.

5 Choose File > Save.

Targeting layers when placing objects

InDesign CS4 lets you place objects on different layers. Think of layers as sheets of transparent film that are stacked on top of each other. By using layers, you can create and edit objects on one layer without affecting—or being affected by—objects on other layers. Layers also determine the stacking position of objects.

Before you import a photograph of an armadillo into your design, you'll make sure that you add the frame to the appropriate layer.

1 In the Pages panel, double-click the page 3 icon to center it in the document window.

2 Choose Window > Layers to display the Layers panel.

3 Click the word "Photos" in the Layers panel to target the Photos layer. Do not click the boxes to the left of the Photos layer because that hides
or
locks the layer.

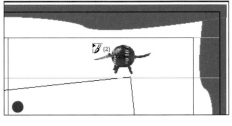

4 Using the Selection tool (↖), click the pasteboard to make sure that nothing is selected.

5 Choose File > Place. If necessary, navigate to the Lesson_02 folder. Click 02_Armadillo.tif, and then Shift+click 02_Gecko.tif. Click Open.

▶ **Tip:** In the Place dialog box, you can select multiple text and graphic files to import. The files are imported in the order they are listed in the dialog box. InDesign lets you import graphics using a variety of file types, including native Photoshop (PSD) and Illustrator (AI) files.

A loaded graphics icon (🖋) appears with a preview of the armadillo. The number 2 next to the pointer indicates how many graphics will be imported.

6 Click in the white area above the word "Mexico" to place the armadillo at the top of the page. You'll move the graphic later, after you crop it.

7 Click at the bottom of the far-right column of text to place the gecko graphic.

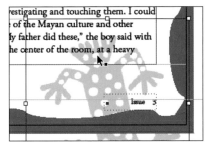

Notice that the two new frames are the same color as the Photos layer in the Layers panel. An object's frame color describes the layer on which it resides.

8 With the gecko graphic still selected in the Control panel, type **15** in the Rotation Angle box. Press Enter or Return.

9 In the Layers panel, click the box to the left of the Text layer name so that the layer lock icon appears.

Locking the Text layer prevents you from selecting or making any changes to it or any objects on the layer. With the Text layer locked, you can edit the frame containing the armadillo without accidentally selecting the frame containing "Hecho en Mexico."

10 Choose File > Save.

Cropping and moving the photograph

You'll now use the Selection tool to crop and move the photo of the armadillo.

1 Choose Edit > Deselect All.

2 Using the Selection tool ( ), click the armadillo.

3 Position the pointer over the middle handle on the right side of the armadillo frame and hold down the mouse button. Drag the frame toward the center of the armadillo to crop it.

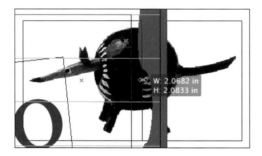

4 Using the Selection tool, position the pointer over the center of the armadillo frame, and drag the object so that it snaps to the bleed guide at the right edge of the page.

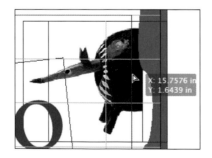

Notice that the edge of the armadillo is behind the decorative border. This is because the Photos layer is below the Graphics layer in the Layers panel.

5 Choose View > Screen Mode > Preview to see the finished pages.

6 Choose File > Save.

7 Choose File > Close.

Exploring on your own

Congratulations! You've completed the InDesign CS4 tour. To learn more about InDesign CS4, you may want to try the following:

*   Continue experimenting with the magazine layout. Add new pages, move items between layers, create text frames, and adjust the graphics using the tools in the Tools panel.

*   Choose Help > InDesign Help to use Adobe InDesign CS4 Help.

*   Go through the lessons in the rest of this book.

Review questions

1 How can you tell if an aspect of a layout will cause output problems?

2 What tool allows you to create text frames? Thread text frames?

3 What symbol indicates that a text frame has more text than it can hold—that is, overset text?

4 What tool allows you to work with both graphics and text?

5 What panel provides options for modifying selected frames, graphics, or text?

Review answers

1 The Preflight panel reports errors when something in the layout does not match the selected preflight profile. For example, if the preflight profile specifies CMYK output and you import an RGB graphic, an error is reported. Preflight errors are also listed in the lower-left corner of the document window.

2 You create text frames with the Type tool and thread text frames with the Selection tool.

3 A red plus sign in the lower-left corner of a text frame indicates overset text.

4 The Position tool, hidden under the Direct Selection tool, allows you to work with graphics or text.

5 The Control panel provides options for modifying the current selection: characters, paragraphs, graphics, frames, tables, and more.

3 SETTING UP A DOCUMENT AND WORKING WITH PAGES

Lesson Overview

In this introduction to setting up a multipage document, you'll learn how to do the following:

- Start a new document.

- Create, edit, and apply multiple master pages.

- Set document defaults.

- Adjust pasteboard size and bleed area.

- Create section markers.

- Override master page items on document pages.

- Add text wrap to a graphic.

- Add graphics and text to document pages.

 This lesson will take approximately 90 minutes.

The flight back from Oaxaca seemed to take forever, but I fear it was only Judith's disgust with me that made it seem interminable. Anyway, we got home and life returned to normal, or even better than normal, even supernormal, if there is such a word. I told Judith I was sorry about the comments I made about her parents and the *Day of the Dead* celebration, and she apologized for her brazen flirting with that good-for-nada bullfighter. Then, in an effort to cement our new-found bond, Judith enrolled us in an *origami* class. "Oh great, I thought, "my marriage has been reduced to folded paper." But now that I've been in the class for a few weeks, I must admit that I love it. Origami is amazing and beautiful.

On the evening of our first class, the instructor, a cheerful gray-haired woman named Alexandra, told us the riveting story of Tsuru no Ox-gaeshi (A Repaying Crane):

"Once upon a time, there was a poor hunter. One day, he came across a trapped crane. He took pity on the crane and released it. A few days later, a lovely woman visited his house, and asked him to shelter for the night. Soon the two got married.

"The bride was sweet in disposition as well as beautiful, so they lived happily. But the hunter couldn't afford to support his new wife. One day, she said she would weave cloth for him to sell at market, but she told him never to see her weaving.

"She stayed in a weaving hut for three days. When she finished weaving, she emerged with a beautiful fabric. He brought the fabric to town, where merchants were surprised and paid gold for it. The fabric was very rare and called Tsuru-no-senba-ori (thousand feathers of crane)."

This story made me feel good inside. I learned to appreciate the art of origami, and I decided to read as much about its history as time allowed.

The name origami was coined in 1880 for the words *ori* (to fold) and *kami* (paper). It started in the first century AD in China. (I thought it started in Japan, but Judith quickly pointed out the error in my thinking.) They say that's when papermaking started, and with papermaking came paper folding. The Chinese developed some simple forms, some of which survive to this day. Buddhist monks brought Origami to Japan in the sixth century AD. It caught on quickly throughout the culture; paper was used in architecture and in many everyday rituals. Many of the earliest designs have been lost, since there was nothing written down about origami until 1797 with the publication of the *Senbazuru Orikata* (How to Fold One Thousand Cranes). *The Kan no mado* (Window of Midwinter), a comprehensive collection of traditional Japanese figures, was published in 1845.

Origami flourished in other parts of the world, as well. Arabs brought the secrets of papermaking to North Africa, and in the eighth century AD, the Moors brought the secrets of Spain. The Moors, devoutly religious, were forbidden to create representational figures. Their paper folding was a study in geometry. After the Moors were driven out of Spain during the Inquisition (Judith gave me a look, but then softened into a smile), the Spanish developed papiroflexia, which sounds to me like some sort of inflammation of the Pope's ligaments. Anyway, this technique is still popular in Spain and Argentina.

Modern origami owes its existence to a man named Akira Yoshizawa. In the 1930's, Yoshizawa designed thousand of models of various subjects. He is the originator of the system of lines and arrows used in modern paper folding. He exhibited his work throughout the west in the 1950's and 1960's and helped inspire many paperfolders in the west as well as Japan.

Origami flourished in other parts of the world, as well. Arabs brought the

There's no place like a sunny beach for summer fun…

secrets of papermaking to North Africa, and in the eighth century AD, the Moors brought the secrets of Spain. The Moors, devoutly religious, were forbidden to create representational figures. Their paper folding was a study in geometry. After the Moors were driven out of Spain during the Inquisition (Judith gave me a look, but then softened into a smile), the Spanish developed papiroflexia, which sounds to me like some sort of inflammation of the Pope's ligaments. Anyway, this technique is still popular in Spain and Argentina.

Modern origami owes its existence to a man named Akira Yoshizawa. In the 1930's, Yoshizawa designed thousand of models of various subjects. He is the originator of the system of lines and arrows used in modern paper folding. He exhibited his work throughout the west in the 1950's and 1960's and helped inspire many paperfolders in the west as well as Japan.

As origami evolves, elaborate folding techniques produce amazing models.

In our class, Judith specialized in creature fish and sea creature origami. During the first two weeks of training, she produced a horseshoe crab, a goldfish, a strikingly beautiful seahorse, a so-so squid, and a lopsided clam, basing her patterns on Barbour, Andreozzi, and Robinson.

As for me, I do not trust the ocean. Origami flourished in other parts of the world, as well. Arabs brought the secrets of papermaking to North Africa, and in the eighth century AD, the Moors brought the secrets of Spain. The Moors, devoutly religious, were forbidden to create representational figures. Their paper folding was a study in geometry. After the Moors were driven out of Spain during the Inquisition (Judith gave me a look, but then softened into a smile), the Spanish developed papiroflexia.

By taking advantage of the features that help you set up the documents you create, you can ensure consistent page layout and simplify your work. In this lesson, you'll learn how to set up a new document, create master pages, and set columns and guides.

Getting started

● **Note:** If you have not already copied the resource files for this lesson onto your hard disk from the Adobe InDesign CS4 Classroom in a Book CD, do so now. See "Copying the Classroom in a Book files" on page 2.

In this lesson, you'll set up a 12-page magazine article and then place text and graphics on one of the spreads.

1 To ensure that the preference and default settings of your Adobe InDesign CS4 program match those used in this lesson, move the InDesign Defaults file to a different folder following the procedure in "Saving and restoring the InDesign Defaults file" on page 2.

2 Start Adobe InDesign CS4. To ensure that the panels and menu commands match those used in this lesson, choose Window > Workspace > [Advanced], and then choose Window > Workspace > Reset Advanced. To begin working, you'll open an InDesign document that is already partially completed.

3 To see what the finished document looks like, open the 03_End.indd file in the Lesson_03 folder, located inside the Lessons folder within the InDesignCIB folder on your hard disk.

● **Note:** As you work, feel free to move panels or change the magnification to meet your needs.

4 Scroll through the document to view the spreads, most of which only have guides and placeholder frames. Navigate to pages 2–3, which is the only spread that you'll complete in this lesson.

5 Close the 03_End.indd file after you have completed examining it, or you can leave this document open for reference.

Creating and saving custom page settings

InDesign lets you save frequently used document settings, including number of pages, page size, columns, and margins. Using these saved document parameters, called *document presets*, lets you create new documents quickly.

1 Choose File > Document Presets > Define.

2 Click New in the Document Presets dialog box.

3 In the New Document Preset dialog box, set the following:

- In the Document Preset box, type **Magazine**.

- In the Number of Pages box, type **12**.

- Make sure that the Facing Pages option is selected.

- In the Width box, type **50p3** (the abbreviation for 50 picas and 3 points).

- In the Height box, type **65p3**.

- In the Columns section, type **5** for Number, and leave the gutter at 1p0.

- In the Margins section, make sure that the Make All Settings The Same icon (✿) in the center of the margin settings is deselected (broken) so that you can enter settings that aren't the same for all four margins. Type **4p** for Bottom; leave the Top, Inside, and Outside margins at 3 picas (3p0).

4 Click More Options, which expands the dialog box. Type **.25 in** the Top box of the Bleed option. Then ensure that the Make All Settings The Same icon is selected (unbroken), so that the same value is used for the Bottom, Inside, and Outside boxes. Click inside the Bottom box and notice that InDesign automatically converts measurements expressed using other measurement units (in this case, inches) to the pica and point equivalents.

Bleed creates an area outside of the page that prints and is used when items extend off of the defined page size, such as a picture or a colored background on a page.

5 Click OK in both dialog boxes to save the document preset.

Creating a new document

When you create a new document, the New Document dialog box appears. You can use a document preset to build the document, or use this dialog box to specify several document settings, including the number of pages, the page size, the number of columns, and more. In this section, you'll use the Magazine preset that you just created.

1 Choose File > New > Document.

2 In the New Document dialog box, choose the Magazine preset from the Document Preset menu if it isn't already selected.

3 Click OK.

InDesign creates a new document using all of the specifications from the document preset, including the page size, margins, and number of pages.

4 Open the Pages panel by choosing Window > Pages, if it is not already open.

In the Pages panel, page 1 is visible and highlighted in blue since it's the page that's currently displayed in the document window. The Pages panel is divided into two sections. The top section displays icons for the master pages. (A master page is

▶ **Tip:** You can use any supported unit of measurement in any dialog box or panel. If you want to use a measurement unit that differs from the default, simply type the indicator for the unit you want to use, such as **p** for picas, **pt** for points, and either **in** or " (inch marks) for inches, after the value you enter into a box. You can change the default units by choosing Edit > Preferences > Units & Increments (Windows) or InDesign > Preferences > Units & Increments (Mac OS).

like a background template that you can apply to many pages in a document.) The lower section displays icons for document pages. In this document, the master page consists of a two-page spread of facing pages.

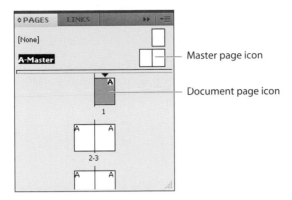

Master page icon

Document page icon

5   Choose File > Save As, name the file **03_Setup.indd** in the Lesson_03 folder, and click Save.

Switching between open InDesign documents

As you work, you may want to switch between your new document and the supplied finished document for reference. If both documents are open, you can bring one or the other to the front.

1   Choose the Window menu. A list of currently open InDesign documents is displayed at the bottom.

2   Choose the document you want to view. That document now appears in front.

Working with master pages

Before you add graphics and text frames to the document, you may want to set up the master pages, which serve as backgrounds for your document pages. Any object that you add to a master page automatically appears on the document pages to which the master page has been applied.

In this document, you'll create two master page spreads—one containing a grid and footer information, and a second containing placeholder frames. By creating multiple master pages, you allow for variation while ensuring consistent design.

▶ **Tip:** By default, page 1 in a new document is a recto page—that is, the page is to the right of the spine. You can also begin a document on a verso page—one that's to the left of the spine. To start on a verso page, create a new document, select page 1 in the Pages panel, and then choose Layout > Numbering & Section Options. In the Numbering & Section Options dialog box, select Start Page Numbering At and enter an even number for the first page in the accompanying box. Click OK to close the dialog box.

Adding guides to the master page

Guides are nonprinting lines that help you lay out a document precisely. Guides placed on a master page appear on any document pages to which that master page has been applied.

For this document, you'll add a series of guides that, along with the column guides, act as a grid that helps you position graphics and text frames.

▶ **Tip:** If the two pages of the master page spread are not centered in the document window, double-click the Hand tool in the Tools panel to center them.

1   In the upper section of the Pages panel, double-click the name A-Master. The master spread's left and right pages appear in the document window.

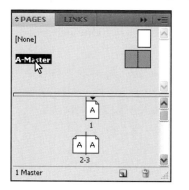

2   Choose Layout > Create Guides.

3   Select Preview.

4   For the Rows option, type **8** in the Number box, and **0** in the Gutter box.

5   For Fit Guides To, select Margins and notice how the horizontal guides appear on your master pages.

▶ **Tip:** Grids can also be added to individual document pages using the same command when working on a document page rather than a master page.

Selecting Margins instead of Page causes the guides to fit within the margin boundaries rather than the page boundaries. You won't add column guides because column lines already appear in your document.

6   Click OK.

Dragging guides from rulers

You can drag guides from the horizontal (top) and vertical (side) rulers to provide additional alignment assistance on individual pages. Pressing Ctrl (Windows) or Command (Mac OS) while dragging a guide applies the guide to the entire spread.

In this lesson, you will place footers below the lower margin of the page where there are no column guides. To position the footers accurately, you will add a horizontal guide and two vertical guides.

1 Double-click the name A-Master in the Pages panel, if it is not already selected. If the A-Master spread is not visible in the top section of the Pages panel, you may need to scroll within the top section of the panel to view additional master pages.

2 Without clicking in your document, move the pointer around the document window and watch the horizontal and vertical rulers as the pointer moves. Notice how the hairline indicators in the rulers correspond to the pointer's position. Also notice that the dimmed X and Y values in the Control panel indicate the position of the pointer.

3 Press Ctrl (Windows) or Command (Mac OS) and position your pointer in the horizontal ruler. Drag a ruler guide down to approximately 62 picas. View the Y value in the Control panel or the Transform panel (Window > Object & Layout > Transform) to see the current position. Don't worry about placing the guide exactly at 62 picas—you'll do that in the next step.

▶ **Tip:** You can also drag the ruler guide without the Ctrl or Command key and release the guide over the pasteboard to have a guide appear across all pages in a spread as well as on the pasteboard.

● **Note:** The controls in the Transform panel are similar to those in the Control panel. You can use either panel to make many common modifications, such as changing position, size, scale, and angle of rotation.

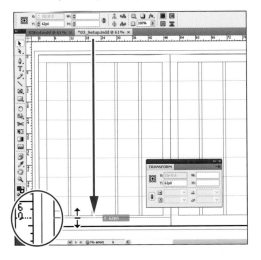

4 To position the guide at exactly 62 picas, select the guide with the Selection tool (▸) if it's not already selected. A selected guide is displayed with a different color than guides that are not selected. When the guide is selected, the Y value is no longer dimmed in the Control or Transform panel. Select the value in the Y box

▶ **Tip:** When working with any panel, you can select the value in a box by clicking the letter or icon that identifies the box. For example, click Y to select the value in the Y box.

in the Control panel and type **62p** to replace the current value. Press Enter or Return to apply the value to the selected guide.

5   Drag a ruler guide from the vertical ruler to the 12p0.6 position. Watch the X value in the Control panel as you drag. The guide snaps to the column guide at that location.

6   Drag another guide from the vertical ruler to the 88p5.4 position.

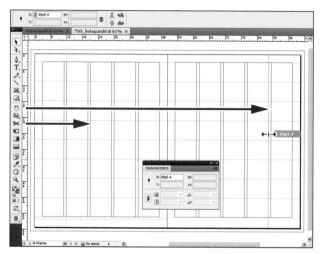

7   Choose File > Save.

Creating a text frame on the master page

Any text or graphic that you place on a master page appears on pages to which the master is applied. To create a footer, you'll add a publication title ("Summer Vacations") and a page number marker to the bottom of both master pages.

● **Note:** When drawing a frame with the Type tool, the frame starts where the horizontal baseline intersects the I beam in the pointer—not the upper corner of the pointer.

1   Make sure that you can see the bottom of the left master page. If necessary, zoom in and use the scroll bars or Hand tool (✋).

2   Select the Type tool (**T**) in the Tools panel. On the left master page, drag to create a text frame below the second column where the guides intersect, as shown. Don't worry about drawing the frame in exactly the right location— you'll snap it into place later.

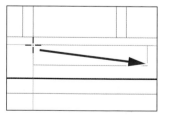

3 With the insertion point in the new text frame, choose Type > Insert Special Character > Markers > Current Page Number.

The letter A appears in your text frame. On document pages that are based on this master page, the correct page number is displayed, such as "2" on document page 2.

4 To add an em space after the page number, right-click (Windows) or Control-click (Mac OS) with the insertion point in the text frame to display a context menu, and then choose Insert White Space > Em Space. Or you can choose this same command from the Type menu.

5 Type **Summer Vacations** after the em space.

Next, you'll change the font and size of the text in the frame.

6 In the Tools panel, select the Selection tool (➤) and make sure that the text frame containing the footer is selected. Make sure that all of the text you just entered is visible. If necessary, enlarge the text frame by dragging the lower-right corner until the text is visible.

7 Choose Type > Character to view the Character panel.

8 In the Character panel, choose Adobe Garamond Pro from the Font Family menu and Regular from the Type Style menu.

9 Make sure that the Font Size box shows 12 pt.

Note: You can edit the attributes of all text in a frame by selecting the frame with the Selection tool. To change the attributes of a portion of text within the frame, use the Type tool.

Note: It's easy to confuse the Font Size menu (🔠) with the Leading menu (🔠). Make sure that you change the font size, not the leading.

10 In the Tools panel, select the Selection tool (➤). If necessary, drag the footer frame so that the upper-left corner snaps to intersection of the horizontal and vertical guides you created earlier.

A   Summer Vacations

Tip: When no objects are selected, changes made in the Character panel or other panels become your default settings for the active document. To avoid modifying your defaults, be certain that an object is selected before making changes in a panel.

11 Click the upper-left corner of the reference point locator (🔳), which is in the upper-left corner of the Control panel. The Control panel should display an X value of 12p0.6 and a Y value of 62p0.

12 Click a blank area of your document window or choose Edit > Deselect All to deselect the text frame.

Next you'll duplicate the footer on the left master page and position the copy on the right master page.

13 Using the Selection tool (▶), select the footer text frame on the left master page. Hold down the Alt key (Windows) or Option key (Mac OS), and drag the text frame to the right master page so that it snaps to the guides, mirroring the left master page as shown.

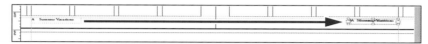

▶ **Tip:** When not selected, a master item is displayed with a dotted line along the edge of its bounding box. This provides a visual distinction between master items and objects created on document pages, whose bounding boxes are displayed with solid lines.

14 Make sure that you can see the bottom of the right master page. If necessary, increase the magnification and scroll as needed to view the text frame on the bottom of the right master page.

15 Select the Type tool (**T**), and click anywhere inside the text frame on the right master page, creating an insertion point.

16 Click Paragraph Formatting Controls (¶) in the Control panel, and then click the Align Right button.

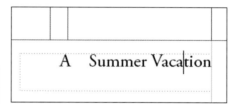

Click Paragraph Formatting Controls at the left side of the Control panel to see the alignment options.

The text is now right-aligned within the footer frame on the right master page. Now you'll modify the right master page, placing the page number on the right side of the words "Summer Vacations."

17 Delete the em space and page number at the beginning of the footer.

18 Place the insertion point at the end of "Summer Vacations" and then choose Type > Insert Special Character > Markers > Current Page Number.

19 Place the insertion point between "Summer Vacations" and the page number character. Right-click (Windows) or Control-click (Mac OS), and then choose Insert White Space > Em Space.

| A | Summer Vacations | Summer Vacations | A |

Left footer and right footer

20 Close or dock the Character panel. Choose Edit > Deselect All, and then choose File > Save.

Renaming the master page

When documents contain several master pages, you may want to rename each master page with a more descriptive name. You will rename this first master page "Grid - Footer."

1 Choose Window > Pages if the Pages panel is not open. Confirm that the A-Master page is still selected. Choose Master Options for "A-Master" from the Pages panel menu (▤).

2 In the Name box, type **Grid - Footer,** and click OK.

Master Options

Prefix: A

Name: Grid - Footer

Based on Master: [None]

Number of Pages: 2

OK

Cancel

▶ **Tip:** In addition to changing the name of master pages, you can also use the Master Options dialog box to change other properties of existing master pages.

Creating additional master pages

You can create multiple master pages within a document. You can build them independently, or base one master page on another master page. By basing master pages on other masters, any change to the parent master appears on the child masters.

For instance, the Grid - Footer master page is useful for most of the pages in the lesson document and can be used as the basis for another set of master pages that share key layout elements, such as margins and the current page number character.

To accommodate different layouts, you will create a separate set of master pages that contains placeholder frames for text and graphics. The Placeholder master will be based on the Grid - Footer master.

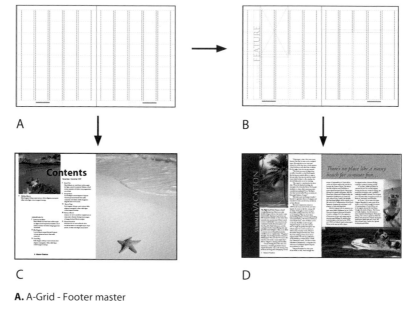

A. A-Grid - Footer master

B. B-Placeholder master

C. Document pages based on A-Grid - Footer

D. Document pages based on B-Placeholder

Creating a placeholder master

Next, you'll create a second master page that will contain placeholders for the text and graphics that will appear in your articles. By creating placeholders on the master pages, you can ensure a consistent layout among articles, and you won't need to create text frames for each page in your document.

1 In the Pages panel, choose New Master from the Pages panel menu.

2 In the Name box, type **Placeholder.**

3 From the Based On Master menu, choose A-Grid - Footer, and click OK.

Notice that the letter A is displayed on the B-Placeholder page icons in the Pages panel. This letter indicates that the A-Grid - Footer master serves as the foundation for the B-Placeholder master. If you were to change the A-Grid - Footer master, the changes would also be reflected in the B-Placeholder master. You may also notice that you cannot easily select objects, such as the footers, from other master pages. You'll learn about selecting and overriding master page items later in this lesson.

▶ **Tip:** If all of the master page icons are not visible in the Pages panel, click the horizontal bar that separates the master page icons from document page icons and drag down until the other master page icons are visible.

Adding a title placeholder frame

The first placeholder contains the title of the article in a rotated text frame.

1 To center the left page in the document window, double-click the left page icon of the B-Placeholder master in the Pages panel.

2 Select the Type tool (**T**). In the pasteboard area off of the left edge of the first column, drag to create a text frame that is slightly wider than the page and approximately as tall as one of the grid blocks. You'll position and resize this frame later.

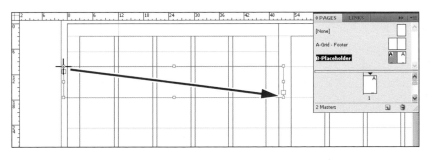

3 With the insertion point inside of the new text frame, type **Season Feature.**

4 Triple-click on the text you typed in the previous step to select all of the characters in the frame.

5 Click Character Formatting Controls (Ⓐ) in the Control panel to view the character formatting options. Choose Trajan Pro from the Font Family menu.

The Trajan font family has only capital letters, so now the text you typed appears in all capitals.

6 Double-click to select the word "SEASON." In the Font Size menu in the Control panel, select 36 pt. Next select the word "FEATURE" and select 60 pt from the Font Size menu.

7 In the Control panel, select Paragraph Formatting Controls (¶) and then click the Align Center button.

8 Select the Selection tool (▶). The text frame is selected. Click and drag the lower-center handle of the text frame until the frame is just large enough to contain the text. If the text disappears, drag the frame handle down again to make the frame larger. When you finish, choose View > Fit Spread In Window to zoom out.

9 In the Control panel, select the upper-left point of the reference point locator (⊞). Click the Rotate 90° Counter-clockwise button (↺) in the middle of the Control panel.

10 Drag the rotated text frame down so that the top edge snaps to the margin guide at the top of the page and the right edge snaps to the right column guide in the far-left column. Then drag the center handle on the bottom of the frame to stretch the frame to the lower margin of the page.

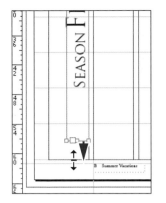

11 Click a blank area of the page or pasteboard to deselect, and then choose File > Save to save the document.

Adding placeholder frames for graphics

You have now created the placeholder text frame for the title of your article. Next, you'll add two graphics frames to the B-Placeholder master. Similar to text frames, these frames act as placeholders on the document pages, helping you to maintain a consistent design.

Although the Rectangle tool (□) and the Rectangle Frame tool (⊠) are more or less interchangeable, the Rectangle Frame tool, which includes a nonprinting X, is commonly used to create placeholders for graphics.

Creating a guide before you draw makes it easier to position the graphics frames.

● **Note:** It's not necessary to build placeholder frames on every document you create. For some smaller documents, you may not need to create master pages and placeholder frames.

1 Choose View > Grids & Guides and confirm that the Snap To Guides option is selected.

2 Drag a ruler guide from the horizontal ruler to the 34-pica location on the left master page. The current location (Y value) is displayed as you drag. Release the mouse when 34p0 is displayed.

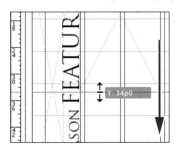

To make sure that the guide is at the 34-pica location, select the Selection tool (▶) and click the guide to select it (the guide changes color). Then type **34p** in the Y box in the Control panel, and then press Enter or Return.

3 Click a blank area of the page or pasteboard to deselect, and then select the Rectangle Frame tool (⊠) in the Tools panel.

4 Position the crosshair pointer on the bleed guide outside the upper-left edge of the page at X 11p0 and Y -1p6. As the crosshair pointer moves, its X and Y coordinates are displayed in the X Location and Y Location boxes in the Control panel.

5 Click and drag to create a frame that extends down from the bleed guide above the top of the page to the horizontal guide you set at the 34-pica location and over to the column guide at the 29p1.8 position.

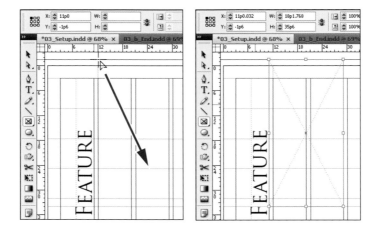

6 Now you'll add a placeholder graphics frame to the master page on the right. Follow the preceding steps 2 through 5, except now drag a guide down to the 46-pica location on the right master page.

7 Draw a rectangular frame that extends horizontally from the spine along the left edge of the right master page to the bleed guide outside the right edge of the page. The top edge of the frame should align with the guide you just created in the previous step; the bottom edge should align with the bleed guide below the bottom of the page.

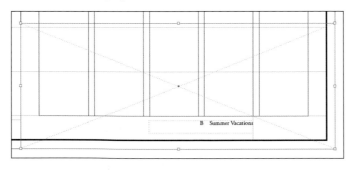

8 Choose File > Save.

Wrapping text around a graphic

You can apply a text wrap to a placeholder frame on a master page to cause text to wrap around the frame on any page to which the master page is applied.

1   Using the Selection tool (➤), select the placeholder graphics frame that you created on the left master page.

2   Choose Window > Text Wrap to open the Text Wrap panel, and then select Wrap Around Bounding Box (▣) so that the text wraps around the frame.

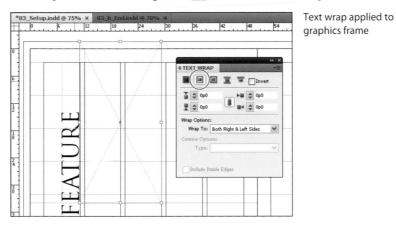

Text wrap applied to graphics frame

3   Make sure that the Make All Settings The Same icon (⚙) is deselected in the Text Wrap panel, and then type **1p0** in the Bottom Offset box. Press Enter or Return. A visible wrap boundary appears at the bottom of the frame.

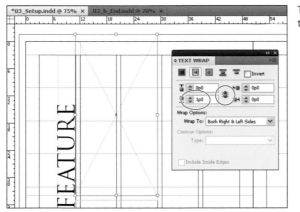

Text wrap offset applied to graphics frame

4   Using the Selection tool (➤), select the placeholder graphics frame that you created on the right master page. Repeat step 3, but this time type **1p0** in the Top Offset box, leaving all of the other offset settings at 0p0. Press Enter or Return. A visible wrap boundary appears at the top of the frame.

5   Close the Text Wrap panel, and choose File > Save.

Drawing colored shapes

You'll now add a background frame for the title bar and another background frame across the top of the right master page. These elements appear on all pages to which the B-Placeholder master has been applied.

1   Choose Edit > Deselect All because the next steps do not require a selected object.

2   Choose View > Fit Page In Window and scroll so that you can see the entire right master page.

3   Select the Selection tool (▸) and drag a new guide from the horizontal ruler to the 16-pica location. Then click a blank area to deselect the guide.

When you are selecting and dragging frames, it's common to accidentally move guides.

▶ **Tip:** The Lock Guides command is also available from the context menu when right-clicking (Windows) or Control-clicking (Mac OS) a blank area of the page or pasteboard.

4   Choose View > Grids & Guides > Lock Guides.

5   Choose Window > Swatches to open the Swatches panel.

6   Select the Rectangle Frame tool (⊠) in the Tools panel. Position the pointer where the bleed guides intersect outside the upper-right corner of the right master page. Click and drag, drawing a frame that extends horizontally to the spine and vertically to the horizontal guide at the 16-pica position.

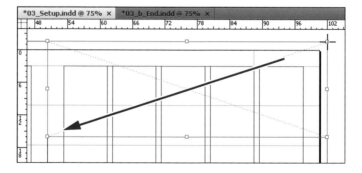

7 In the upper-left corner of the Swatches panel, click the Fill box (■), and then click [Paper] in the list of swatches to set [Paper] as the placeholder color for the frame. Notice that the Fill box is also in front of the Stroke box in the Tools panel.

8 Scroll so that you can see the entire left master page.

9 Still using the Rectangle Frame tool (⊠), position the pointer where the bleed guides intersect outside the upper-left corner of the left master page. Click and drag, drawing a frame that extends horizontally to the right edge of the first column and vertically to the blecd guide below the bottom of the page. Repeat step 7 to fill the frame with [Paper]. Notice that the new frame blocks the placeholder text from view.

10 With the new frame still selected, choose Object > Arrange > Send To Back.

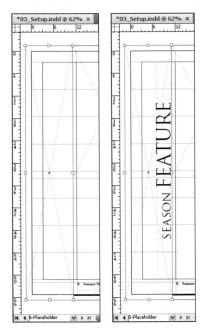

11 Choose Edit > Deselect All, and then choose File > Save.

Creating text frames with columns

You have added placeholders for the title, graphic, and two background frames for the B-Placeholder master pages. To finish the B-Placeholder master, you'll create the text frames for the story text.

1 Select the Type tool (**T**), and on the left master page, position your pointer at the intersection of the right and bottom margin guides. Drag to draw a text frame that is eight rows tall and four columns wide. The frame should extend vertically to the top margin and horizontally to the left margin of the second column.

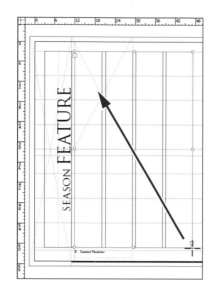

2   Choose View > Fit Spread In Window. Close or hide any panels, as necessary, to view the spread.

3   On the right master page, position your pointer at the intersection of the left margin and the top of the third row, and then drag to create a text frame that is six rows tall and four columns wide, snapping to the guides as shown.

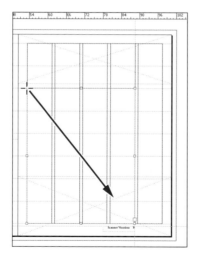

Next, you'll make sure that each of the main story text frames has two columns.

4   Select the Selection tool (![arrow]), and Shift-click to select the two text frames you just created on the left and right master pages.

5   Choose Object > Text Frame Options. In the Columns section of the Text Frame Options dialog box, change the value in the Number box to 2. Click OK to close the Text Frame options dialog box and apply your change.

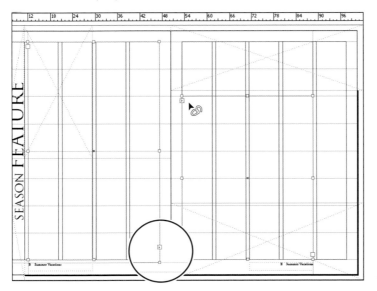

Each of the main story text frames includes two columns of text. To make the text flow from one text frame to the next, you will thread the frames.

6 With the Selection tool (✸), click the out port in the lower-right corner of the text frame on the left master page. Position the pointer over the text frame on the master page on the right so that it changes from a loaded text icon (▦) to a thread icon (⌘), and then click. The text frames are now linked.

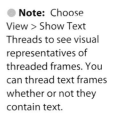

● **Note:** Choose View > Show Text Threads to see visual representatives of threaded frames. You can thread text frames whether or not they contain text.

7 Choose File > Save.

Applying the masters to document pages

Now that you have created all of the master pages, it's time to apply them to the pages in your layout. By default, all of the document pages are formatted with the A-Grid - Footer master. You will apply the B-Placeholder master to the appropriate pages. You can apply master pages to document pages by dragging master page icons onto document page icons or by using a Pages panel menu option. In large documents, you may find it easier to display the page icons horizontally in the Pages panel.

1 Choose Panel Options from the Pages panel menu.

2 In the Pages section of the Panel Options dialog box, deselect Show Vertically, and choose Small from the Size menu. Click OK.

3 If all master page icons are not visible, position your pointer over the horizontal bar, located beneath the master pages. Click and drag down so that you can see all of the master pages. Then position the pointer in the lower-right corner of the Pages panel; click and drag the lower-right corner of the Pages panel down as far as necessary until you can see all of the pages.

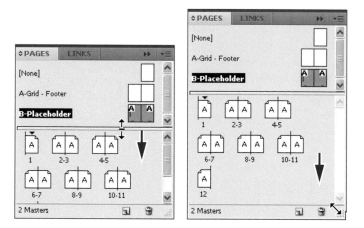

Now that you can see all of the page icons in the Pages panel, you'll apply the B-Placeholder master to pages in the document that will contain articles.

4 Click the B-Placeholder name, drag the name down, and position it on the lower-left corner of the page 6 icon or the lower-right corner of the page 7 icon. When a box appears around both page icons representing the spread, release the mouse button.

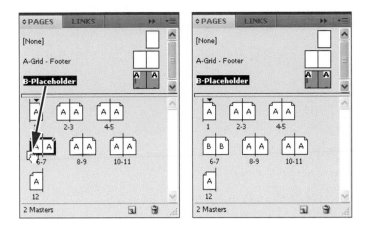

The B-Placeholder master pages are applied to pages 6 and 7, as indicated by the letter B in the page icons. Instead of dragging the B-Placeholder master to the remaining spreads, you'll use a different method to apply master pages.

5 Choose Apply Master To Pages from the Pages panel menu. From the Apply Master menu, choose B-Placeholder. In the To Pages box, type **8-11**. Click OK.

Notice that pages 6–11 in the Pages panel are now formatted with the B-Placeholder master. Page 12 requires individual formatting without page numbering, so no master page formatting is required for this page.

6 In the Pages panel, click and drag the [None] master page down onto the page 12 icon. Release the mouse button when a box appears around the page icon.

Make sure that the A-Grid - Footer master is assigned to pages 1–5 and the B-Placeholder master is assigned to pages 6–11; page 12 should have no master page assigned to it.

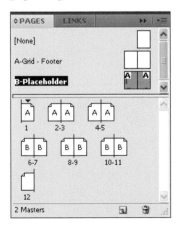

7 Choose File > Save.

Adding sections to change page numbering

The magazine you're working on requires introductory material that is numbered with lowercase Roman numerals (i, ii, iii, and so on). You can use different kinds of page numbering by adding a section. You'll start a new section on page 2 to create Roman-numeral page numbering, and then you'll start another section on page 6 to revert to Arabic numerals and restart the numbering sequence.

1 In the Pages panel, double-click the page 2 icon.

2 Choose Numbering & Section Options from the Pages panel menu. In the New Section dialog box, make sure that Start Section and Automatic Page Numbering are selected.

3 Choose i, ii, iii, iv. . . from the Style menu in the Page Numbering section of the dialog box. Click OK.

4 Examine the page icons in the Pages panel. Starting with page 2, the numbers now appear as Roman numerals in the footers of the pages.

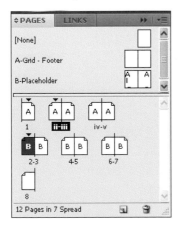

The triangle above page ii indicates the start of a section.

Now you'll specify that the document uses Arabic numbers from page 6 through the end of the document.

5 Select page 6 (vi) in the Pages panel by clicking once.

6 Choose Numbering & Section Options from the Pages panel menu.

7 In the New Section dialog box, make sure that Start Section is selected.

8 Select Start Page Numbering At, and type **2** to start the section numbering with page 2.

9 In the Style menu, select 1, 2, 3, 4. . . and click OK.

● **Note:** Single-clicking a page icon targets the page for editing purposes. If you want to navigate to a page, double-click the page in the Pages panel.

Now your pages are properly renumbered. Notice that a black triangle appears above pages 1, ii, and 2 in the Pages panel, indicating the start of a new section.

10 Choose File > Save.

Adding new pages

You can add new pages to your existing document. You're going to add two additional pages.

1 In the Pages panel menu, choose Insert Pages.

2 Type **2** in the Pages box, choose At End Of Document from the Insert menu, and then choose B-Placeholder from the Master menu.

3 Click OK. Two pages are added to the end of the document, using B-Placeholder as the master.

Arranging and deleting pages

In the Pages panel, you can arrange the sequence of pages and delete extra pages.

1 In the Pages panel, double-click the page 8 icon, and then click and drag it to the right of the page 10 icon. When you see a black bar to the right of page 10, release the mouse button. Page 8 is moved to the position of page 10, and page 9 and 10 are moved to the positions of 8 and 9, respectively.

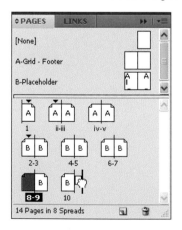

2 Double-click the page numbers beneath the spread icon for pages 8 and 9 to select both pages.

3 Click the Delete Selected Pages button at the bottom of the panel. Pages 8 and 9 are deleted from the document.

Placing text and graphics on the document pages

Now that the framework of the 12-page publication is in place, you're ready to format the individual articles. To see how the changes you made to the master pages affect the document pages, you'll add text and graphics to the spread on pages 2 and 3.

1   In the Pages panel, double-click the page 2 icon (not page ii) to center it in the document window.

Notice that since the B-Placeholder master is assigned to page 2, the page includes the grid, the footer, and the placeholder frames from the B-Placeholder master.

To import text and graphics from other applications, such as images from Adobe Photoshop or text from Microsoft Word, you'll use the Place command.

2   Choose File > Place. Open the Lesson_03 folder in your InDesignCIB folder, and double-click the 03_d.psd file.

The pointer becomes a loaded graphics icon (📷) and shows a preview of the image.

3   Position the loaded graphics icon over the graphics frame placeholder on page 2 so that the icon appears in parentheses (📷), and then click. You may need to move the loaded graphics icon toward the top of the placeholder frame to see the icon in parentheses.

4   To position the image correctly, choose Object > Fitting > Center Content. Click a blank area of the page to deselect all objects or choose Edit > Deselect All.

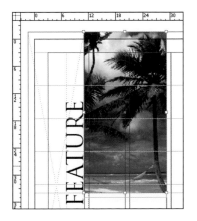

▶ **Tip:** Parentheses appear when InDesign recognizes a preexisting frame beneath the icon when importing text or graphics into your layout. InDesign uses the existing frame rather than create a new text or graphics frame.

5 Repeat steps 2 through 4, except this time place the image 03_e.psd into the bottom placeholder frame on page 3. You may need to move the loaded graphics icon toward the right of the placeholder frame to see the icon in parentheses. Instead of centering content, choose Object > Fitting > Fill Frame Proportionally.

6 To be sure that nothing is selected, choose Edit > Deselect All. Then choose File > Place and double-click 03_c.doc, which is a text file that was created in Microsoft Word.

Tip: If a frame is selected when you place a file, the contents of the file are added to the selected frame. You can avoid this by deselecting objects prior to importing or by deselecting Replace Selected Item in the Place dialog box when importing a file.

The pointer changes to a loaded text icon (⯐), with a preview of the first few lines of text that you are placing.

With the loaded text icon, you can drag to create a text frame or click inside an existing text frame. When you move the loaded text icon over an existing text frame, the icon appears in parentheses.

You can click to insert the text into an individual, unthreaded frame, or you can click to autoflow the text into threaded frames, which you'll do next.

Note: In previous versions of InDesign, it was necessary to hold down the Shift key when placing text to automatically flow the text into threaded placeholder frames. The new Smart Text Reflow controls in the Type pane of the InDesign CS4 Preferences dialog let you control how text flows when placed.

7 Position the loaded text icon anywhere inside the text frame on the bottom of page 2. Notice that parentheses are displayed around the icon. Click the mouse.

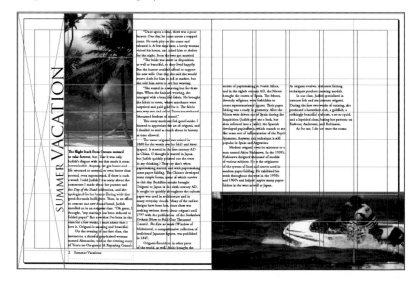

The text flows into the threaded text frames on pages 2 and 3, wrapping around the images according to how you have set up text wrap on the master pages. If these frames had not been threaded, the text would have flowed only into the text frame on page 2 and would have resulted in overset text. In that situation, you could still manually flow the text from page 2 to 3.

● **Note:** If your text did not flow as indicated, choose Edit > Undo Place and reposition the pointer so that it is in the two-column text frame.

8 Choose Edit > Deselect All.

9 Choose File > Save.

Overriding master page items on document pages

The placeholders you added to the master pages appear on the document pages. InDesign prevents you from accidentally moving or deleting these objects by requiring you to override or detach the master items to select and edit those items on document pages. You'll now replace the word "SEASON" with "SUMMER" and "FEATURE" with "VACATION." Editing this text requires you to select the master page frame that contains the text "SEASON FEATURE." You'll also color the text.

1 To make sure that you're on page 2, select page 2 from the page box in the lower-left corner of the document window.

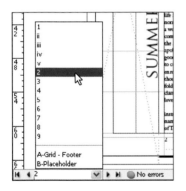

2 If necessary, adjust your view so that you can see the "SEASON FEATURE" text on page 2. With the Selection tool (▶), try to select this text frame by clicking it.

You cannot select master page items on the document pages simply by clicking. However, by holding down a modifier key on your keyboard, you can then select a master page object such as this text frame.

3 Hold down Shift+Ctrl (Windows) or Shift+Command (Mac OS), and click the title placeholder frame on the left side of page 2 to select it.

4 Using the Type tool (**T**), double-click the word "SEASON" to select it, and then type **SUMMER.**

5 Double-click the word "SUMMER" to select it. In the Swatches panel, select the Fill box (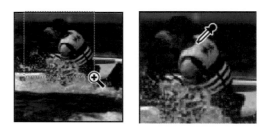), then choose [Paper] to make the text white.

6 Using the Type tool (**T**), double-click the word "FEATURE," and type **VACATION**. Select the word VACATION by double-clicking it.

Next you'll use the Eyedropper tool to choose a color in an imported graphic and apply it to the selected text, and then you'll use the Eyedropper tool to apply color to other elements.

7 Double-click the page 3 icon in the Pages panel to center the page in the window. In the Tools panel, select the Zoom tool (🔍) and drag a marquee around the image of the man with the life vest to magnify the image.

8 In the Tools panel, make sure that the Text Fill box (📝) is showing, and then select the Eyedropper tool (🖊). Move the tip of the Eyedropper tool over the yellow area in the life vest and click to select it. The color you click becomes the fill color that is applied to the text you have selected.

9 Choose View > Fit Spread In Window. Notice that even though you've used other tools, the text is still selected. Choose Edit > Deselect All.

⬤ **Note:** Although you created these frames on a master page, they appear on the document page you are currently formatting because the master page was applied to this document page.

10 Select the Selection tool (▶), and press Shift+Ctrl (Windows) or Shift+Command (Mac OS) and click the wide rectangle frame you created at the top of page 3 to select it. Use the Eyedropper tool as you did in step 8 to fill the frame with the same yellow color. Choose Edit > Deselect All.

11 Again, select the Selection tool (▶). Press Shift+Ctrl (Windows) or Shift+Command (Mac OS) and click the tall rectangular frame at the leftmost edge of page 2 to select it. This time use the Eyedropper tool to select a dark blue color from the palm tree image on page 2 as the fill color.

12 Choose Edit > Deselect All.

13 Choose File > Save.

Rotating Spreads

In some cases, you may want to rotate all content on a page or spread to make it easier for readers to view a particular layout. For example, a standard-sized magazine with portrait-oriented pages might require a calendar page with a landscape orientation. You could lay out such a page by rotating all objects 90°, but then you would have to turn your head or rotate your monitor to modify the layout and edit text. To make editing easier, you can rotate—and unrotate—spreads. For an example of this feature, open the 03_End.Indd document in the Lesson _03 folder.

1   In the Pages panel, double-click page 4 to select it, and center it in the document window.

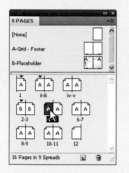

2   Choose View > Rotate Spread > 90° CW.

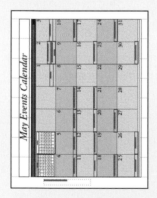

After you rotate the spread (right), it's easier to work with the objects on the page.

3   Choose View > Rotate Spread > Clear Rotation.

4   Close the document without saving changes.

Viewing the completed spread

Now you'll hide guides and frames to see what the completed spread looks like.

1 Choose View > Fit Spread In Window and hide any panels, if necessary.

▶ **Tip:** To hide or show all panels, including the Tools panel and Control panel, press Tab.

2 Choose View > Screen Mode > Preview to hide all guides, grids, frame edges, and the pasteboard.

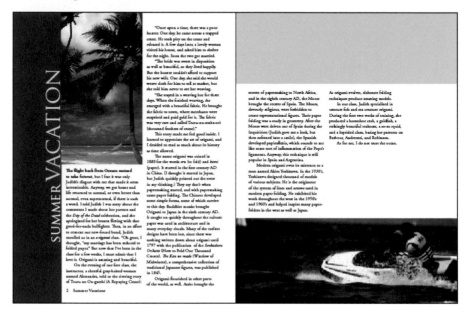

You have formatted enough of the 12-page document to see how adding objects to the master pages helps you maintain a consistent design throughout your document.

3 Choose File > Save.

Congratulations. You have finished the lesson.

Exploring on your own

A good way to reinforce the skills you've learned in this lesson is to experiment with them. Try some of the following exercises. They'll give you more practice with InDesign techniques.

1 Place another photograph in the third column on page 3. Use the 03_f.psd image that is inside the Lesson_03 folder. To see how to complete this step, open the 03_End.indd file in the Lesson_03 folder and use the Pages panel to display page 3.

2 Add a pull quote. Using the Type tool (**T**), drag a text frame over the yellow rectangle on page 3. Type **There's no place like a sunny beach for summer fun...**. Triple-click the text, and use the Control panel or Character panel to format the text using the font, size, style, and color of your choice.

3 Use the Rotate tool in the Tools panel to rotate the "title" text frame, experimenting with different corners or edges of the reference point locator (⊞) in the Control panel, and notice the difference in the results.

4 Create a new set of master pages for a spread that you could use for the continuation of this story. Name the new master page **C-Next** and choose A-Grid - Footer from the Based On Master menu. Then create placeholder frames for the text and graphics, giving the spread a different arrangement from the B-Placeholder master pages. When you finish, apply the C-Next master pages to pages 4 and 5 of your document.

Review questions

1 What are the advantages of adding objects to master pages?

2 How do you change the page numbering scheme?

3 How do you select a master page item on a document page?

Review answers

1 By adding objects such as guides, footers, and placeholder frames to master pages, you can maintain a consistent layout on the pages to which the master is applied.

2 In the Pages panel, select the page icon where you want new page numbering to begin. Then choose Numbering & Section Options from the Pages panel menu and specify the new page numbering scheme.

3 Hold down Shift+Ctrl (Windows) or Shift+Command (Mac OS), and then click the object to select it. You can then edit, delete, or manipulate the object.

Getting started

● **Note:** If you have not already copied the resource files for this lesson onto your hard disk from the Adobe InDesign CS4 Classroom in a Book CD, do so now. See "Copying the Classroom in a Book files" on page 2.

In this lesson, you'll work on a pair of spreads that make up a four-page newsletter. You'll add text and images and adjust the layout to get just the design you want.

1 To ensure that the preference and default settings of your Adobe InDesign CS4 program match those used in this lesson, move the InDesign Defaults file to a different folder following the procedure in "Saving and restoring the InDesign Defaults file" on page 2.

2 Start Adobe InDesign CS4. To ensure that the panels and menu commands match those used in this lesson, choose Window > Workspace > [Advanced], and then choose Window > Workspace > Reset Advanced. To begin working, you'll open an InDesign document that is already partially completed.

3 Choose File > Open, and open the 04_a_Start.indd file in the Lesson_04 folder, located inside the Lessons folder within the InDesignCIB folder on your hard disk.

● **Note:** As you work through the lesson, move panels or change the magnification to a level that works best for you.

4 Choose File > Save As, rename the file 04_Frames.indd, and save it in the Lesson_04 folder.

5 To see what the finished document looks like, open the 04_b_End.indd file in the same folder. You can leave this document open to act as a guide as you work. When you're ready to resume working on the lesson document, choose Window > 04_Frames.indd.

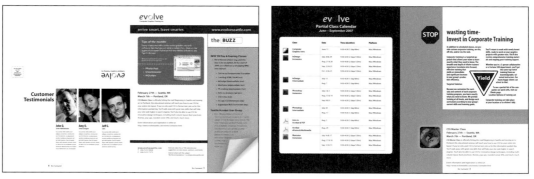

The newsletter in this lesson contains two facing-page spreads: The spread on the left contains pages 4 (the back page) and page 1 (the cover); the spread on the right contains pages 2 and 3 (the center spread). (The Numbering & Section Options command [Layout menu] was used to start the layout on an even-numbered page.)

Working with layers

By default, a new document contains just one layer (named Layer 1). You can rename the layer and add more layers at any time as you create your document. Placing objects on different layers lets you organize them for easy selection and editing. In the Layers panel, you can select, display, edit, and print different layers individually, in groups, or all together.

The 04_Frames.indd document has two layers. You'll experiment with these layers to learn how the order of the layers and the placement of objects on layers can greatly affect the design of your document.

About Layers

Every InDesign document includes at least one named layer, and you can add as many layers as you want. Think of layers as transparent sheets stacked on top of each other. When you create an object, you can place it on the layer of your choice, and you can move objects between layers. Each layer contains its own set of objects.

By using multiple layers, you can create and edit specific areas or kinds of content in your document without affecting other areas or kinds of content. For example, if a document prints slowly because it contains many large graphics, you can use one layer for only the text in the document; then, when it's time to proofread the text, you can hide all other layers and quickly print only the text layer. You can also use layers to display alternate design ideas for the same layout, or different versions of advertisements for different regions.

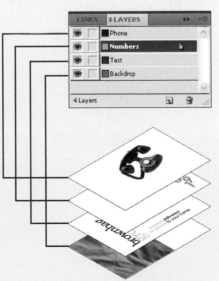

1 Click the Layers panel tab, or choose Window > Layers.

2 If the text layer is not selected in the Layers panel, click to select it. Notice that a pen icon (✒) appears to the right of the layer name. The pen icon indicates that this layer is the target layer, and anything you import or create is placed on this layer. The highlight indicates that the layer is selected.

3 Click the eye icon (👁) to the far left of the Graphics layer name. All the objects on the Graphics layer are hidden. The eye icon lets you hide or display individual layers. When you turn the visibility of a layer off, the eye disappears. Click the empty box again to display the layer contents.

Click to hide layer contents.

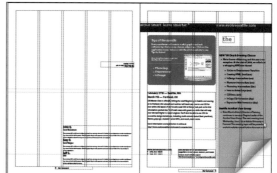
The spread with hidden content.

4 Using the Selection tool (▶), click the screen shot image in the orange box of the "Tips of the month!" area on the right page.

In the Layers panel, you'll notice that the Text layer is selected and a small blue square appears to the right of the layer name. This indicates that the selected object belongs to this layer. You can move objects from one layer to another by dragging this square between layers in the panel.

5 In the Layers panel, drag the small blue square from the Text layer to the Graphics layer. The image now belongs to the Graphics layer and appears at the top of the stacking order in the document.

Select the image and drag its icon.   Result.

6 Click the layer lock box (🔒) to the left of the Graphics layer to lock the layer.

7 Using the Selection tool (⬉), click to select the evolve logo at the top of the right page. You cannot select the graphic because it is on the Graphics layer, and the Graphics layer is locked.

Next you will make a new layer and move existing content to it.

8 At the bottom of the Layers panel, click the Create New Layer button.

9 Double-click the name of the new layer (it is most likely named Layer 3) to open the Layer Options dialog box. Change the name to **Background**, and click OK.

10 In the Layers panel, drag the Background layer to the bottom of the layer stack. A line appears when you move the cursor below the Text layer, indicating that the layer is moved to the bottom.

► **Tip:** To create a new layer and name it at the same time, hold down the Alt key (Windows) or Option key (Mac OS) and click the Create New Layer button in the Layers panel. This opens the New Layer dialog box automatically.

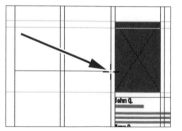

The Background layer has no content yet, which you will address later in the lesson.

11 Choose File > Save.

Creating and editing text frames

In most cases, text is placed inside a frame. The size and location of a text frame determine how the text appears on a page. Text frames can be created with the Type tool and edited using a variety of tools—as you'll try out in this part of the lesson.

Creating and resizing text frames

Now you'll create your own text frame, adjust its size, and then resize another frame.

1 In the Layers panel, click the Text layer to select it. Any content created will be placed on the Text layer now.

2 Select the Type tool ($\mathbf{T}$) in the Tools panel. Open the Pages panel by clicking its tab on the right side of the workspace. Double-click the page icon for the back page (page 4). (It's the left page of the first facing-page spread.)

▶ **Tip:** InDesign CS4 displays live Width and Height values as you drag. These values, as well as X and Y values, are also displayed in the Control panel and the Transform panel (Window > Object & Layout > Transform).

3 Position the pointer where the left edge of the first column meets the horizontal guide at approximately 34p on the vertical ruler. Drag to create a frame that snaps to the right edge of the second column and has a height of about 8p.

Using Smart Guides

New in InDesign CS4, the Smart Guides feature gives you great flexibility in precisely creating and positioning objects. With Smart Guides, you can snap objects to the edges and centers of other objects, to the vertical and horizontal centers of pages, and to the midpoints of columns and gutters. Plus, Smart Guides draw dynamically to provide visual feedback while you work.

You can enable four Smart Guide options in the Guides & Pasteboard preferences (Edit > Preferences > Guides & Pasteboard [Windows] or InDesign > Preferences > Guides & Pasteboard [Mac OS]):

*   Align To Object Center. Causes object edges to snap to the center of other objects on a page or spread when you create or move an object.

*   Align To Object Edges. Causes object edges to snap to the edge of other objects on a page or spread when you create or move an object.

*   Smart Dimensions. Causes the width, height, or rotation of an object to snap to the dimensions of other objects on a page or spread when you create, resize, or rotate an object.

*   Smart Spacing. Lets you quickly arrange objects so that the space between them is equal.

The Smart Guides command (View > Grids & Guides > Smart Guides) lets you turn Smart Guides on and off. Smart Guides are enabled by default.

To familiarize yourself with Smart Guides, create a new multicolumn one-page document. (In the New Document dialog box, specify a value greater than 1 in the Columns Number field.)

1   In the Tools panel, select the Rectangle Frame tool (). Click the left margin guide and drag to the right. As the pointer moves across the page, notice that a guide is displayed when the pointer reaches the middle of a column, the midpoint between a gutter, and the horizontal center of the page. Release the mouse button when a Smart Guide appears.

2   With the Rectangle Frame tool still selected, click the top margin guide and drag downward. Notice that when the pointer reaches the top edge, center, and bottom edge of the first object you created, as well as the vertical center of the page, a Smart Guide appears.

3   In an empty area of the page, create one more object with the Rectangle Frame tool. Drag the mouse slowly and watch carefully. Smart Guides appear when the pointer reaches the edge or center of any of the other objects. Also, when the height or width of the new object equals the height or width of either of the other two objects, a vertical or horizontal (or both) line appears next to the object you're creating and the object with the matching height or width.

4   Close the document without saving changes.

4 In the new text frame, type **Customer**, press Shift+Enter (Windows) or Shift+Return (Mac OS) to create a forced line break, and then type **Testimonials**. Click four times to select all the text in the frame.

Now you'll apply a paragraph style to the text.

5 Click the Paragraph Styles panel tab or choose Type > Paragraph Styles. Alt-click (Windows) or Option-click (Mac OS) the style named Testimonials.

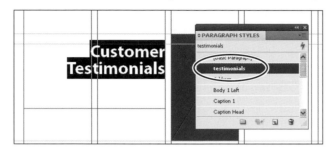

Read more about styles in Lesson 8, "Working with Styles."

6 Using the Selection tool (↖), double-click the bottom center handle of the selected text frame to fit the frame to the text vertically.

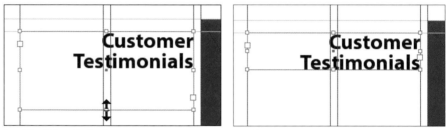

Double-click to fit the frame.   Result.

7 On the page to the right (page 1; the cover of the newsletter), use the Selection tool (↖) to select the text frame below "The Buzz" text. The frame contains the text, "NEW '09. . .".

8 Drag the center bottom handle downward to resize the height of the frame until the bottom edge snaps to the margin guide at the bottom of the page. When the pointer approaches the margin guide, the arrows change in appearance, indicating that the frame edge is about to snap to the guide. When you release the mouse button, the previously hidden overset text appears.

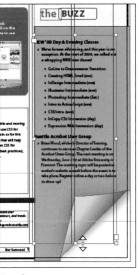

Resize the frame by
dragging the center point.

Result.

9 Choose File > Save.

Reshaping a text frame

So far, you've resized a text frame with the Selection tool by dragging a handle.
Now, you'll reshape the frame using the Direct Selection tool to adjust an anchor
point.

1 If the text frame in the rightmost column on the newsletter's cover (page 1) is
still not selected, use the Selection tool (▶) to select it now.

2 In the Tools panel, select the Direct Selection tool (▷). Four very small anchor
points now appear at the corners of the selected text frame. The anchor points
are hollow, indicating that none of them is selected.

▶ **Tip:** To resize a text
frame and the text
characters inside it
simultaneously, use the
Scale tool (▦), or hold
down Ctrl (Windows) or
Command (Mac OS) as
you drag a text frame
handle.

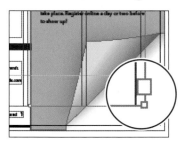
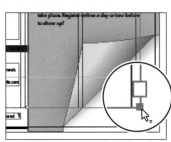

Unselected anchor point.

Selected anchor point.

3 Select the anchor point in the lower-right corner of the text frame and drag it
upward until it snaps to the horizontal guide at 48p0. (After you start dragging,
you can hold down the Shift key to restrict any horizontal movement.)

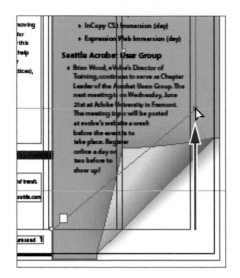

Be sure to drag only the anchor point—if you drag just above or to the left of the anchor point, you'll move other corners of the text frame too.

4   Press the V key to switch to the Selection tool.

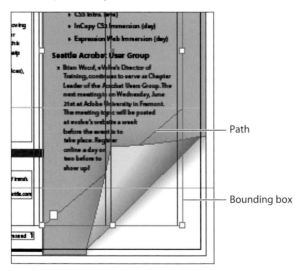

Path

Bounding box

Tip: By pressing the A or V key, you can toggle between the Selection and Direct Selection tools. These are just two of the many keyboard shortcuts available in InDesign. For more shortcuts, refer to "Keyboard shortcuts" in InDesign Help.

5   Deselect all objects, and then choose File > Save.

Creating multiple columns

Now you'll take an existing text frame and convert it to a multiple-column text frame.

1   Use the Selection tool (➤) to select the text frame on the back page of the newsletter (page 4) that begins with "John Q." If you want, use the Zoom tool (🔍) to magnify the area you're working on.

2   Double-click the text frame to select the Type tool. This places the insertion point within the frame where you double-click. Choose Object > Text Frame Options.

3   In the Text Frame Options dialog box, type **3** in the Number box and **0p11** in the Gutter box if necessary. The gutter controls the distance between the columns. Click OK.

4   To balance the three columns of text, with the Type tool still selected, place the insertion point in front of the name "Amy O." and choose Type > Insert Break Character > Column Break. This forces "Amy O." to the top of the second column. Repeat this step after placing the insertion point before "Jeff G."

5   Choose Type > Show Hidden Characters to see the break characters (unless Show Hidden Characters is already displayed in the Type menu).

Adjusting text inset within a frame

You'll now finish the blue title bar on the cover by fitting the text nicely into the frame. By adjusting the inset between the edge of the frame and the text, you make the text easier to read.

1 Select the Selection tool (⬏), and then select the blue text frame at the top of page 1 with the text "arrive smart. leave smarter."

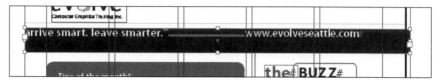

2 Choose Object > Text Frame Options. If necessary, drag the Text Frame Options dialog box aside so that you can still see the bar as you set options.

● **Note:** The Make All Settings The Same icon lets you change all of the inset values at the same time. Sometimes, however, you need to deselect it when you want to change values independently.

3 In the Text Frame Options dialog box, make sure that the Preview option is selected. Then, in the Inset Spacing section, click to deselect the Make All Settings The Same icon (🔗) so that you can change the left setting independently. Change the Left value to 3p0 to move the left margin of the text 3 picas to the right and away from the left edge of the frame.

Text Frame Options dialog box:

General | Baseline Options

Columns
Number: 1   Gutter: 1p0
Width: 48p9
☐ Fixed Column Width

Inset Spacing
Top: 0p0   Left: 3p0
Bottom: 0p0   Right: 3p9

Vertical Justification
Align: Top
Paragraph Spacing Limit: 0p0

☐ Ignore Text Wrap

☑ Preview   OK   Cancel

Vertically aligning text within a frame

You'll now align the text vertically in the blue bar.

1 Using the Selection tool (⬏), select the blue bar on the cover of the newsletter, if it is not still selected.

2 Choose Object > Text Frame Options. In the Vertical Justification section of the Text Frame Options dialog box, choose Center from the Align menu. Click OK.

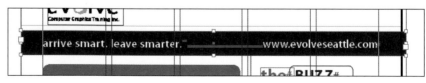

3 Choose File > Save.

Note: At times, choosing center for vertical justification may not exactly center an object in the text frame, especially for smaller text frames. You can make the object "look" centered by specifying Inset Spacing or the First Baseline settings in the Text Frame Options dialog box.

4 Click OK to save your changes and close the Text Frame Options dialog box.

Creating and editing graphics frames

Now you're ready to start adding the employees' images to the spread. In this section, you'll focus on different techniques for creating and modifying graphics frames and their contents. To start, you'll import an image and place it in your document.

Because you'll be working on graphics rather than text, your first step is to make sure that the graphics appear on the Graphics layer rather than on the Text layer. Isolating items on different layers streamlines your workflow and makes it easier to find and edit elements of your design.

Drawing a new graphics frame

To begin, you'll create a frame for the first graphic on the back page (page 4).

1 If the Layers panel is not visible, click the Layers panel tab, or choose Window > Layers.

2 In the Layers panel, click the lock icon (🔒) to unlock the Graphics layer. Lock the Text layer by clicking the box to the left of the layer name. Select the Graphics layer by clicking the name of the layer so that the new elements are assigned to this layer.

3 Display page 4 in the document window by choosing it from the page box at the bottom of the document window.

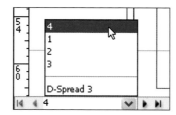

Using the guides for references, you'll add a graphics frame for the image you'll place in the next section.

4 In the Tools panel, select the Rectangle Frame tool (⊠). In the far-right column on page 4, start dragging from where the left guide of the column meets the horizontal guide halfway down the page. Continue dragging to the right edge of the column just above the "Jeff G." text.

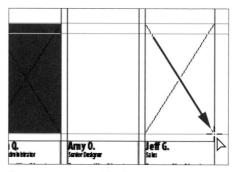

Drag to create a graphics frame.

5 Switch to the Selection tool and make sure that the graphics frame is still selected.

Placing graphics within an existing frame

Now, you'll place the first employee's image within the selected frame.

1 With the graphics frame still selected, choose File > Place and then double-click JeffG.tif in the Links folder in the Lesson_04 folder. The image appears in the graphics frame.

● **Note:** If the graphics frame isn't selected when you place the image, the pointer changes to the loaded graphics icon (🔬). In this case you could click within the frame to place the image.

Next, you'll create a copy of the graphics frame and use it as a placeholder frame for a different graphic. You'll replace the graphic of the copied frame later in the lesson.

2 Select the Selection tool (➤). Hold down the Alt key (Windows) or the Option key (Mac OS), and drag the JeffG graphic to the left until it snaps into the column directly to the left. Duplicating the graphics frame rather than creating a new frame with the Rectangle Frame tool ensures that both frames are exactly the same size.

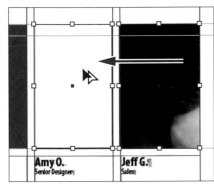

Drag-copy a graphics frame.

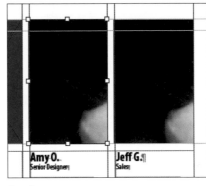

Result.

Resizing a graphics frame

The design for this page calls for the image of JeffG to extend across to the right edge of the page. Although this image is not yet the right size or shape to do that, you'll start making those adjustments now.

First, you'll stretch the frame.

1 Choose View > Fit Spread In Window so that you can see the back page (page 4) and the cover of the newsletter (page 1) in the document window. If necessary, scroll horizontally so that you can see the right edge of the back page, and hide the Layers panel by clicking the Layers tab.

2 Using the Selection tool (➤), click the JeffG graphic. Drag the right handle until the right side of the frame snaps into place against the spine (the vertical line between the back page and the cover).

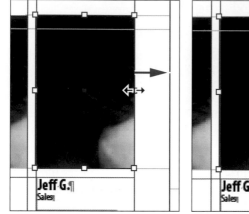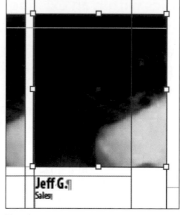

Drag the right side
of the frame to resize.

Result.

Notice that only the frame bounding box changes, when you move the edge. Within the frame, the image is cropped differently but is not affected by moving a frame edge.

3 Choose File > Save.

Resizing and moving an image within a frame

▶ **Tip:** In addition to the methods used here, you can use the context menu to resize pictures by right-clicking (Windows) or Control-clicking (Mac OS) and choosing Fitting > Fit Content Proportionally.

You have just finished resizing the graphics frame, but the image within the frame remains unchanged. You'll now resize only the image so that it fills the designated area.

The content and frame for any placed graphic are separate elements. Unlike text objects, the frame and its content each has its own bounding box. Resizing the graphic content is exactly like resizing the frame, except that you work with the bounding box for the content using the Direct Selection tool (⬚).

1 Press the A key to switch to the Direct Selection tool (⬚), and then position the pointer over the image of JeffG until the pointer appears as a hand icon (✋). Click to select the frame contents (the image itself). The bounding box changes to another color, indicating that the frame is no longer selected but the contents are.

2 Select the handle in the lower-right corner of the graphic bounding box, and then hold down the Shift key and drag to make the image smaller. Continue dragging until the image dimensions are just a bit larger than the frame.

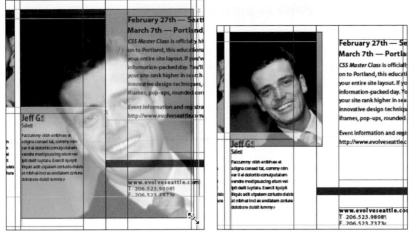

Drag bounding box of contents.   Result.

3 Position the Direct Selection tool over the JeffG image so that you see the hand icon. Drag the image with the hand icon, and notice how the area of the image that is visible within the frame changes as you drag. If you drag too far to the right, the image no longer covers the left side of the frame area. Drag the image so that the right edge of the image aligns with the right edge of the frame.

If you want to see an entire image as you move it, hold down the mouse button before dragging with the Direct Selection tool. Begin dragging when the hand icon turns into an arrow (↳). After you start dragging, you'll see a ghosted image of the hidden areas of the graphic contents, a feature called Dynamic Preview. If you don't wait for the pointer to change, you'll still see the bounding box of the graphic as you drag.

As an alternative to steps 2 and 3, you can simultaneously resize a graphics frame and its content by using the Selection tool and holding down Shift+Ctrl (Windows) or Shift+Command (Mac OS) as you drag a handle of the frame. The Shift key maintains the proportions of the bounding box so that the graphic is not distorted. Using the Shift key is optional if distorting the graphic doesn't matter to your design.

4 Make sure that the image entirely fills the frame.

5 Choose File > Save.

▶ Tip: Images resized more than 120% of their original size may not contain enough pixel information for high-resolution offset printing. Check with your print service provider if you're unsure of the resolution and scaling requirements for any documents you plan to have printed.

Replacing the contents of graphics frames

After you create the two frames, it's easy to replace the contents with other graphics or text. Your next task is to replace the copied JeffG image with another image. Because the frame and contents are independent, it's easy to swap out one image for another.

1   Using the Selection tool, click the JeffG image (the one above "Amy O.") to select it. Choose File > Place and then double-click AmyO.tif to place the new image directly into the selected frame, replacing the JeffG image. Remember that you created this frame as a placeholder earlier in the lesson by drag-copying an existing frame.

▶ **Tip:** You can also access the fitting commands from the context menu by right-clicking (Windows) or Control-clicking (Mac OS).

2   With the frame still selected, choose Object > Fitting > Fill Frame Proportionally. The graphic is resized so that it fits into the frame.

3   Choose Object > Fitting > Center Content to center the AmyO image in the frame.

Now you'll place a picture into the blue frame to the left of the AmyO image.

● **Note:** If the icon appears with a line through it (⟋⟍), the current layer is selected but locked. You cannot add objects to a locked layer. Make sure that the Graphics layer in the Layers panel is both unlocked and selected. The pointer should then appear as a loaded graphics icon so that you can proceed with this step.

4   Choose Edit > Deselect All to deselect the frame.

5   Choose File > Place, and select JohnQ.tif in the Links folder in the Lesson_04 folder. Click Open. The pointer changes to a loaded graphics icon (🖋).

6   Hover over the blue frame to the left of the AmyO image. The loaded graphics icon is surrounded by parentheses (🖋), indicating that if you click, the image will be placed in that frame. A thumbnail of the image appears under the icon. Click to place the image in the frame filled with blue.

● **Note:** If you click a blank area of the page, the image is placed on the page where you click. The image is typically placed at 100% of its original size.

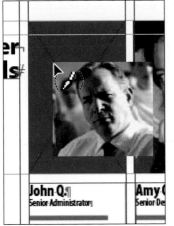

Click to place the image.

7 With the JohnQ graphic still selected, choose Object > Fitting > Fill Frame Proportionally. InDesign resizes the graphic so that it fits into the frame. To center the content, choose Object > Fitting > Center Content.

8 Choose File > Save.

Now you've placed images in several different ways in three different frames to complete the roster of images on the back page (page 4).

Changing the shape of a frame

When you resized the graphics frame using the Selection tool, the frame maintained its rectangular shape. Now you'll use the Direct Selection tool and the Pen tool to reshape a frame on page 3 (the right page of the center spread).

1 Choose 3 from the page box at the bottom of the document window. Choose View > Fit Page In Window.

2 Click the Layers panel tab, or choose Window > Layers. In the Layers panel, click the lock icon for the Text layer to unlock it.

Next, you'll change the shape of a rectangular frame and by doing so, change the background of the page.

3 Press the A key to switch to the Direct Selection tool (↖). Move the tip of the pointer over the right edge of the green frame that covers the page, and click when the pointer appears with a small diagonal line (↖). This selects the path and reveals the anchor points and center point for the frame. Leave the path selected.

4 Press the P key to switch to the Pen tool (✒).

5 Carefully position the pointer over the top edge of the frame path where it intersects with the vertical guide in the first column on page 3. When you see the Add Anchor Point tool (🖊⁺), click. A new anchor point is added. The Pen tool automatically changes to the Add Anchor Point tool when it moves over an existing path.

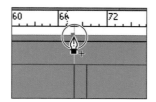

6 Move the pointer to where the horizontal guide below the text intersects with the bleed guide. Using the Pen tool, click again to add another new anchor point, then choose Edit > Deselect All.

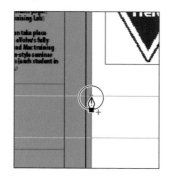

This point and the point you created in the previous step will form the corners of the irregular shape you're creating. Repositioning the anchor point at the upper-right corner of the green frame will complete the reshaping of the frame.

7 Switch to the Direct Selection tool. Click to select the upper-right corner point of the green frame. Drag the point down and to the left. When the anchor point snaps into place at the intersection of the first column and the first horizontal guide from the top of the page (at 40p9 on the vertical ruler), release the mouse button.

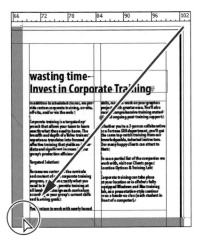

The graphics frame is now properly shaped and sized for the design.

8 Choose File > Save.

Wrapping text around a graphic

You can wrap text around the frame of an object or around the object itself. As you wrap text around the Yield sign in this exercise, you'll see the difference between wrapping text around the bounding box and around the graphic.

Your first task is to move the Yield sign graphic. For precise positioning, you can use the Smart Guides that are displayed dynamically when you create, move, or resize objects.

1 Using the Selection tool (➤), select the graphics frame with the image of a Yield sign that is off the right edge of the center spread (page 3).

2 Being careful not to select one of the handles, hold down the Shift key and move the frame to the left so that the center point of the graphic is aligned with the middle of the gutter between the two columns of text. When the center point aligns with the middle of the gutter between the first and second columns, you should see a vertical Smart Guide appear. When this guideline appears, release the mouse button.

Make sure that you have moved the frame onto the page without changing its size. Notice that the text overlaps the image. You'll change this by applying a text wrap.

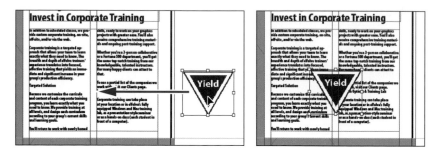

3   Choose Window > Text Wrap. In the Text Wrap panel, select Wrap Around
    Bounding Box to wrap the text around the bounding box, not around the Yield
    graphic's shape. If necessary, choose Show Options from the panel menu to
    display all of the controls in the Text Wrap panel.

Wrap text around a bounding box.   Result.

The option leaves too much white space for your desired design, so you'll try
another Text Wrap option.

● **Note:** The Wrap To
menu in the Text Wrap
panel menu is available
only if you selected the
Wrap Around Bounding
Box or Wrap Around
Object Shape at the top
of the panel.

4   Select Wrap Around Object Shape so that the text wraps around the contour
    of the graphic shape instead of the bounding box. In the Wrap Options section,
    choose Both Right & Left Sides from the Wrap To menu if it isn't already
    selected. In the Contour Options section, choose Detect Edges from the Type
    menu. Click a blank area to deselect all, or choose Edit > Deselect All.

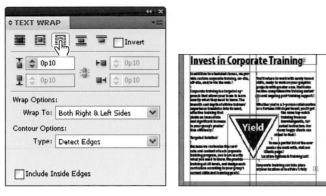

Wrap text around an object.   Result.

5 Close the Text Wrap panel, and choose File > Save.

Working with frames

In this section, you'll use various features that adjust the orientation of objects on the page and in relationship to each other. To begin, you'll use the Pathfinder panel to subtract the area of one shape from another. Then you'll work with rotation techniques and the alignment of selected objects.

Working with compound shapes

You can change the shape of an existing frame by adding to or subtracting from its area. The shape of a frame can also be changed, even if the frame already contains text or graphics. Now you'll subtract a shape from the green background, to create a new white background.

1 Choose View > Fit Page In Window to fit page 3 in the window.

2 Using the Rectangle Frame tool (⊠), draw a frame from where the right edge of the first column meets the horizontal guide at 46p6 on the vertical ruler, to the lower-right corner of the page where the red bleed guides intersect.

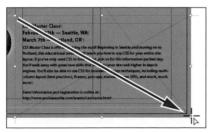

Draw a rectangle, and snap to the bleed guide corner.

3 With the Selection tool (⬉) selected, hold down the Shift key and click the green box (outside of the frame you just created) that covers a good part of page 3 to simultaneously select the new rectangle and the green box.

4 Choose Object > Pathfinder > Subtract to subtract the top shape (the new rectangle) from the green shape. The text frame at the bottom of the page is now on a white background.

CSS Master Class¶
February 27th — Seattle, WA¶
March 7th — Portland, OR¶
CSS Master Class is officially hitting the road! Beginning in Seattle and moving on to Portland, this educational seminar will teach you how to use CSS for your entire site layout. If you've only used CSS to format text, join us for this information-packed day. You'll walk away with great new skills that will help your site rank higher in search engines. You'll also be able to use CSS for innovative design techniques, including multi-column layout (best practices), iframes, pop-ups, rounded corner DIVs, and much, much more!

Event information and registration is online at:
http://www.evolveseattle.com/events/cssmaster.html¶

5 With the green box still selected, choose Object > Lock Position. This helps avoid accidental repositioning of the frame.

Converting shapes

You can change the shape of an existing frame, even if the frame already contains text or graphics. You'll try this out by adding a frame around the Stop sign, and then adjusting it.

1 In the Tools panel, hold down the mouse button on the Rectangle tool (▭) until you see hidden tools. Select the Polygon tool (⬡).

2 Click anywhere on page 3 to the left of the text "wasting time." In the Polygon dialog box, change the Polygon Width and Polygon Height to 9p0. Change the Number Of Sides to 5, and click OK.

3 With the shape on the page selected, choose File > Place, and select StopSign.tif in the Links folder in the Lesson_04 folder. Click Open.

4 Choose Object > Fitting > Center Content to center the picture in the frame.

Change the Polygon settings.

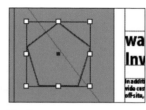

The frame.

The placed picture.

Next you'll change the shape to an eight-sided polygon, to match the Stop sign.

5 Make sure that the polygon you created is still selected, and then double-click the Polygon tool (⬠) in the Tools panel to open the Polygon Settings dialog box. Do the following, and then click OK:

• Type 8 in the Number Of Sides box.

• Leave the Star Inset at 0%.

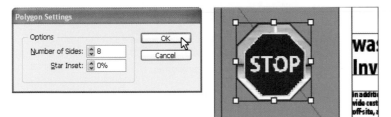

6 Using the Selection tool, select the blue world graphic on page 3. Choose Object > Convert Shape > Rounded Rectangle. Choose Edit > Deselect All.

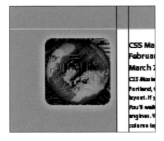

7 Choose File > Save.

Using the Position tool

The Position tool lets you manipulate a frame and its graphic content using one tool. Typically, you would use the Direct Selection tool to move a graphic within a graphics frame. You could then manipulate the position of the frame by switching to the Selection tool and moving the frame to its new position.

With the Position tool, you can perform either task without switching between two tools. You can still use the Direct Selection tool to select and modify individual points of frames.

1 Using the Selection tool (▶), click in the middle of the Stop sign image to select it. If you want, use the Zoom tool (🔍) to magnify the area you're working on.

2 Drag the upper-left corner of the selected frame so that the top and left frame edges coincide with the edges of the Stop sign. Similarly, drag the lower-right corner of the frame so that the bottom and right frame edges coincide with the Stop sign.

Dragging the upper-left corner.   Dragging the lower-right corner.

3 Hold down the mouse button on the Direct Selection tool (↖) and select the Position Tool (✋) from the menu of hidden tools that appears.

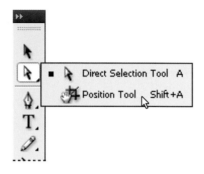

▶ **Tip:** To move an object in small increments, hold down Shift+Ctrl (Windows) or Shift+Command (Mac OS) and press an arrow key. To move an object in larger increments, hold down just the Shift key and press an arrow key.

4 Click the Stop sign image on page 3. Notice that your pointer changes to the Hand tool (✋) when your pointer is over the graphic contents of the frame. Using the arrow keys, move the image within the frame so that it looks more centered.

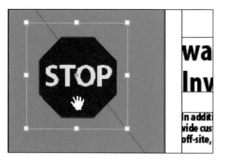

● **Note:** If you accidentally resize the frame, choose Edit > Undo and try again. You just want to move the frame closer to the right edge of the green box.

5 Position the pointer over the edge of the red Stop sign image. The pointer now has a dot (↖.), indicating that if you click, a frame will be selected. Click the frame and drag it to the right so that it is closer to the edge of the green box.

Transforming and aligning objects

Various tools and commands in InDesign let you modify an object's size or shape, and change its orientation on the page. All transformations—rotating, scaling, shearing, and reflecting—are available in the Transform and Control panels, where you can precisely specify transformations. You can also align or distribute objects horizontally or vertically along the selection, margins, page, or spread.

You'll experiment with some of these features now.

Rotating an object

InDesign features several options for rotating objects. In this part of the lesson, you'll use the Control panel to rotate the world image.

1   Using the Selection tool (▸), select the blue image of the world at the bottom of page 3.

2   In the Control panel, make sure that the center point is selected on the reference point locator (⊞) so that the object rotates around its center. Choose 90° from the Rotation Angle menu.

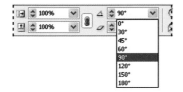

Rotating an image within its frame

You can rotate both the frame and contents in one action by selecting the object with the Selection tool and then dragging one of the handles with the Rotate tool.

When you rotated the image of the world, you used the Control panel to set a precise rotation angle. Now you'll use the Rotate tool to freely rotate the image of JeffG.

1   Choose View > Fit Page In Window, and then select page 4 in the page box at the bottom of the document window.

2   Press the A key to switch to the Direct Selection tool ($\mathbb{k}$), position the pointer over the image above the Jeff G. text, and then click.

3   In the Control panel, make sure that the center point in the reference point locator (⊞) is selected.

4   Press the R key to select the Rotate tool (⟳). Position the crosshair over one of the corner handles.

● **Note:** After you rotate the graphic, you may need to use the Direct Selection tool to reposition the graphic so that it fills the frame.

5   Hold down the mouse button until the crosshair becomes a solid arrow, to get a preview of the contents as you rotate; then drag the handle clockwise to rotate the image until you like the result. (If you don't wait for the solid arrow, only the bounding box remains visible as you drag to rotate.)

The sample uses a rotation of −20°.

Aligning multiple objects

Precise alignment is easiest when you use the Align panel. Now you'll use the Align panel to center an image on the cover of the newsletter (page 1), and then align multiple images to a selected image.

1 Choose View > Fit Page In Window, and then choose page 2 in the page box at the bottom of the document window. Using the Selection tool (▶), Shift-click the text frame at the top of the page containing the "Partial Class Calendar" text and the evolve logo above it.

2 Choose Window > Object & Layout > Align.

3 In the Align panel, choose Align To Page from the Alignment Location Options menu, and then click the Align Horizontal Centers button (⬒). The objects are now aligned to the center of the page.

Select the text frame and logo.   Align the objects.   Result.

4 Click a blank area or choose Edit > Deselect All.

5 Choose the Selection tool (▶), and then Shift-click the eight icons on the left side of the page.

6 In the Align panel, choose Align To Selection from the Alignment Location Options menu, then click the Align Horizontal Centers button (⬒).

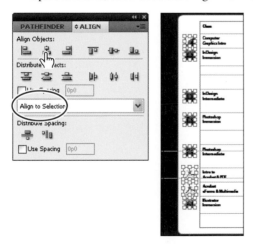

7 Choose Edit > Deselect All, and then choose File > Save.

Scaling grouped objects

When objects are grouped together, InDesign allows you to edit individual objects without ungrouping. InDesign also allows you to resize a group of objects all at once. Next you'll select two of the icons and group them together. Then you'll resize the entire group to resize both images at once.

1   Using the Selection tool (![pointer]), Shift-click each of the two Acrobat PDF icons on the left side of page 2.

2   Choose Object > Group to group them together. Hold down Shift+Ctrl (Windows) or Shift+Command (Mac OS), and with the Selection tool, drag from the upper-right corner of the group down and to the left to make the group of images roughly the same width as the orange icon below the group.

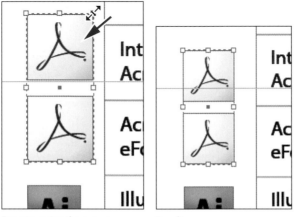

Drag to resize the group.   Result.

3   Choose Edit > Deselect All, and then choose File > Save.

Selecting and modifying grouped objects

Now that you've aligned the evolve logo at the top of page 2 to the center of the page, you'll change the fill color of some of the logo's shapes. Because they're grouped, you can select and modify them as a unit. You'll now change the fill color of just a few of the shapes without ungrouping or changing the other objects of the group.

The Direct Selection tool or menu commands lets you select individual objects in a grouped object.

● **Note:** You can choose Object > Select > Content, or right-click (Windows) or Control-click (Mac OS) the group and choose Select > Content from the context menu.

1   With the Selection tool (↖), click the evolve group at the top of page 2. If you want, use the Zoom tool (🔍) to magnify the area you're working on.

2   Click the Select Content button (⊕) in the Control panel to select one object in the group without ungrouping.

Select the group with the Selection tool.   Choose Select Content.   Result.

3   Click the Select Previous Object button (◀⊞) in the Control panel six times to select the first "e" in the word "evolve." Note the Select Next Object button that selects in the opposite direction.

Clicking Select Previous Object six times.   Result.

4   Using the Direct Selection tool (↖), hold down the Shift key and click the "v," "l," "v," and "e" letters in the logo to simultaneously select them.

5   Click the Swatches panel tab or choose Window > Swatches. Click the Fill box in the Swatches panel and choose [Paper] to fill the letter shapes with a white color.

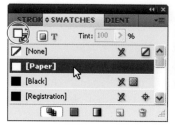

Changing the fill of the
selected shapes to [Paper].

Result.

Finishing up

Now it's time to admire your work.

1 Choose Edit > Deselect All.

2 Choose View > Fit Spread In Window.

3 At the bottom of the Tools panel, hold down the current mode button and
choose Preview from the hidden menu that appears.

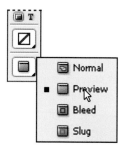

4 Press the Tab key to close all the panels at the same time. Press the Tab key
again when you are ready to show all the panels.

5 Choose File > Save.

Congratulations. You have finished the lesson.

Exploring on your own

One of the best ways to learn about frames is to experiment on your own.

In this section, you'll learn how to nest an object inside a shape you create. Follow these steps to learn more about selecting and manipulating frames.

1 Using the Direct Selection tool (☞), select and copy any image.

2 Navigate to page 2 by choosing Layout > Go To Page, type **2**, and click OK.

3 To create a new page, choose Layout > Pages > Add Page. This adds a page directly after the page you are currently on.

4 Use the Polygon tool (⬡) to draw a shape on the new page (use any number of sides and any value for the star inset). Select the shape using the Direct Selection tool, and then choose Edit > Paste Into to nest the image inside the frame. (If you choose Edit > Paste, the object is not pasted inside the selected frame.)

5 Use the Direct Selection tool to move and scale the image within the frame.

6 Use the Direct Selection tool to select and change the shape of the polygon frame.

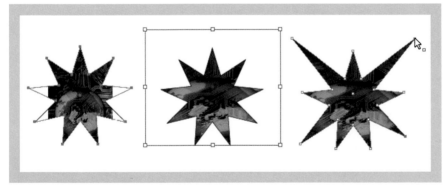

Left: Image pasted into frame, with the Direct Selection tool selected.
Center: Image moved and scaled within the frame.
Right: Polygon frame reshaped.

7 Use the Selection tool (☜) to rotate both the frame and the image. Use the Direct Selection tool to rotate only the image within the frame.

8 When you have finished experimenting, close the document without saving.

Review questions

1 When should you use the Selection tool to select an object, and when should you use the Direct Selection tool to select an object?

2 How do you resize a frame and its contents simultaneously?

3 How do you rotate a graphic within a frame without rotating the frame?

4 Without ungrouping objects, how do you select an object within a group?

Review answers

1 Use the Selection tool for general layout tasks, such as positioning and sizing objects. Use the Direct Selection tool for tasks involving drawing and editing paths or frames, for example, to select frame contents or to move an anchor point on a path.

2 To resize a frame and its contents simultaneously, select the Selection tool, hold down Ctrl (Windows) or Command (Mac OS), and then drag a handle. Hold down the Shift key to maintain the object's proportions.

3 To rotate a graphic within a frame, use the Direct Selection tool to select the graphic within the frame. Select the Rotate tool, and drag one of the handles to rotate only the graphic, not the frame.

4 To select an object within a group, select it using the Direct Selection tool.

5 IMPORTING AND EDITING TEXT

In this introduction to importing and editing text, you'll learn how to do the following:

- Enter and import text into text frames.

- Thread text frames and flow text.

- Load styles from another document.

- Apply styles to text.

- Handle a missing font.

- Find and change text and formatting.

- Add a page continuation note.

- Check the spelling in a document.

- Automatically correct misspelled words.

- Edit a spelling dictionary.

- Move text by dragging and dropping.

- Use the Story Editor.

 This lesson will take approximately 60 minutes.

Welcome to the

EXPEDITION TEA COMPANY™

Take an extraordinary adventure into the world of tea. EXPEDITION TEA COMPANY™ carries an extensive array of teas from all the major tea growing regions with some of the very best these estates have to offer. Choose from our selection of teas, gift collections, teapots, or read up on information to make your tea drinking experience more enjoyable.

Loose Leaf Teas

Browse our wide selection of premium loose leaf teas from around the world including black, green, oolong, white, rooibos and chai. Try a few samples or stock up on your favorite.

Teapots

View our collection of teapots, chosen to satisfy every taste including ceramic, cast-iron Tetsubin, stainless, silver-plate, Kyusu, and more.

Tea Gift Collections

Our tea collections are packaged in golden tins within a felt-lined keepsake wooden box with a leather handle and brass latches. Give it as a gift to your favorite tea lover or to yourself!

Tea Accessories

Tea timers, tea bags, tea strainers, scoops and a variety of other tea things to make your tea time absolutely perfect.

EXPEDITION TEA COMPANY™
www.expeditiontea.com

tea@expeditiontea.com

phone: (206) 463-9292

Expedition
TEA COMPANY

Extraordinary Adventures
into the World of Tea

2008 Premium Tea Catalog

With Adobe InDesign CS4, you can import text, thread text through frames, and edit text within the frames. Once you import text, you can create and apply styles, find and replace text and formatting, and use dynamic tools to correct spelling errors.

Getting started

In this lesson, you'll work on a 12-page catalog. Several pages of the catalog have already been completed. The final text for the catalog has been written, and you're ready to flow the copy into the document and add the finishing touches to the catalog.

Note: If you have not already copied the resource files for this lesson onto your hard disk from the Adobe InDesign CS4 Classroom in a Book CD, do so now. See "Copying the Classroom in a Book files" on page 2.

1 To ensure that the preferences and default settings of your Adobe InDesign CS4 program match those used in this lesson, move the InDesign Defaults file to a different folder following the procedure in "Saving and restoring the InDesign Defaults file" on page 2.

2 Start Adobe InDesign CS4. To ensure that the panels and menu commands match those used in this lesson, choose Window > Workspace > [Advanced], and then choose Window > Workspace > Reset Advanced.

Managing fonts

To begin working, you'll open an existing InDesign document. If this document contains fonts that are not active on your system—a common problem—you'll receive an error message about missing fonts.

Note: When you open a file that uses fonts not installed on your system, an alert message appears that indicates which fonts are missing. The text that uses missing fonts is also highlighted in pink in the document, making it clear which fonts may cause problems when printing. InDesign provides several opportunities to correct the situation.

1 Choose File > Open, and open the 05_Start.indd file in the Lesson_05 folder, located inside the Lessons folder within the InDesignCIB folder on your hard disk.

2 Click OK to close the alert message.

You will fix the problem of the missing font in the next section by replacing it with a font that is installed on your system.

3 Using the Pages panel, navigate through the pages in the document. Pages 6 through 10 have already been completed. In this lesson, you'll replace any missing fonts and complete the first five pages of the catalog, as well as pages 11 and 12.

4 Choose File > Save As, rename the file **05_Working.indd**, and save it in the Lesson_05 folder.

5 To see what the finished document looks like, open the 05_End.indd file in the same folder. If you prefer, you can leave the document open to use as a guide as you work.

6 When you're ready to resume working on the lesson document, display it by clicking its tab in the upper-left corner of the document window.

Finding and changing a missing font

When you opened the document in the previous exercise, the CaslonAntT font may have been listed as missing. If this font is active on your computer, you did not receive an alert message; but you can still follow the steps, or you can skip ahead to the next section. You will now search for text that is formatted with the CaslonAntT font and replace it with the Adobe Garamond Pro font.

1 If necessary, click the 05Working.indd tab in the upper-left corner of the window to display the catalog in progress.

2 In the Pages panel, double-click the page 2 icon (you may need to scroll in the Pages panel to see page 2). The pink highlighted text in the headline on that page indicates that the text is formatted with a missing font.

3 Choose Type > Find Font. The Find Font dialog box lists the fonts used in the document and the type of font, such as PostScript, TrueType, or OpenType. An alert icon (⚠) appears next to any missing fonts.

●**Note:** For your own projects, you may need to add the missing font to your system instead of using a different font. You can do this by installing the font on your system, using font management software to activate the font, or adding the font files to the InDesign Fonts folder. For more information, see InDesign Help.

4 Select CaslonAntT in the Fonts In Document list.

5 For the Replace With option, choose Adobe Garamond Pro from the Font Family menu. Although the font's name is Adobe Garamond Pro, you will find it alphabetized under "G" rather than "A."

6 Choose Regular from the Font Style menu.

7 Click Change All. Click Done to close the dialog box and see the replaced font in the document.

8 Choose File > Save.

Creating and entering text

You can use InDesign to enter text into your documents, or you can import text created in other applications, such as word-processing software.

You'll start by creating a text frame in which to enter text. In the gold area beneath the logo "Expedition Tea Company" on page 1, you'll create a text frame for the catalog title, "2008 Premium Tea Catalog." You'll then apply a style to this title.

1 While viewing page 1, double-click the Zoom tool (🔍) in the Tools panel to change the magnification to 100%.

2 To mark the location of the top of the headline frame that you are about to create, drag down from the horizontal ruler to create a guide at the 39p0 location. To help you position the guide, watch the Y value shown in the box next to the pointer as you drag.

3 Using the Type tool (T), position the I-bar pointer next to the left margin where it intersects with the 39p0 guide.

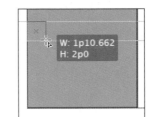

4 Drag to create a text frame in the blank area below the guide down to the bottom of the gold box. The text frame spans the first column, and the top of the frame snaps to the 39p0 guide.

After you draw a text frame using the Type tool (T), an insertion point appears, ready for you to begin typing.

▶ **Tip:** If you need to resize the frame, drag the frame handles with the Selection tool and snap to the guides. Select the Type tool and click in the frame to place an insertion point.

5 In the text frame you just created, type **2008 Premium Tea Catalog**.

To format this type, you will apply the Catalog Title style. When you apply a paragraph style, you can place an insertion point anywhere in the paragraph or select any part of the paragraph.

6 Click the Paragraph Styles panel tab to open the Paragraph Styles panel. With the insertion point anywhere in the text you just typed, select Catalog Title in the Paragraph Styles panel.

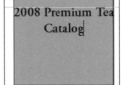

7 Choose File > Save.

Vertically aligning text

To evenly distribute the space on the top and bottom of the text frame, you will center the text vertically using vertical justification.

1 With the insertion point anywhere in the text frame you just created, choose Object > Text Frame Options.

2 In the Vertical Justification section of the Text Frame Options dialog box, choose Center from the Align menu, and click OK.

3 Choose File > Save.

Flowing text manually

The process of taking imported text, such as that from a word-processing program, and flowing it across several connected text frames is called threading text. InDesign lets you flow text manually for greater control, flow text automatically to save time, and flow text while adding pages.

You'll start by flowing text manually. First you select a file to import. You can then drag to create a frame, or you can click anywhere on the page to create a text frame in a column. In this exercise you'll use both methods to flow the text into the columns on the first page of the catalog.

1 In the Pages panel, double-click the page 1 icon to center that page in the document window. Click a blank part of the page to deselect all items.

2 Drag a guide down from the horizontal ruler to approximately the 7p3 position, which is where the bottom of your first text frame will be.

3 Choose File > Place. In the Place dialog box, make sure that Show Import Options is selected.

4 Locate and select 05_Intro.doc in the Lesson_05 folder, and click Open.

5 In the Microsoft Word Import Options dialog box, make sure that Preserve Styles And Formatting From Text And Tables is selected. This retains the formatting applied in the word-processing application. Click OK.

Using the loaded text icon, you will now create a text frame spanning the width of the middle and far-right columns. This text frame will hold the text "Welcome to the Expedition Tea Company."

6 Position the loaded text icon () in the upper-left corner of the middle column.

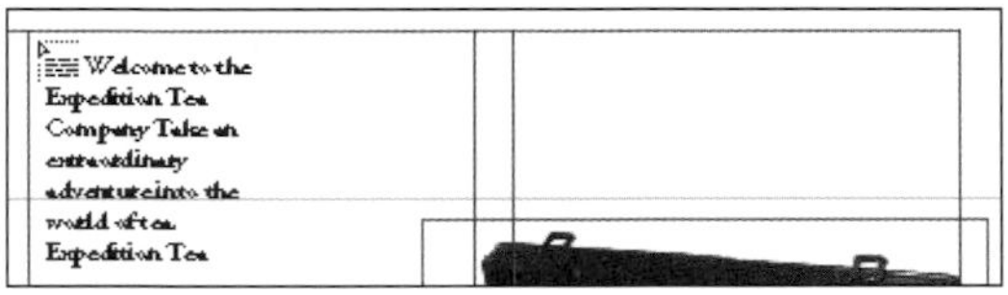

7 Drag to create a text frame across the width of the middle and far-right columns and down to the guide at 7p3.

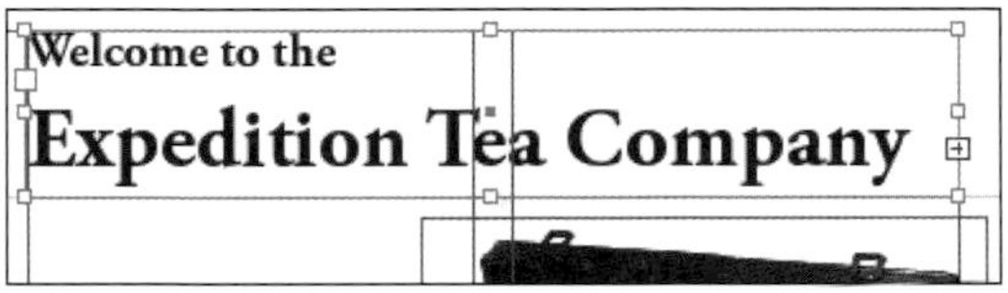
Welcome to the
Expedition Tea Company

Notice that the text frame includes an out port in the lower-right corner. The red plus sign indicates that some of the text you imported is overset, meaning that not all of the text fits into the existing text frame. You will now flow the additional text into another text frame in the middle column on page 1.

8 Using the Selection tool (), click the out port of the frame you just created.

9 Position the loaded text icon in the middle column directly below the text frame you just created, and click.

▶ **Tip:** If you change your mind and decide you don't want to flow overset text, you can click any tool in the Tools panel to cancel the loaded text icon. No text will be deleted.

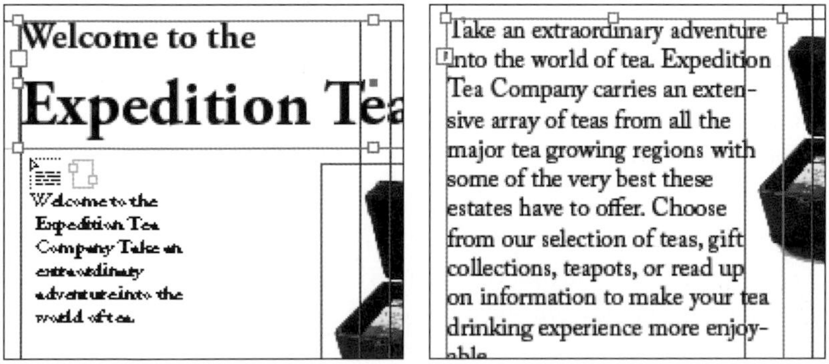
Welcome to the
Expedition Te
Take an extraordinary adventure into the world of tea. Expedition Tea Company carries an extensive array of teas from all the major tea growing regions with some of the very best these estates have to offer. Choose from our selection of teas, gift collections, teapots, or read up on information to make your tea drinking experience more enjoyable

The text flows into a new frame from where you clicked to the bottom of the middle column. The out port in the new text frame contains a red plus sign, again indicating that there is still overset text.

10 Using the Selection tool (▸), click the out port of the frame you just created and then click directly under the image of the wooden tea box to flow the rest of the text into the far-right column.

● **Note:** While you can thread text into separate frames for each column, you can also work with one large frame that is divided into multiple columns using Object > Text Frame Options. (You do this in a later exercise in this lesson.) Each method has its advantages depending on the document type.

Loading the Type tool with multiple text files

In the Place dialog box, you can "load" the Type tool with multiple text files and then place them individually. Loading the Type tool works as follows:

- Ctrl-click (Windows) or Command-click (Mac OS) to select multiple files.
- Shift-click to select a continuous range of files.
- You can navigate to different folders and continue to select files.
- When you click Open, the loaded text icon shows in parentheses how many files are loaded, such as (4).
- Click to place the text files one at a time.

Working with styles

Styles provide an efficient, easy way to apply consistent formatting across an entire document. For example, to keep all headlines formatted in the same way throughout your document, you can create a headline style that contains the necessary formatting attributes.

To make the appearance of the article consistent with the other articles in the catalog, you will apply a paragraph style called Body Copy. This style has already been created for formatting the body text of the main descriptive copy in the catalog.

1 If necessary, click the Paragraph Styles panel tab to open the Paragraph Styles panel. To keep it handy, drag the Paragraph Styles tab out of its panel group.

The Paragraph Styles panel for this document includes Body Copy, Catalog Title, Headline 1, Headline 2, Headline 3, Headline Reverse, Tab, Normal, and Body Text. The Normal and Body Text styles have a disk icon (🖫) next to them, indicating that the styles were imported from a different application. In this case, Normal and Body Text are Microsoft Word styles that were imported when you placed the article. You'll now apply the InDesign style, Body Copy, to the text.

● **Note:** The [Basic Paragraph] style is the only paragraph style available when you first create a document with InDesign. You can create new styles or add styles from other InDesign documents. Importing text with styles from Microsoft Word also adds styles to InDesign documents.

2 In the Pages panel, double-click the page 1 icon to center the page in the document window.

3 Using the Type tool (T), click to place an insertion point in the first paragraph beginning with "Take an extraordinary."

4 Select Body Copy in the Paragraph Styles panel. This paragraph is now formatted in a different font.

Take an extraordinary adventure into the world of tea. Expedition Tea Company carries an extensive array of teas from all the major tea growing regions with some of the very best these estates have to offer. Choose from our selection of teas, gift collections, teapots, or read up on information to make your tea drinking experience more enjoyable.

Take an extraordinary adventure into the world of tea. Expedition Tea Company carries an extensive array of teas from all the major tea growing regions with some of the very best these estates have to offer. Choose from our selection of teas, gift collections, teapots, or read up on information to make your tea drinking experience more enjoyable.

Before (left) and after (right) the paragraph style is applied.

5 Repeat steps 3 and 4, but this time, place an insertion point in each body paragraph following the four headlines.

6 Choose File > Save.

Adding a jump line page number

Because the Black Tea category heading continues from page 3 to page 4, you can let readers know where they can resume reading when they get to the bottom of the page. To indicate this, you will add a jump line, "(Continued on page x)." A jump line page number automatically reflects the number of the next page in the text flow.

1 Double-click the page 3 icon in the Pages panel to center the page in the document window. Scroll to the right to view a portion of the pasteboard.

2 Select the Type tool (T). Working on the pasteboard, drag to create a text frame that is approximately 17p6 by 1p10.

3 Using the Selection tool (↖), drag the new text frame to the bottom of the second column on page 3.

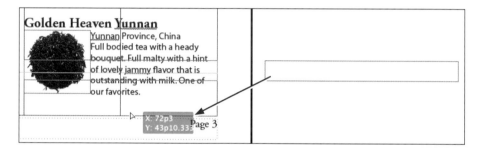

4 Using the Type tool (T), click to place an insertion point in the new frame. Type **(Black tea continued on page)**, including the space and the parentheses. Then use the Left Arrow key to move the insertion point to the left of the closing parenthesis.

● **Note:** For the Next Page Number character to work properly, the text frame containing the jump line must touch or overlap the threaded frame.

5 Right-click (Windows) or Control-click (Mac OS) the text frame, and choose Insert Special Character > Markers > Next Page Number from the context menu. The jump line now reads "(Black tea continued on page 4)."

6 Choose File > Save.

Formatting paragraph text

The jump line, "(Black tea continued on page 4)," is probably formatted with a different paragraph style than you want to use. You'll reformat that text now.

1 Select the Type tool (T), and then triple-click "(Black tea continued on page 4)" to select the text.

2 In the Paragraph Styles panel, click Body Copy to apply the style to the selected text.

3 With Character Formatting Controls selected in the Control panel, choose Italic from the Type Style menu.

Notice that the Body Copy style has a plus sign (+) next to it in the Paragraph Styles panel. The plus sign indicates that the selected paragraph has additional formatting applied to it that isn't part of the applied style, which in this case is the Italic type style you just applied. This additional formatting is called an override.

Changing horizontal and vertical text alignment

Next, you'll adjust the alignment of the jump line.

1 In the Control panel, select Paragraph Formatting Controls (¶), and click the Align Right (≡) button.

Now you will align the jump line to the bottom of the frame.

2 Choose Object > Text Frame Options.

3 Choose Bottom from the Align menu in the Vertical Justification section of the Text Frame Options dialog box. Click OK.

4 With the Selection tool (➤), click the text frame containing the jump line text, and then Shift-click to select the text frame immediately above it.

5 Choose Object > Group. This keeps the story and its jump line together if you move them.

6 Choose File > Save.

Using semi-autoflow to place text frames

Now you will use semi-autoflow to place a text file into multiple columns on page 5. Semi-autoflow lets you create text frames one at a time. The pointer becomes a loaded text icon that automatically reloads after each column is placed, until there is no more overset text. The loaded text icon changes slightly in appearance, depending on whether you are threading text manually, or using semi-autoflow or autoflow.

1 In the Pages panel, double-click the page 5 icon to center the page in the document window. Click a blank part of the page to deselect all items.

2 Choose File > Place. In the Place dialog box, deselect Replace Selected Item. Locate and double-click 05_Greentea.doc in the Lesson_05 folder. If the Import Options dialog box displays, click OK.

3 Hold down the Alt (Windows) or Option (Mac OS) key, and position the loaded text icon (⯊) in the first column at the horizontal 6p7 guide, and click.

The text flows into the first column. Because you held down Alt or Option, the pointer is still a loaded text icon, ready for you to flow text into another frame.

4 Release the Alt or Option key, and position the loaded text icon (⯊) in the second column on page 5 at the 6p7 guide, and click. You now have text in both columns.

GREEN TEA

Green Tea
Green teas are best with water heated to slightly below boiling (180ºF) and steeped for three minutes.

Green Tea Collection

A collection of great green teas. Five 2 oz. tins in an elegant wooden case. Includes: Dragonwell (Lung Ching), Sencha Kyoto Cherry Rose, Genmaicha (popcorn tea), Green Tea Chai, Mint Green.

Genmaicha (Popcorn Tea)
Japan

Green tea blended with fire-toasted rice with a natural sweetness and almost chewy character. During the firing the rice may pop not unlike popcorn, hence the pet name Ïpopcorn tea.Ï

Kapchorua Green
Kenya

Surprisingly good body in the cup with classic Kenya tea flavorÛalmost peach-like fruitiness. A fine example of a high-quality Kenyan tea. Bright amber with greenish highlights.

Mint Green
Sri Lanka

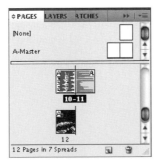

Peppermint oil gives this tea refreshing cool mint flavor that makes for a delicious and heady cup. Deliciously refreshing day or night.

Sencha Kyoto Cherry Rose
China

Fresh, smooth sencha tea with depth and body. The cherry flavoring and subtle rose hints give the tea a wonderful exotic character not to mention a joy to behold.

Superior Gunpowder
Taiwan

This is a strong dark-green brew with a mcmorable fragrance, slightly bitter and long lasting finish with surprising body and captivating green tea taste.

Premium Green Teas

Dragonwell (Lung Ching)
China

Distinguished by its beautiful shape, emerald color, fragrance and sweet floral character. Full-bodied tending astringent (brisk) with a slight heady bouquet.

Gyokuro (Pearl Dew)
Japan
Considered the best tea in Japan, this full-flavored green tea has a satisfying light refreshing character. Tending pleasantly vegetative with some briskness.

Expedition Tea Company   Page 5

● **Note:** If the words "Sencha Kyoto Cherry Rose" appear at the bottom of the first column, using the Type tool, click to place an insertion point before the word "Sencha," and choose Type > Insert Break Character > Column Break to push the text to the top of the second column.

5 Choose File > Save.

Changing the number of columns in a frame

You can change the number of columns within a text frame, as opposed to creating separate text frames for each column on a page. You will now change the number of columns within the text frame on page 11.

1 In the Pages panel, double-click the page 11 icon to center the page in the document window.

2 Using the Selection tool (⬤), select the text frame on page 11.

3 Choose Object > Text Frame Options, and type **2** in the Number box in the Columns section of the Text Frame Options dialog box. Click OK.

The text now flows into two columns.

● **Note:** If the words "Shipping Information" appear at the bottom of the first column, using the Type tool, click to place an insertion point before the word "Shipping," and choose Type > Insert Break Character > Column Break to push the text to the top of the second column.

Text Frame Options

General | Baseline Options

Columns
Number: 2 Gutter: 1p0
Width: 17p6
☐ Fixed Column Width

Inset Spacing
Top: 0p0 Left: 0p0
Bottom: 0p0 Right: 0p0

Vertical Justification
Align: Top
Paragraph Spacing Limit: 0p0

☐ Ignore Text Wrap

☐ Preview   Cancel   OK

About Us
Expedition Tea Company was started by a small group of folks who not only love tea, but who are also fascinated by the regional differences in teas, teapots, and the rituals that surrounded this great beverage.

More than Just the Tea
Tea is more than just a great beverage. We are committed to providing you not only with the best teas, but also to infuse your life with the story

Shipping Information
We ship our products via USPS Priority Mail. Shipping rates are as follows:
Free shipping for orders $75 and over
For orders up to $9.99 $3.85
For orders up to $39.99 $6.85
For orders up to $74.99 $10.85

Orders are typically shipped the next day, ensuring a prompt and timely delivery of all your packages.

4 Choose File > Save.

Loading styles from another document

Styles appear only in the document in which you create them. However, it's easy to share styles between InDesign documents by loading, or importing, styles from other InDesign documents. In this exercise, you will load styles from another document. This other document has a style that works well for some text in this catalog.

1 If necessary, open the Paragraph Styles panel. From the Paragraph Styles panel menu, choose Load Paragraph Styles.

2 In the Open A File dialog box, double-click 05_Styles.indd in the Lesson_05 folder.

3 Deselect the [Basic Paragraph] style, because you only want to import the Tab With Leader style. Click OK.

4 In the Paragraph Styles panel, notice that the new style Tab With Leader appears. You may need to scroll through the list or resize the panel to see this additional style.

5 In the Pages panel, double-click the page 11 icon to center the page in the document window, if it is not already. Click a blank part of the page to deselect all items.

6 Using the Type tool (T), drag to select the three lines of text in the second column starting with "For orders up to."

7 In the Paragraph Styles panel, click the Tab With Leader style. The new style is applied to the selected text.

Before (left) and after (right) applying the Tab With Leader paragraph style.

Shipping Information
We ship our products via USPS Priority Mail. Shipping rates are as follows:
Free shipping for orders $75 and over
For orders up to $9.99 $3.85
For orders up to $39.99 $6.85
For orders up to $74.99 $10.85

Orders are typically shipped the next day, ensuring a prompt and timely delivery of all your packages.

Shipping Information
We ship our products via USPS Priority Mail. Shipping rates are as follows:
Free shipping for orders $75 and over
For orders up to $9.99 . . . . $3.85
For orders up to $39.99 . . . . $6.85
For orders up to $74.99 . . . . $10.85

Orders are typically shipped the next day, ensuring a prompt and timely delivery of all your packages.

8 Choose File > Save.

Flowing text into an existing frame

When you place text, you can flow the text into a new frame or an existing frame. To flow text into an existing frame, click to place an insertion point to flow text at that point, or click the loaded text icon in an existing frame, which replaces that frame's contents.

The last page of the catalog includes a placeholder frame for the address. You'll place a new text story in this frame.

1   In the Pages panel, double-click the page 12 icon to center the page in the document window.

2   Choose File > Place. In the Place dialog box, deselect both Show Import Options and Replace Selected Item if necessary. Locate and double-click 05_CompanyAddress.doc in the Lesson_05 folder.

The pointer becomes a loaded text icon (⬚), previewing the first few lines of text in the story you are placing. When you move the loaded text icon over an empty text frame, parentheses enclose the icon (⬚).

3   Position the loaded text icon (⬚) over the placeholder text frame below the logo, and click. If necessary, resize the text frame to fit the text.

4   Choose File > Save.

Adding pages while flowing text

The catalog you are working on in this lesson reflects a common workflow—the graphic designer creates a layout and adds the copy to the sections as it becomes available. Another common workflow, particularly for longer documents, is for the graphic designer to receive all the copy for a project at once. In this case, InDesign CS4 makes it easy to flow text and automatically add new pages with a new feature called Smart Text Reflow.

With Smart Text Reflow, flowing text or typing into a master text frame automatically adds pages with threaded text frames to contain all the text. If text becomes shorter through editing or reformatting, any extra pages can be deleted as well. Now you'll try out this feature.

1   Choose File > New > Document.

2   In the New Document dialog box, select Master Text Frame. Click OK.

3   Choose Edit > Preferences > Type (Windows) or InDesign > Preferences > Type (Mac OS) to open the Type preferences.

The options in the Smart Text Reflow section of the Type preferences let you specify how pages are handled when you use Smart Text Reflow: where pages are added (to the end of a story, section, or document), whether Smart Text Reflow applies only to master text frames or to other text frames in a document, how pages are inserted into facing-page spreads, and whether empty pages are deleted as text becomes shorter.

4   Make sure that Smart Text Reflow is selected. It is on by default. Click OK.

5   Choose File > Place. In the Place dialog box, locate and select 05_CatalogCopy.doc in the Lesson_05 folder, and click Open.

6   On the first page of the new document, hold down Ctrl+Shift (Windows) or Command+Shift (Mac OS) and click to select the master text frame.

7   Click the loaded text icon to flow all the text into the master text frame, adding pages as necessary. Note the number of pages in the Pages panel.

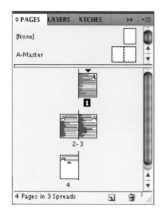

8   Choose File > Close. When the alert displays, click Don't Save.

Finding and changing text and formatting

Like most popular word-processing software, InDesign lets you find text and replace it. You can also search for and change formatting and special characters.

In this part of the lesson, you'll search for occurrences of the words "Expedition Tea Company" in the catalog and change all instances to include the trademark symbol (™) at the end and change the case to small capital letters.

1   If necessary, make sure that you can easily read the text and see the formatting on the page by zooming in. Click in the pasteboard to make sure nothing is selected.

2   Choose Edit > Find/Change. Click the Text tab at the top of the Find/Change dialog box to display the text search options.

3 Type **Expedition Tea Company** in the Find What box.

4 Press Tab to navigate to the Change To box.

5 Type **Expedition Tea Company** again, but add the trademark symbol by choosing Symbols > Trademark Symbol from the Metacharacters menu (@) to the right of the Change To box.

A ^d (a caret and the letter d) is inserted after the company name. This is the code for the trademark symbol.

6 In the Search menu, select Document. In the row of icons below the Search menu, select the Include Master Pages icon (⊞), because the company name also appears on these pages.

These settings tell InDesign to search all text frames in the document, including the master pages, for the phrase "Expedition Tea Company" and replace it with "Expedition Tea Company™." Next you'll change the format of the words found.

7 Click More Options to display additional formatting options. If you see Fewer Options, it has already been selected.

8 Leave the area in the Find Format section unchanged, but select the Specify Attributes To Change icon (⚲) to the right of the Change Format section.

9 On the left side of the Change Format Settings dialog box, select Basic Character Formats. Then, in the main part of the dialog box, choose Small Caps from the Case menu.

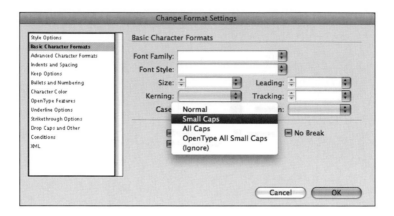

10 Leave the other options blank. Click OK to return to the Find/Change dialog box.

Notice the alert icon (●) that appears above the Change To box. This icon indicates that InDesign will change text to the specified formatting.

11 Click Change All. A message appears, telling you how many instances were found and changed.

12 Click OK to close the message, and then click Done to close the Find/Change dialog box.

13 In the Pages panel, double-click page 1 to view the results.

● **Note:** If a "Cannot find match" message appears, you may have typed the text incorrectly, selected Whole Word or Case Sensitive, or failed to clear formatting used in a previous search. Another possibility is that you selected Story from the Search menu but the text you're looking for is in a different story.

14 Choose File > Save.

Checking spelling

Much like those used in word-processing programs, InDesign has features for checking spelling. You can check the spelling in selected text, an entire story, all stories in a document, or all stories in several open documents at once. You can also check spelling dynamically—as you type the words. To expand or limit what words are permitted or flagged for misspelling, you can also add words to your document's dictionary.

Now you'll check the spelling of the catalog copy and see how to customize your dictionary.

1   Using the Pages panel, navigate to page 1. Select the Type tool (T) in the Tools panel, and click to place an insertion point before the word "Welcome" in the first paragraph.

2   Choose Edit > Spelling > Check Spelling.

3   In the Check Spelling dialog box, choose Document from the Search menu to check the spelling in the entire catalog document.

4   Click Start to find the first misspelled word in the document. The word "oolong" appears in the Not In Dictionary box.

5   Scan the choices offered in the Suggested Corrections list. If you wanted to replace the word, you could select an alternate spelling from this list or simply type the corrected spelling into the Change To box. You can then choose whether to change just this instance of the word (by clicking Change), or all instances of the word (by clicking Change All).

6   Because "oolong" is the correct name for a type of tea, click Ignore All to ignore this assumed misspelling. Ignore All skips all instances of the word, and "oolong" won't come up again as misspelled. Clicking Skip would skip only the first instance of the word.

If you choose to ignore all instances of a word, InDesign ignores the misspelling only until it is restarted.

7   Click Done.

8   Choose File > Save.

Adding words to a dictionary

To prevent a word from being repeatedly identified as a misspelling in other InDesign documents, you can add it to a user dictionary. The user dictionary can either apply to all documents or to a specific document.

1   Click the Type tool (T) anywhere in the text.

2 Choose Edit > Spelling > Check Spelling.

3 From the Search menu, choose Document to check the spelling in the entire catalog document.

4 Click Start to find the first misspelled word in the document. The word "rooibos" appears in the Not In Dictionary box.

5 Click Add to add this word to the external user dictionary file, ENG.UDC. An external dictionary can be used by all InDesign documents. InDesign now recognizes "rooibos" as being correctly spelled.

6 Click Done.

7 Choose File > Save.

Adding words to a document-specific dictionary

You may want to limit the specific spelling of a word to a single document. Storing a word in an open document's internal dictionary restricts its use to that document only.

Here you'll delete a word from the external user dictionary, and then add it to the document's internal dictionary.

▶ **Tip:** If a word is not specific to one language—such as a person's name—you can choose All Languages to add the word to every language's spelling dictionary.

1 Choose Edit > Spelling > Dictionary to display the Dictionary dialog box.

The target dictionary is the external user dictionary. English: USA is the current language. Since Added Words is selected in the Dictionary List menu, the words that have been added to the external user dictionary appear in the Text box.

2 Select the word "rooibos" that appears in the text box.

3 Click Remove to remove the word from the external user dictionary.

Now you'll add the word to the document's internal dictionary.

4 From the Target menu, choose the file 05_Catalog.indd.

5 Type the word **rooibos** in the Word box, and click Add.

The word is added to the Dictionary List for this document only. The word is recognized only within this document, and subsequent InDesign documents will continue to flag the word as misspelled.

6 Click Done.

7 Choose File > Save.

Checking spelling dynamically

It's not necessary for you to wait until a document is finished before checking the spelling. Enabling dynamic spelling allows you to see misspelled words in text while you type or flow imported text.

1 Choose Edit > Preferences > Spelling (Windows) or InDesign > Preferences > Spelling (Mac OS) to display Spelling preferences.

2 In the Find section, select the possible errors you want highlighted.

3 Make sure that Enable Dynamic Spelling is selected.

4 In the Underline Color section, use the menus to customize how possible errors are highlighted.

● **Note:** To disable dynamic spelling, choose Edit > Spelling > Dynamic Spelling.

5 Click OK to close the Preferences dialog box and return to your document.

Words that may be misspelled words (according to the default user dictionary) are immediately underlined. Underlining also highlights any misspelled words you add to the document when Dynamic Spelling is selected.

Teapots
View our collection of teapots, chosen to satisfy every taste including ceramic, cast-iron Tetsubin, stainless, silver-plate, Kyusu, and more.

6 Try typing the word **snew** somewhere in the text to see this feature in action. Delete the word before continuing.

7 Choose File > Save.

Automatically correcting misspelled words

Autocorrect takes the concept of dynamically checking spelling to the next level. With Autocorrect activated, InDesign automatically corrects misspelled words as you type them. Changes are made based on an internal list of commonly misspelled words. You can change this list to include additional commonly misspelled words, including in other languages.

1 Choose Edit > Preferences > Autocorrect (Windows) or InDesign > Preferences > Autocorrect (Mac OS) to display Autocorrect preferences.

2 Make sure that the Enable Autocorrect option is selected. You can also select Autocorrect Capitalization Errors.

By default, the list of commonly misspelled words and the language is English: USA.

3 Change the language to French and note the commonly misspelled words in that language.

4 Try other languages, if you'd like. Change the language back to English: USA before proceeding.

5 Click Add. In the Add To Autocorrect List dialog box, type the word **snew** in the Misspelled Word box, and **snow** in the Correction box.

6 Click OK to add the word, and then click OK again in the Preferences dialog box.

7 Using the Type tool (T), type the word **snew** into the first column on page 1. Press the spacebar to make a space.

Notice the Autocorrect feature in action.

8 Choose File > Save.

Editing text by dragging and dropping

For misplaced words in your document, InDesign allows you to drag and drop text within and between frames, layout windows, and documents. You'll now use drag and drop to move text from one paragraph to another in your catalog.

1 Choose Edit > Preferences > Type (Windows) or InDesign > Preferences > Type (Mac OS) to display Type preferences.

2 In the Drag And Drop Text Editing section, select Enable In Layout View. This option lets you move text into and out of open document windows, and within documents in the Layout View. Click OK

3 In the document window, navigate to page 11. If necessary, adjust your view until you can comfortably read the paragraphs at the top of the first column.

The sentence "Tea is more than just a great beverage." was mistakenly placed at the beginning of the first paragraph titled "More than Just the Tea."

4 Using the Type tool (T), drag to select this sentence.

● **Note:** The default Layout View displays the full layout of text and graphics. Alternately, you can view only the text in the separate Story Editor window.

5 Hover the I-bar pointer over the highlighted words until it changes to the drag and drop icon (▶ᴛ).

6 Drag the words to their correct location at the end of the paragraph after the word "well."

The sentence moves to the new location.

More than Just the Tea
Tea is more than just a great beverage. We are committed to providing you not only with the best teas, but also to infuse your life with the story behind the tea. This might include information about the history, health benefits, rituals, accessories, environmental influence as well as ways to improve not only your own experience with tea but that of others as well.

More than Just the Tea
We are committed to providing you not only with the best teas, but also to infuse your life with the story behind the tea. This might include information about the history, health benefits, rituals, accessories, environmental influence as well as ways to improve not only your own experience with tea but that of others as well. Tea is more than just a great beverage.

Using the Story Editor

If you're more comfortable working with an editing interface that isolates the text, try using the Story Editor.

1 With page 11 of the catalog in the document window, select the Type tool (T) and click inside the first column to place an insertion point.

2 Choose Edit > Edit In Story Editor.

The Story Editor window shows plain text with no formatting applied. Any graphics and other non-text elements are omitted to make editing easier.

3 If necessary, drag the vertical scroll bar to view all the text in the selected story.

The column to the left of the text displays a vertical depth ruler and the name of the paragraph styles that are applied to each paragraph.

```
  O O O   □ 05_Catalog.indd: About Us Expedition ...
Body Copy  │ EXPEDITION TEA COMPANY™ was started by a small group
           │ of folks who not only love tea, but who are
           │ also fascinated by the regional differences in
           │ teas, teapots, and the rituals that surrounded
        5.8│ this great beverage.
Headline 3 │ More than Just the Tea
Body Copy  │ We are committed to providing you not only with
           │ the best teas, but also to infuse your life
           │ with the story behind the tea. This might
       12.2│ include information about the history, health
           │ benefits, rituals, accessories, environmental
           │ influence as well as ways to improve not only
           │ your own experience with tea but that of others
           │ as well.  Tea is more than just a great
       16.2│ beverage.
Headline 3 │ Ask Us
Body Copy  │ Our staff includes a professionally certified
           │ Grade Three Tea Specialist (Specialty Tea
           │ Institute). We love to suggest teas based on
       22.6│ what you currently like to help expand your
           │ options. Or tell you the history of a
           │ particular teapot. And we'll certainly be
           │ drinking a cup of one of our favorites while we
           │ do the research.
```

4 Place an insertion point in the Story Editor window, and type the word **accessories** in the first paragraph after "teapots," and before "and." If necessary, move the Story Editor window aside, so you can see that the corresponding text has also been changed in the document window.

To make viewing and editing type easier, you can change the display characteristics of the Story Editor window.

5 Choose Edit > Preferences > Story Editor Display (Windows) or InDesign > Preferences > Story Editor Display (Mac OS) to display Story Editor Display preferences.

6 Change the font size to 14 points and the line spacing to Doublespace to see if it makes editing easier for you. Click OK.

7 Close the Story Editor.

8 Choose File > Save to save your work.

9 When you're finished looking at your work, choose File > Close.

Congratulations. You have finished the lesson.

● **Note:** The Story Editor displays line numbers for reference purposes, and uses dynamic spelling to highlight misspelled words, just like in the document window. If the Enable In Story Editor option is selected in Type preferences, you can also drag and drop type in the Story Editor, just as you did in this exercise.

Exploring on your own

In this lesson, you covered the basics of creating and applying styles. If you do a significant amount of writing in InDesign, you'll want to learn how Next Style works and how to apply styles using keyboard shortcuts.

1 With no text selected, double-click the Headline 3 style in the Paragraph Styles panel.

2 In the Paragraph Style Options dialog box, click to place an insertion point in the Shortcut box.

3 Using the number keys on the numeric keypad, press Ctrl+Alt+3 (Windows) or Command+Option+3 (Mac OS) to create the keyboard shortcut. Keep the following in mind:

- If text does not appear in the Shortcut box, be sure that you are using the numbers from the numeric keypad.

- In Windows, make sure that Num Lock is on.

- If you are using a laptop computer that does not include a numeric keypad, select the style names in the Paragraph Styles panel.

4 Choose Body Copy from the Next Style menu, and then click OK.

5 Practice applying the Headline 3 style using your keyboard shortcut. Notice that when you press Enter or Return at the end of a Headline 3 paragraph, the next paragraph is automatically formatted with the Body Copy style.

Review questions

1 How do you autoflow text? How do you flow text one frame at a time?

2 How does using styles save time?

3 While checking the spelling in your document, InDesign flags words that are not in the dictionary—but may not actually be misspelled. How can you fix this problem?

Review answers

1 When the loaded text icon appears after using the Place command or clicking an out port, hold down the Shift key and click. To flow text one frame at a time, you can hold down Alt (Windows) or Option (Mac OS) to reload the loaded text icon after you click or drag to create a frame.

2 Styles save time by letting you keep a group of formatting attributes together that you can quickly apply to text. If you need to update the text, you don't have to change each paragraph formatted with the style individually. Instead, you can simply modify the style.

3 Add those words to the document's or InDesign's default spelling dictionary for the language or languages of your choice.

6 WORKING WITH TYPOGRAPHY

In this lesson, you'll learn how to do the following:

- Customize and use the baseline grid.

- Adjust vertical and horizontal text spacing.

- Change fonts and spacing.

- Insert special characters from OpenType fonts.

- Hang punctuation outside a margin.

- Add and format drop caps.

- Apply the Adobe Paragraph and Adobe Single-line composers.

- Specify a tab with a leader and hanging indent.

- Add a rule to a paragraph.

 This lesson will take approximately 60 minutes.

*Restaurant*Profile

Assignments Restaurant

Sure, you can get Caesar salad prepared tableside for two at any of the higher-end restaurants in town—for $25 plus another $40 (just for starters) for a single slab of steak. Or you can visit Assignments Restaurant, run by students of the International Culinary School at The Art Institute of Colorado, where tableside preparations include Caesar salad for $4.50 and steak Diane for $19. No, this isn't Elway's, but the chefs in training create a charming experience for patrons from start to finish.

Since 1992, the School of Culinary Arts has trained more than 4,300 chefs—all of whom were required to work in the restaurant. Those chefs are now working in the industry all over the country says Chef Instructor Stephen Kleinman, CEC, AAC. "Whether I go to a restaurant in Manhattan or San Francisco, people know me," Kleinman says, describing encounters with former students. Although he claims to be a "hippy from the '60s," Kleinman apprenticed in Europe, attended a culinary academy in San Francisco and had the opportunity to cook at the prestigious James Beard House three times. He admits that his experience lends him credibility, but it's his warm, easygoing, approachable style that leads to his success as a teacher.

"Some of the best restaurants in the world serve tableside; chefs are more grounded this way," claims Kleinman, who would never be mistaken for a snob. "By having the students come to the front of the house—serving as waitpeople and preparing tableside—we break a lot of barriers.

IF YOU GO
Name .... Assignments Restaurant
Address......... 675 S. Broadway, Denver
Reservations ... call 303 770-0023 or visit www.opentable.com
Hours .... Wednesday–Friday, 11:30 a.m.–1:30 p.m. and 6–8 p.m.

THE RESTAURANT

Assignments Restaurant, tucked back by the Quest Diagnostics lab off South Broadway near Alameda Avenue, seats 71 at its handful of booths and tables. The blissful quiet, a welcome change from the typical hot spot, is interrupted only by solicitous servers dressed in chef attire. Despite decor that is on the edge of institutional with its cream-coloredwalls, faux cherry furniture and kitschy cafe artwork, this is a spot that welcomes intimate conversation with friends and family.

A perusal of the menu, while munching fresh bread and savoring a glass of wine, tempts you with its carefully planned variety. "The menu is all designed to teach cooking methods," says Kleinman. "It covers 80 to 85 percent of what students have been learning in class—saute, grill, braise, make vinaigrettes, cook vegetables, bake and make desserts." In a twist on "You have to know the rules to break them," Kleinman insists that students need to first learn the basics before they can go on to create their own dishes.

For our "test dinner," an amuse bouche, a crab-stuffed mushroom cap, arrives followed by an appetizer of chorizo-stuffed prawns wrapped in applewoodsmoked bacon. The tableside Caesar preparation is a wonderful ritual that tastes as good as it looks. Entrees, all under $20, include grilled trout, sweet and sour spareribs, spinach lasagna, seared duck breast, flatiron steak, steak Diane prepared tableside and pesto-crusted lamb chops. We opted for a succulent trout and tender spareribs, and notice that a $10 macaroni and cheese entree makes Assignments kid-friendly for special occasions.

THE GOALS

The purpose of this unique restaurant is to give students practical experience so they can hit the ground running. "The goal is to make the students comfortable, thinking on their feet, getting ready for reality," says Kleinman. He wants students to be able to read tickets, perform, and recover and learn getting valuable front-of-the-house and business experience in addition to cooking.

Five to seven students work in the kitchen at one time, covering stations. Students work toward an associate of applied science degree in culinary arts or a bachelor of arts degree in culinary management.

With degree in hand, the school places 99 percent of its students. While many students are placed at country clubs and resorts that prefer formal training, chefs from all over town—Panzano or Jax Fish House—have trained at Assignments as well. Or try O's Restaurant, whose recent media darling chef Ian Kleinman is not just a former student but Stephen Kleinman's son. Make a reservation, and maybe the next celebrity chef to hit town will whip up a tableside bananas Foster for you.

Kelly Kordes Anton is the editor of Colorado Expression magazine and the co-author of various books on publishing technologies, including Adobe InDesign How-To: 100 Essential Techniques.

> *"Maybe the next celebrity chef to hit town will whip up a tableside bananas Foster for you."*

CAESAR SALAD
2 cloves garlic
Taste kosher salt
2 anchovy fillets, chopped
1 coddled egg
½ lemon
½ Tbsp Dijon mustard
¼ cup red wine vinegar
¾ cup virgin olive oil
¼ tsp Worcestershire sauce
Romaine lettuce heart, washed and dried
¼ cup croutons
¼ cup Parmesan cheese
Taste cracked black pepper

Grind together the garlic and salt. Add the chopped anchovies. Stir in the egg and lemon. Add the vinegar, olive oil and Worcestershire sauce, and whip briefly. Pour over lettuce and toss with croutons, Parmesan and black pepper.

CHORIZO-STUFFED PRAWNS
3 prawns, butterflied
3 Tbsp chorizo sausage
3 slices bacon, blanched
1 bunch parsley, fried
2 oz morita mayonnaise (recipe follows)
½ oz olive oil

Heat oven to 350°. Stuff the butterflied prawns with chorizo. Wrap a piece of the blanched bacon around each prawn and place in the oven. Cook until the chorizo is done. Place the fried parsley on a plate and place the prawns on top. Drizzle with the morita mayonnaise.

MORITA MAYONNAISE
1 pint mayonnaise
1 tsp smoked morita powder
1 Tbsp lemon juice
Salt and pepper to taste

Mix all the ingredients together and serve.

InDesign CS4 offers many features for fine-tuning typography, including drop caps for leading the eye into a paragraph, Optical Margin Alignment for hanging punctuation outside the edge of a frame, and precision line and character spacing controls.

Getting started

● **Note:** If you have not already copied the resource files for this lesson onto your hard disk from the Adobe InDesign CS4 Classroom in a Book CD, do so now. See "Copying the Classroom in a Book files" on page 2.

In this lesson, you'll fine-tune the typography in a restaurant review for a high-end lifestyles magazine. For the rich look of the magazine, the type is precisely spaced and formatted: it uses a baseline grid for aligning text across columns, actual fractions in the recipes, and decorative touches such as drop caps and pull quotes.

1 To ensure that the preferences and default settings of your Adobe InDesign CS4 program match those used in this lesson, move the InDesign Defaults file to a different folder following the procedure in "Saving and restoring the InDesign Defaults file" on page 2.

2 Start Adobe InDesign CS4. To ensure that the panels and menu commands match those used in this lesson, choose Window > Workspace > [Advanced], and then choose Window > Workspace > Reset Advanced.

3 Choose File > Open, and open the 06_Start.indd file in the Lesson_06 folder, located inside the Lessons folder within the InDesignCIB folder on your hard disk. If missing font alert displays, click OK.

4 Choose File > Save As, rename the file **06Working.indd**, and save it in the Lesson_06 folder.

5 If you want to see what the finished document looks like, open the 06_End.indd file in the same folder. You can leave this document open to act as a guide as you work. When you're ready to resume working on the lesson document, click its tab in the upper-left corner of the document window.

In this lesson, you will be working with text a great deal. You can use the Character Formatting Controls and the Paragraph Formatting Controls in the Control panel, or you can use the Character panel and Paragraph panel. Using the individual Character and Paragraph panels can be easier for formatting text because you can drag the panels to where you need them.

6 Choose Type > Character and Type > Paragraph to open the two primary text-formatting panels. Leave these panels open until you finish this lesson.

● **Note:** Drag the Paragraph panel tab into the Character panel tab to create a panel group, if you prefer.

Adjusting vertical spacing

InDesign provides several options for customizing and adjusting the vertical spacing of text in a frame. You can:

- Set the space between all lines of text using a baseline grid.

- Set the space between each line using the Leading menu in the Character panel.

- Set the space between each paragraph using the Space Before and Space After options in the Paragraph panel.

- Use the Vertical Justification options in the Text Frame Options dialog box to align text within a frame.

In this section of the lesson, you will use the baseline grid to align text.

Using the baseline grid to align text

Once you've decided on the font size and leading for your document's body text, you may want to set up a baseline grid (also called a leading grid) for the entire document. The baseline grid represents the leading for your document's body text and is used to align the baseline of type in one column of text with the baseline of type in neighboring columns.

Before you set up the baseline grid, you need to check the margin value for the top of your document and the leading value for the body text. (Normally, you would write the values down to remember them. The values are repeated in the steps here.) These elements work together with the grid to create a cohesive design.

1 To view the top margin value for the page, choose Layout > Margins And Columns. The top margin is set to 6p0 (6 picas, 0 points). Click Cancel.

2 To view the leading value, select the Type tool (T) in the Tools panel and click to place an insertion point in a body-text paragraph. Check the Leading value (🅐) in the Character panel. The leading is set to 14 pt (14 points).

3 Choose Edit > Preferences > Grids (Windows) or InDesign > Preferences > Grids (Mac OS) to set the baseline grid options.

● **Note:** To see the default baseline grid in action, you can select all the text (Edit > Select All) and click Align To Baseline Grid in the lower-right corner of the Paragraph panel. Notice how much the line spacing changes, then choose Edit > Undo.

4 In the Baseline Grid section, type **6** in the Start box to match your top margin setting of 6p0. This option sets the location of the first grid line for the document. If you use the default value of 3p0, the first grid line would appear above the top margin.

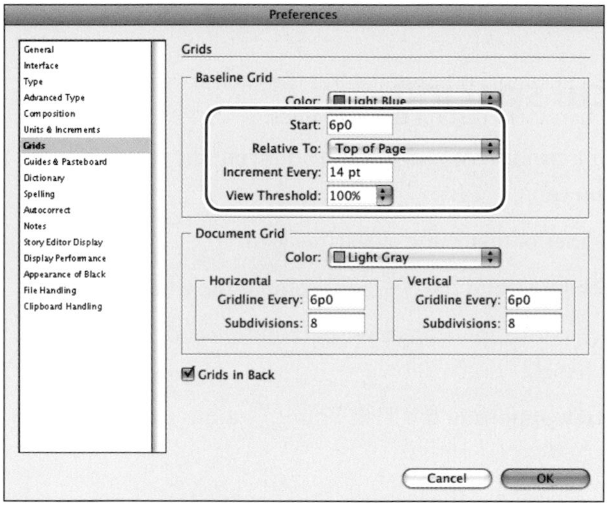

5 In the Increment Every box, type **14 pt** to match your leading.

6 Choose 100% from the View Threshold menu.

The View Threshold menu sets the minimum value at which you can see the grid onscreen. At 100%, the grid appears in the document window only at magnifications of 100% or higher.

7 Click OK.

8 Choose File > Save.

Viewing the baseline grid

Now you'll make the grid that you just set up visible onscreen.

Note: If the grid does not appear, it is because the document view is smaller than the grid's view threshold value. Choose View > Actual Size to change the view scale to 100%, the view threshold.

1 To view the baseline grid in the document window, choose View > Grids & Guides > Show Baseline Grid.

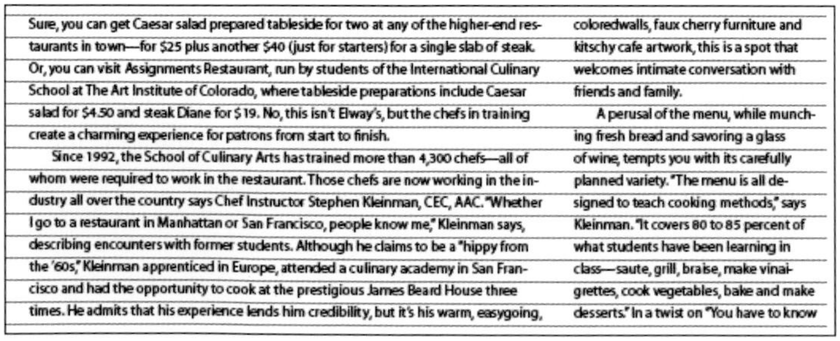

You can align one paragraph, selected paragraphs, or all the paragraphs in a story to the baseline grid. (A story is all the text in a series of threaded text frames.) In the following steps, you will use the Paragraph panel to align the main story to the baseline grid.

▶ Tip: When applying paragraph attributes, it isn't necessary to select an entire paragraph with the Type tool. Just select part of the paragraph or paragraphs you want to format. If you are formatting only one paragraph, you can simply click in the paragraph to place an insertion point.

2   Using the Type tool (T), click to place an insertion point anywhere in the first paragraph on the spread, and then choose Edit > Select All to select all of the text in the main story.

3   If the Paragraph panel isn't visible, choose Type > Paragraph.

4   In the Paragraph panel, click Align To Baseline Grid (≣≣). The text shifts so that the baselines of the characters rest on the grid lines.

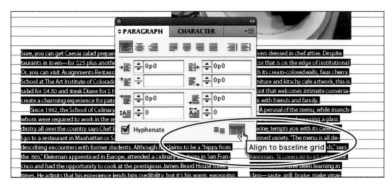

In this magazine, the pull quotes, boxed text, and recipes do not snap to the baseline grid. For a creative touch, the designer allows them to "float."

5   Click the pasteboard to deselect the text. Choose File > Save.

Changing the spacing between paragraphs

When you apply a space before or after a paragraph that you have previously aligned to the baseline grid, the space automatically adjusts to the next highest multiple of the grid's Increment Every value. For example, if the Increment Every value is set to 14 points (1p2) and you specify Space After of any value greater than 0 pt and less than 14 pt, InDesign automatically increases the space value to 14 pt. If you specify a value greater than 14 pt, such as 16 pt, InDesign increases it to the next higher multiple, or 28 pt.

Here you'll make the subheads in the main story stand out more by inserting space above them. Then, you'll update the paragraph style to automatically apply the new space above to all the subheads.

1   Using the Type tool (T), click anywhere in the subhead "The Restaurant" on the left-facing page.

2   In the Paragraph panel, type **6 pt** in the Space Before box (⁺≣), and press Enter or Return.

The points are automatically converted to picas, and the text in the subhead shifts automatically to the next grid line.

3 Choose Type > Paragraph Styles to open the Paragraph Styles panel.

4 With the insertion point still in "The Restaurant" subhead, notice that a plus sign (+) appears after the Subhead style name in the panel.

This sign indicates that the formatting of the selected text has been modified from the original formatting of the applied style.

5 Choose Redefine Style from the Paragraph Styles panel menu. The Subhead style takes on the formatting—specifically, the new space above—of the selected paragraph.

Notice that the plus sign (+) no longer appears after the style name, and that space is added above "The Goals" subhead on the right-facing page as well.

6 Choose View > Grids & Guides > Hide Baseline Grid.

7 Choose File > Save.

Changing fonts and type style

Changing the fonts and type styles of text can make a dramatic difference in the appearance of your document. Here you'll change the font family, type style, size, and leading for the text in the pull quote on the right-facing page. In addition, you will insert "alternate glyphs"—fancier characters—available in the OpenType font in use. You'll make these changes in the Character panel and the Glyphs panel.

1 Zoom in on the pull quote on the right-facing page.

2 If the Character panel isn't visible, choose Type > Character.

3 Using the Type tool (T), click inside the pull quote on the right-facing page; then click four times to select the entire paragraph.

4 In the Character panel, set the following options:

- Font: Adobe Caslon Pro (alphabetized under "C")
- Style: Bold Italic
- Size: 14 pt
- Leading: 30 pt

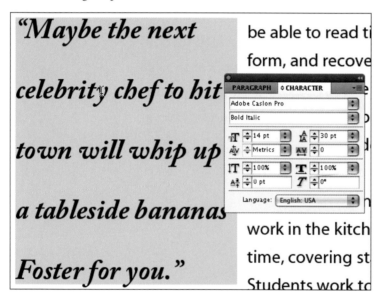

Replacing a character with an alternate glyph

Because Adobe Caslon Pro is an OpenType font, which typically provides multiple glyphs for standard characters, you can select alternatives for many characters. A glyph is a specific form of a character. For example, in certain fonts, the capital letter A is available in several forms, such as swash and small cap. You use the Glyphs panel to select alternatives and locate any glyph in a font.

1 Using the Type tool (T), select the first "M" in the pull quote.

2 Choose Type > Glyphs.

3   In the Glyphs panel, choose Alternates For Selection from the Show menu to see the alternates for the letter M. Depending on the version of Adobe Caslon Pro that is active, your options may look different.

4   Double-click the more script-like "M" to replace the original character in the pull quote.

"Maybe the next celebrity chef to town will whip a tableside bananas Foster for you."

5   Repeat this process to replace the "F" in "Foster," lower in the pull quote, with a fancier letter F.

"Maybe the next celebrity chef to hit town will whip up a tableside bananas Foster for you."

6   Choose File > Save.

Adding a special character

Now you'll add a decorative font character and a right-indent tab to the end of the story—also known as an "end-of-story character." This lets the reader know that the story is finished.

1 If necessary, scroll or zoom to see the last body paragraph of the story, ending with the words "bananas Foster for you."

2 Using the Type tool (T), click to place an insertion point in the last paragraph, just after the final period.

3 If the Glyphs panel is not open, choose Type > Glyphs.

You can use the Glyphs panel to view and insert OpenType attributes such as ornaments, swashes, fractions, and ligatures.

4 At the bottom of the panel, choose Adobe Caslon Pro from the Font menu.

5 In the Glyphs panel, choose Ornaments from the Show menu.

6 From the scrollable list, select any decorative character you prefer and double-click to insert it. The character appears at the insertion point in the document.

▶ **Tip** Some of the more commonly used glyphs, such as the copyright and trademark symbols, also appear in the context menu. To access the context menu, right-click (Windows) or Control-click (Mac OS) at the insertion point.

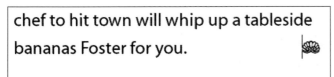

7 Using the Type tool (T), click to place an insertion point between the final period and the decorative character.

8 Right-click (Windows) or Control-click (Mac OS) to display the context menu, and choose Insert Special Character > Other > Right Indent Tab.

Note: The Adobe Caslon Pro font may display many more glyphs than you are accustomed to seeing, because it is an OpenType font. OpenType fonts can contain many more characters and glyph alternates than earlier PostScript typefaces. Adobe OpenType fonts are built on the same foundation as PostScript. For more information on OpenType fonts, visit Adobe.com/type.

9 Choose File > Save.

chef to hit town will whip up a tableside bananas Foster for you.

Inserting fraction characters

► **Tip:** If you are working on a cookbook or other document that requires a variety of fractions, the fractions built into most fonts will not cover all the values you need. You will need to research using the numerator and denominator formatting available in some OpenType fonts or purchasing a specific fraction font.

The recipes in the story do not use actual fraction characters—rather, the 1/2 is built with a numeral 1, a slash, and a numeral 2. Most fonts contain individual characters for common fractions such as ½, ¼, and ¾. When available, these elegant fractions look much more professional than using numerals and slashes.

1 Using the Zoom tool (🔍), zoom in on the recipes at the bottom of the right-facing page.

2 Using the Type tool (T), select the first instance of "1/2" ("1/2 lemon" in the Caesar Salad recipe).

3 If the Glyphs panel is not open, choose Type > Glyphs.

4 Resize the panel so you can see more characters. Scroll as necessary to locate the ½ fraction.

5 Double-click the ½ fraction to replace the selected "1/2" in the text.

Notice that the ½ fraction is stored in the Recently Used boxes at the top of the Glyphs panel.

Now you'll change instances of the "1/4" and "3/4" fractions.

6 In the Caesar Salad recipe, locate and select "1/4" ("1/4 cup red wine vinegar").

7 In the Glyphs panel, locate and double-click the ¼ fraction.

8 Repeat steps 6 and 7, locating and selecting "3/4" ("3/4 cup virgin olive oil"), and in the Glyphs panel, replacing it with the ¾ fraction.

9 If you wish, replace the remaining instances of "1/2" and "1/4" in the recipes by selecting the text and double-clicking the respective glyphs in the Recently Used boxes.

CAESAR SALAD
2 cloves garlic
Taste kosher salt
2 anchovy fillets, chop
1 coddled egg
½ lemon
½ Tbsp Dijon mustard
¼ cup red wine vinega
¾ cup virgin olive oil
¼ tsp Worcestershire :
Romaine lettuce hear
¼ cup croutons
¼ cup Parmesan chee
Taste cracked black pe

CHORIZO-STUFFED PRAWNS
3 prawns, butterflied
3 Tbsp chorizo sausage
3 slices bacon, blanched
1 bunch parsley, fried
2 oz morita mayonnaise (recipe follows)
½ oz olive oil

Heat oven to 350°. Stuff the butterflied prawns with chorizo. Wrap a piece of the blanched bacon around each prawn and place in the oven. Cook until the chorizo is done. Place the fried parsley on a plate and place the prawns on top. Drizzle with the morita mayonnaise.

10 Close the Glyphs panel.

11 Choose File > Save.

Changing paragraph alignment

You can easily manipulate how a paragraph fits within its text frame by changing the horizontal alignment. You can align text with one or both edges of a text frame or you can apply inset spacing. Justifying text aligns both the left and right edges. In this exercise, you'll align the author's biographical information—otherwise known as the "bio"—with the right margin.

1 Scroll and zoom as necessary to view the author's bio under the last paragraph of the story.

2 Using the Type tool (T), click to place an insertion point in the bio.

3 In the Paragraph panel, click Align Right (≣).

Because the text in the bio is so small, the line spacing from the baseline grid looks too big. To fix this, you will unlock this paragraph from the grid.

4 With the insertion point still in the bio paragraph, in the Paragraph panel, click Do Not Align To Baseline Grid. If the text no longer fits, use the Selection tool to make the text frame slightly longer.

Kelly Kordes Anton is the editor of *Colorado Expression* magazine and the co-author of various books on publishing technologies, including *Adobe InDesign How-Tos: 100 Essential Techniques*.

5 Choose Edit > Deselect All to deselect the text frame.

6 Choose File > Save.

Hanging punctuation outside the margin

Expert typographers often prefer to align text visually rather than numerically. Sometimes, particularly with punctuation at the beginning and end of lines, margins that are in fact even may appear uneven. To fix this visual discrepancy, designers "hang" punctuation slightly outside the text frame. Called Optical Margin Alignment, this hanging punctuation allows some of the text, such as punctuation and quotation marks, to be positioned outside of the text frame.

In this exercise, you will apply Optical Margin Alignment to the pull quote.

1 Scroll and zoom as necessary to view the pull quote on the right-facing page.

2 Using the Type tool (T), click in the pull quote.

● **Note:** Optical Margin Alignment applies to all of the text in a story—defined as all the text in a series of threaded text frames—hence the **use of the** Story panel.

3 Choose Type > Story to open the Story panel.

4 Select Optical Margin Alignment, and then close the Story panel.

Notice how the left edges of the opening quotation marks now hang outside the text frame. The text looks more visually aligned.

"*Maybe the next celebrity chef to hit town will whip up a tableside bananas Foster for you.*"

"*Maybe the next celebrity chef to hit town will whip up a tableside bananas Foster for you.*"

Without (left) and with (right) Optical Margin Alignment.

5 Choose File > Save.

Creating a drop cap

You can add creative touches to your document using the special InDesign font features. For example, you can make the first character or word in a paragraph a drop cap, apply a gradient or color fill to text, or create superscript and subscript characters, along with ligatures and old-style numerals. Here you'll create a five-character drop cap out of the first word in the first paragraph of the story.

1 Scroll to view the first paragraph in the left-facing page. Using the Type tool (T), click to place an insertion point anywhere in that paragraph.

2 In the Paragraph panel, type **3** in the Drop Cap Number Of Lines box (🔳) to make the letters drop down three lines.

3 Type 5 in the Drop Cap One Or More Characters box (🔳) to enlarge the first five characters: "Sure,". Press Enter or Return.

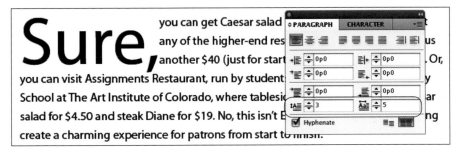

4 Using the Type tool, select the five drop-cap characters.

Now, you can apply any character formatting you wish. In many magazines, the drop caps in the regular stories are formatted the same way with more ornate formatting used in features.

5 Choose Type > Character Styles to open the Character Styles panel.

6 Click the Drop Cap style to apply it to the selected text.

> *Sure,* you can get Caesar salad prepared tableside for two at any of the higher-end restaurants in town—for $25 plus another $40 (just for starters) for a single slab of steak. Or, you can visit Assignments Restaurant, run by students of the International Culinary School at The Art Institute of Colorado, where tableside preparations include Caesar salad for $4.50 and steak Diane for $19. No, this isn't Elway's, but the chefs in training create a charming experience for patrons from start to finish.

7 Choose File > Save.

Applying a stroke to text

Next, you'll add a stroke to the drop cap characters you just created.

1 With the Type tool (T) still selected, select the drop cap characters.

2 In the Swatches panel, select the Stroke box (🔲) and then click Black. A stroke appears around each of the letters.

The default size of the stroke is 1 point. You'll change the stroke to 1.5 points.

3 Choose Window > Stroke.

4 In the Stroke panel, type **1.5 pt** in the Weight box, and press Enter or Return.

5 Press Shift+Ctrl+A (Windows) or Shift+Command+A (Mac OS) to deselect the text so that you can view the stroke effect.

To see how the stroke and drop caps are retained even as the text is edited, you will replace the "S" in "Sure" with an alternate glyph.

6 Close the Stroke panel. Then choose Type > Glyphs.

7 Using the Type tool, select the "S" in "Sure."

8 In the Glyphs panel, choose Alternates for Selection from the Show menu.

9 Double-click the fancy "S" to replace the italic "S."

10 Close the Glyphs panel.

11 Choose File > Save.

Adjusting the drop cap alignment

You can adjust the alignment of the drop cap letters as well as scale the size of the drop cap if it has a descender such as a "y." In this section, you'll adjust the drop cap so that it aligns better with the left margin.

1 Using the Type tool (T), click to place an insertion point anywhere in the first paragraph with the drop cap.

2 In the Paragraph panel, choose Drop Caps And Nested Styles from the panel menu.

3 Select Align Left Edge to move the drop cap so that it aligns better to the left edge. Click OK.

4 Choose File > Save.

Adjusting letter and word spacing

You can change the spacing between letters and words using kerning and tracking. You can also control the overall spacing of text in a paragraph by using the Single-line and Paragraph Composers.

Adjusting the kerning and tracking

In InDesign, you can control the space between letters by using kerning and tracking. By adjusting kerning, you can add or subtract space between specific letter pairs. Tracking creates an equal amount of spacing across a range of letters. You can use both kerning and tracking on the same text.

Here you'll manually kern some letters in the drop cap. Then you'll track the heading "If You Go" in the purple box.

1 To distinguish the amount of space between letters more easily and to see the results of the kerning more clearly, select the Zoom tool (🔍) in the Tools panel and drag a marquee around the drop caps.

2 Select the Type tool (T) and click to place an insertion point between the "u" and the "r" in "Sure."

3 Press Alt+Right Arrow (Windows) or Option+Right Arrow (Mac OS) to increase the amount that the letter "r" moves to the right. Continue to press this key combination until the spacing between the two adjacent letters looks visually pleasing to you.

▶ **Tip:** When kerning text, the Right Arrow key adds space and the Left Arrow key removes space when combined with the Alt (Windows) or Option (Mac OS) key.

The example shows the key combination pressed twice. You can see the new kerning values in the Character panel as well.

Now you'll set a tracking value for the entire "If You Go" heading to increase the overall spacing. To set tracking, you must first select the entire range of characters you want to track.

4   Choose Edit > Deselect All. Scroll down to view the "If You Go" heading in the purple box below the word "Sure."

5   Using the Type tool (T), click three times on "If You Go" to select the entire heading. (If you have trouble selecting the text, first use the Selection tool to select the purple text frame.)

6   In the Character panel, type **40** in the Tracking box (**AV**). Press Enter or Return.

7   Click on the pasteboard to deselect the text.

8   Choose View > Fit Spread In Window to see the overall effect of your latest changes.

9   Choose File > Save.

Applying the Adobe Paragraph and Single-line composers

The density of a paragraph (sometimes called its color) is determined by the composition method used. When composing text, InDesign considers the word spacing, letter spacing, glyph scaling, and hyphenation options you've selected, and then evaluates and chooses the best line breaks. InDesign provides two options for composing text: the Adobe Paragraph Composer, which looks at all of the lines in the paragraph, or the Adobe Single-line Composer, which looks separately at each individual line.

When you use the Paragraph Composer, InDesign composes a line while considering the impact on the other lines in the paragraph, to set the best overall arrangement of the paragraph. As you change type in a given line, previous and subsequent lines in the same paragraph may break differently, making the overall paragraph appear more evenly spaced. When you use the Single-line Composer, which is the standard for other layout and word-processing software, InDesign recomposes only the lines following the edited text.

The text in this lesson was composed using the default, the Adobe Paragraph Composer. To see the difference between the two, you'll recompose the body text using the Single-line Composer.

1 Using the Type tool (T), click to place an insertion point anywhere in the main story.

2 Choose Edit > Select All.

3 In the Paragraph panel, choose Adobe Single-line Composer from the panel menu. If necessary, increase the view scale to see the difference.

The Single-line Composer handles each line individually. As a result, some lines in a paragraph appear more dense or sparse than others. Because the Paragraph Composer looks at multiple lines at once, it makes the density of the lines in a paragraph more consistent.

4 Click a blank area of the page to deselect the text and look at the different spacing and line endings.

The Adobe Paragraph
Composer (left) and
the Adobe Single-line
Composer (right).

A perusal of the menu, while munching fresh bread and savoring a glass of wine, tempts you with its carefully planned variety. "The menu is all designed to teach cooking methods," says Kleinman. "It covers 80 to 85 percent of what students have been learning in class—saute, grill, braise, make vinaigrettes, cook vegetables, bake and make desserts." In a twist on "You have to know the rules to break them," Kleinman insists that students need to first learn the basics before they can go on to create their own dishes.

A perusal of the menu, while munching fresh bread and savoring a glass of wine, tempts you with its carefully planned variety. "The menu is all designed to teach cooking methods," says Kleinman. "It covers 80 to 85 percent of what students have been learning in class—saute, grill, braise, make vinaigrettes, cook vegetables, bake and make desserts." In a twist on "You have to know the rules to break them," Kleinman insists that students need to first learn the basics before they can go on to create their own dishes.

5 To restore the story to the Adobe Paragraph Composer, choose Edit > Undo.

6 Choose File > Save.

Setting tabs

You can use tabs to position text in specific horizontal locations in a frame. In the Tabs panel, you can organize text and create tab leaders, indents, and hanging indents.

Aligning text to tabs and adding tab leaders

Here you'll format the tabbed information in the "If You Go" box on the left-facing page. The tab markers have already been entered in the text, so you will be setting the final location of the text.

1 Scroll and zoom as necessary to view the "If You Go" box.

2 To view the tab markers in the text, choose Type > Show Hidden Characters, and make sure that Normal Mode (⊟) is selected in the Tools panel.

3 Using the Type tool (T), click in the "If You Go" box and choose Edit > Select All to select all of the text.

4 Choose Type > Tabs to open the Tabs panel.

When a text frame has an insertion point and enough space at the top, the Tabs panel snaps to the top of the frame so that the measurements in the panel's ruler exactly match the text. Regardless of the position of the Tabs panel, you can enter values to set tabs with precision.

● **Note:** If you change the view scale, the Tabs panel may no longer snap to the text frame containing the text insertion point. To realign the Tabs panel, click the magnet icon in the panel.

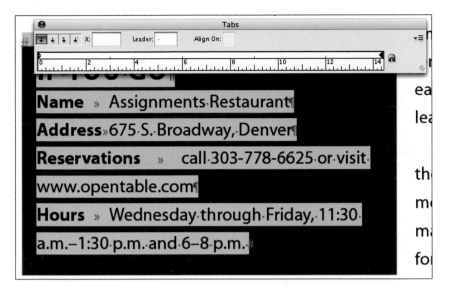

5 In the Tabs panel, click Left-Justified Tab (⬇) so that text aligns to the left of the tab stop.

6 Type **5p5** in the X box and press Enter or Return.

The information following each tab marker in the selected text now aligns to the new tab stop, which is positioned just above the ruler in the Tabs panel.

7 With the text still selected and the Tabs panel still open, click the new tab stop to select it. Type a period (.) and a space in the Leader box. Using a space between periods creates a more open dot sequence in the tab leader.

8 Press Enter or Return to apply the tab leader. Leave the Tabs panel open and in position for the next exercise.

The Leader box specifies the character or characters that fill the space between the text and the tab stop. Tab leaders are commonly used in tables of contents.

▶ **Tip:** To insert a tab character in a table, choose Type > Insert Special Character > Other > Tab.

9 Choose File > Save.

Working with tabs

The controls for creating and customizing tabs in InDesign are fairly similar to those in a word processor. You can precisely position tabs, repeat tabs across a column, create leaders for tabs, specify how text aligns with tabs, and easily modify the tabs you've created. Tabs are paragraph formats, so they apply to the paragraph containing the text insertion point or any selected paragraphs. All the controls are in the Tabs panel, which you open by choosing Type > Tabs. Here's how the tabs controls work.

- **Enter tabs:** To enter a tab in text, press the Tab key.

- **Specify tab alignment:** To specify how text aligns with a tab stop—for example, to the left of the tab stop (the traditional setting) or on a decimal point—click one of the tab buttons in the upper-left corner of the Tabs panel: Left-Justified Tab, Center-Justified Tab, Right-Justified Tab, or Align To Decimal (Or Other Specified Character) Tab.

- **Position tabs:** To position a tab stop, click one of the tab buttons and then type a value in the X box and press Enter or Return. You can also click a tab button and then click in the space just above the ruler.

- **Repeat tabs:** To create multiple tab stops the same distance apart, select a tab on the ruler. Choose Repeat Tab from the Tabs panel menu. This creates tab stops across the column based on the distance between the selected tab stop and the previous tab stop (or the left indent).

- **Specify a character to align text on:** To align text on a character such as a decimal point, click the Align To Decimal (Or Other Specified Character) Tab button and then type or paste a character into the Align On box. (If the text does not contain that character, text will align to the left of the tab stop.)

- **Create a tab leader:** To fill the white space between text and tabs—for example, to add periods between text and page numbers in a table of contents—enter up to eight characters to repeat in the Leader box.

- **Move tabs:** To change the position of a tab stop, select the tab on the ruler, type a new position in the X box. On Windows, press Enter on the keyboard; on Mac OS, press Return. Or, drag the tab on the ruler to a new location.

- **Delete tabs:** To delete a tab, drag it off the tab ruler. Or, select the tab on the ruler and choose Delete tab from the Tabs panel menu.

- **Reset default tabs:** To return to the default tab stops, choose Clear All from the Tabs panel menu. The default tab stop positions vary depending on the document's settings in the Units & Increments panel of the Preferences dialog box. For example, if the Horizontal Ruler units is set to Inches, default tab stops are placed at every half-inch.

- **Change tab alignment:** To change a tab stop's alignment, select it on the ruler and then click a different tab button. Or, press the Alt (Windows) or Option (Mac OS) key while clicking the tab on the ruler to cycle through the four alignment options.

▶ Tip: When working with tabs, it helps to view the tab characters by choosing Type > Show Hidden Characters. It is very common to receive word-processing files in which the writer or editor has entered multiple tabs to align the text onscreen—or worse, entered spaces rather than tabs. The only way to see what you're dealing with (and fix it) is to view hidden characters.

● Note: On Mac OS, when entering a new position for a tab, pressing Enter on the numeric keypad creates a new tab stop rather than moving the selected tab stop.

Creating a hanging indent

In a "hanging indent," text before the tab marker hangs to the left—as you will often see in a bulleted or numbered list. To create a hanging indent for the information in the "If You Go" box, you will use the Tabs panel. You can also use the Left Indent (◀▤) and First Line Left Indent (▼▤) boxes in the Paragraph panel.

1   Using the Type tool (T), select all the text in the "If You Go" box.

2   Make sure that the Tabs panel is still aligned directly above the text frame. If it has moved, click the magnet button (🧲) in the Tabs panel.

3   In the Tabs panel, drag the bottom indent marker on the left side of the ruler to the right until the X value is 5p5. Dragging the bottom marker moves both indents at once. Notice how all the text shifts to the right, and the Left Indent value in the Paragraph panel changes to 5p5. Keep the text selected.

Now you'll bring just the category headings back to their original location in the frame to create a hanging indent.

4   In the Paragraph panel, type **−5p5** in the First Line Left Indent (▼▤) box. Deselect the text, and view the hanging indent.

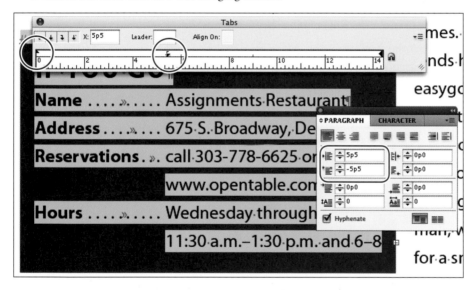

▶ **Tip:** You can also adjust the first-line indent for selected paragraphs by dragging the top indent marker on the tab ruler. However, it can be difficult to select the marker without accidentally creating or modifying a tab stop.

5   Close the Tabs panel.

Notice that the text now overflows the text frame (as indicated by the red plus sign in the lower-right corner of the text frame). There are many ways to remedy this, including expanding the text frame, tracking the text, or editing the text. In this case, you will edit the text.

6   Using the Type tool, double-click the word "through" in the "Hours" section.

7 Choose Type > Insert Special Character > Hyphens And Dashes > En Dash. Delete any extra spaces around the dash.

An en dash looks better in ranges than a hyphen.

8 Choose File > Save.

Adding a rule above a paragraph

You can add a rule, or line, above or below a paragraph. The advantage to using rules rather than simply drawing a line is that rules can be applied with a paragraph style; and they travel with the paragraph when text reflows. Here you'll add a rule above the author bio at the end of the story.

1 Scroll to view the third column on the right-facing page containing the italicized author bio.

2 Using the Type tool (T), click to place an insertion point in the author bio.

3 Choose Paragraph Rules from the Paragraph panel menu.

4 At the top of the Paragraph Rules dialog box, choose Rule Above from the menu, and select Rule On to activate the rule.

5 Select the Preview option. Move the dialog box so that you can see the paragraph.

6 In the Paragraph Rules dialog box, set these options:

- From the Weight menu, choose 1 pt.

- From the Color menu, choose Pantone 584 PC.

- From the Width menu, choose Column.

- In the Offset box, type **0p9.**

7 Click OK to apply the changes.

A lime green rule now appears above the author bio.

8 To view your results:

- Choose View > Fit In Window.
- Choose Preview from the Screen Mode menu (■ ▼) in the Application bar at the top of the screen.

9 Choose File > Save.

Congratulations, you have finished the lesson. To finalize this article, you would likely spend time with an editor or proofreader to fix any tight or loose lines, awkward line breaks, widows, and orphans.

Exploring on your own

Now that you have learned the basics of formatting text in an InDesign document, you're ready to apply these skills on your own. Try the following tasks to improve your typography skills.

1 Place an insertion point in various paragraphs and experiment with turning hyphenation on and off in the Paragraph panel. Select a hyphenated word and choose No Break from the Character panel menu to stop an individual word from hyphenating.

2 Experiment with different hyphenation settings. First, select all the text in the main story. Then, choose Hyphenation from the Paragraph panel menu. Select Preview, and then experiment with the settings. For example, Hyphenate Capitalized Words is selected for this text, but an editor would probably want to turn it off to prevent the chef's name from hyphenating.

3 Experiment with different justification settings. First, select all the text, and then click Justify With Last Line Aligned Left (▤) in the Paragraph panel. Choose Justification from the Paragraph panel menu. Select Preview and experiment with the settings. For example, look at the difference that the Adobe Single-line Composer and the Adobe Paragraph Composer makes when applied to justified (rather than left-aliged) text.

4 Choose Type > Insert Special Character and view all the options available, such as Symbols > Bullet Character and Hyphens And Dashes > Em Dash. Using these characters rather than hyphens significantly enhances how professional the typography looks. Choose Type > Insert White Space and notice the Nonbreaking Space. Use this to "glue" two words together so they cannot split at the end of a line (such as "Mac OS").

Review questions

1 How do you view the baseline grid?

2 When and where do you use a right-indent tab?

3 How do you hang punctuation outside the edges of a text frame?

4 What is the difference between the Paragraph Composer and the Single-line Composer?

Review answers

1 To view the baseline grid, choose View > Grids & Guides > Show Baseline Grid. The current document view must be at or above the view threshold set in the baseline grid preferences. By default, that value is 75%.

2 A right-indent tab, which automatically aligns text with the right margin of a paragraph, is useful for placing end-of-story characters.

3 Select the text frame and choose Type > Story. Select Optical Margin Alignment, which will apply to all the text in the story.

4 The Paragraph Composer evaluates multiple lines at once when determining the best possible line breaks. The Single-line Composer looks at only one line at a time when determining line breaks.

7 WORKING WITH COLOR

Lesson Overview

In this introduction to working with colors and color management, you'll learn how to do the following:

- Add colors to the Swatches panel.

- Apply colors to objects.

- Create dashed strokes.

- Create and apply a gradient swatch.

- Adjust the direction of the gradient blend.

- Create a tint.

- Create a spot color.

- Specify a color management engine.

- Specify default source ICC profiles.

- Assign ICC profiles in InDesign CS4.

- Embed ICC profiles in images created in other Adobe applications.

 This lesson will take approximately 90 minutes.

You can create, save, and apply process and spot colors, including tints, mixed inks, and blended gradients. When your document must meet high-end color printing standards, a color management system reconciles color differences among devices so that you can be reasonably certain of the colors your system ultimately produces.

Getting started

● **Note:** If you have not already copied the resource files for this lesson onto your hard disk from the Adobe InDesign CS4 Classroom in a Book CD, do so now. See "Copying the Classroom in a Book files" on page 2.

In this lesson, you'll work on and set up color management for an advertisement for a fictitious chocolate company called Tifflins Truffles. Color management is important in environments where you must evaluate image color reliably in the context of the final output. Color correction is a different issue that involves images with tonal or color-balance problems, and is usually handled in the original graphics application, such as Photoshop CS4.

The ad will run in a variety of publications, so getting consistent and predictable color is your goal. You will set up the color management system using a CMYK press-oriented workflow, build the document using images from other Adobe software, and specify ICC profiles for individual images to ensure color integrity.

The ad consists of images created in InDesign CS4 and other Adobe applications. You will color-manage those images to achieve consistent color output from InDesign CS4.

1 To ensure that the preferences and default settings of your Adobe InDesign CS4 program match those used in this lesson, move the InDesign Defaults file to a different folder following the procedure in "Saving and restoring the InDesign Defaults file" on page 2.

2 Start Adobe InDesign CS4.

3 Choose File > Open, and open the 07_Start.indd file in the Lesson_07 folder, located inside the Lessons folder in the InDesignCIB folder on your hard disk.

4 Choose File > Save As, rename the file **07_Color.indd**, and save it in the Lesson_07 folder.

5 Choose Window > Workspace > Advanced to make sure all the commands you need are available. Then choose Window > Wordspace > Reset Advanced.

● **Note:** This lesson is designed for users who work with InDesign CS4 in environments that also have Adobe Illustrator (version 9 or later) and Adobe Photoshop (version 5 or later) installed. If you do not have those applications installed on your computer, skip the instructions for color-managing graphics from Illustrator and Photoshop.

6 If you want to see what the finished document looks like, open the 07_End.indd file located in the same folder. You can leave this document open to act as a guide as you work. When you're ready to resume working on the lesson document, click its tab in the upper-left corner of the document window.

CMYK image already placed in document

InDesign CS4 object

Illustrator PDF file
Photoshop file

Defining printing requirements

It's a good idea to know printing requirements before you start working on a document. For example, meet with your prepress service provider and discuss your document's design and use of color. Because your prepress service provider understands the capabilities of their equipment, they may suggest ways for you to save time and money, increase quality, and avoid potentially costly printing or color problems. The ad used in this lesson was designed to be printed by a commercial printer using the CMYK color model.

To confirm that your document matches the printing requirements, you can use a preflight profile, which contains a set of rules regarding the document's size, fonts, colors, images, bleeds, and more. The Preflight panel can then alert you to issues in the document that do not follow the rules set in the profile. In this exercise, you will import a preflight profile provided by the printer of a magazine that will publish the ad.

▶ **Tip:** Your output provider or commercial printer may provide a preflight profile with all the necessary specifications for output. You can import the profile and use it to check your work against these criteria.

1 Choose Window > Output > Preflight.

2 Choose Define Profiles from the Preflight panel menu.

3 In the Preflight Profiles dialog box, click the Preflight Profile Menu button (▤) below the list of preflight profiles at left. Choose Load Profile.

4 Select the Magazine Profile.idpp in the Lesson_07 folder, located inside the Lessons folder within the InDesignCIB folder on your hard disk. Click Open.

5 With the Magazine Profile selected, look through the settings specified for the output of this ad. Checked options are those that InDesign will flag as incorrect—for example, since RGB is checked, any RGB images will be reported as errors.

6 Click OK to close the Preflight Profiles dialog box.

7 Choose Magazine Profile from the Profile menu on the Preflight panel. Notice that the profile detects one issue with an imported Illustrator file. If you were actually going to send this ad to the magazine, the error would need to be resolved.

8 Choose File > Save.

Creating and applying colors

For maximum design flexibility, InDesign provides a variety of methods for creating and applying colors and gradients. The software makes it easy to experiment while helping to ensure proper output. In this section, you will learn a variety of methods for creating and applying colors.

Adding colors to the Swatches panel

You can add color to objects using a combination of panels and tools. The InDesign CS4 color workflow revolves around the Swatches panel. Using the Swatches panel to name colors makes it easy to apply, edit, and update colors for objects in a document. Although you can also use the Color panel to apply colors to objects, there is no quick way to update these colors, which are considered unnamed colors. Instead, you'd have to update the unnamed color of each object individually.

You'll now create most of the colors you'll use in this document. Because this document is intended for a commercial press, you'll be creating CMYK process colors.

1 Make sure that no objects are selected, and then open the Swatches panel. (If the Swatches panel is not visible, choose Window > Swatches.)

The Swatches panel stores the colors, tints, and gradients you can create and store for reuse.

2 Choose New Color Swatch from the Swatches panel menu.

3 Deselect Name With Color Value, and for Swatch Name, type **Brown**. Make sure that Color Type and Color Mode are set to Process and CMYK, respectively.

New Color Swatch		
Swatch Name: Brown		OK
☐ Name with Color Value		Cancel
Color Type: Process		Add
Color Mode: CMYK		
Cyan	0	%
Magenta	76	%
Yellow	76	%
Black	60	%

4 For the color percentages, type the following values:
Cyan (C) = **0**, Magenta (M) = **76**, Yellow (Y) = **76**, Black (K) = **60**

5 Click Add to include this new color in the Swatches panel and keep the dialog box open, ready to create two more colors.

● **Note:** As you work through the lesson, you can move panels around or change the magnification to a level that works best for you. For more information, see "Changing the magnification of a document" in Lesson 1.

● **Note:** The Name With Color Value option names a color using the CMYK color values that you enter, and automatically updates the name if you change the value. This option is available only for process colors and is useful when you want to use the Swatches panel to monitor the exact composition of process-color swatches. For this swatch, you deselected Name With Color Value so that you can use a name (Brown) that's easier to read.

6 Repeat the previous three steps to name and create the following colors:

- **Blue:** Cyan (C) = **60**, Magenta (M) = **20**, Yellow (Y) = **0**, Black (K) = **0**

- **Tan:** Cyan (C) = **5**, Magenta (M) = **13**, Yellow (Y) = **29**, Black (K) = **0**

7 When finished, click Done in the New Color Swatch dialog box.

▶ **Tip:** If you forget to type the name for a color or if you type an incorrect value, double-click the swatch, change the name or value, and then click OK.

New colors added to the Swatches panel are stored only with the document in which they are created—although you can import them into other documents. You'll apply these colors to text, images, and strokes in the layout.

8 Choose File > Save.

Applying colors to objects

There are three general steps to applying a swatch color: (1) selecting the text or object, (2) selecting the stroke or fill in the Tools panel, depending on what you want to change, and (3) selecting the color in the Swatches panel. You can also drag swatches from the Swatches panel to objects. In this exercise, you will apply colors to strokes and fills using both the Swatches panel and the Eyedropper tool.

1 Select any one of the diamond shapes in the upper right of the page with the Selection tool (▶). Because these three objects are grouped, they all are now selected.

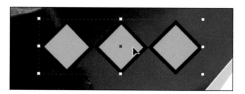

You will ungroup these objects and lock them in place. Locking objects prevents you from accidentally moving them.

2 With the group of objects still selected, choose Object > Ungroup. Then, choose Object > Lock Position.

3 Choose Edit > Deselect All or click a blank area on the document window to deselect all objects.

▶ **Tip:** To increase magnification, press Ctrl+= (Windows) or Command+= (Mac OS). To zoom out, press Ctrl+- (Windows) or Command+- (Mac OS).

4 Select the Zoom tool (🔍) in the Tools panel and drag to draw a marquee around the diamonds. The view magnification changes so that the area defined by the marquee now fills the document window. Make sure that you can see all three diamond shapes.

5 Select the Selection tool (▶), and click in the center diamond. Select the Stroke box (◪) in the Swatches panel, and then select the Green swatch (you may need to scroll down in the list of swatches).

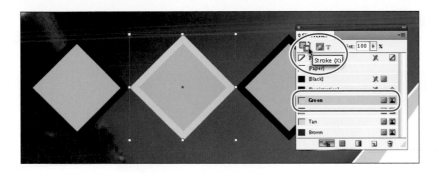

The stroke of the diamond shape is now green.

6 Deselect the object.

7 Select the diamond on the left. Select Brown in the Swatches panel to apply a brown stroke.

8 With the diamond on the left still selected, select the Fill box (⊞) in the Swatches panel, and then select the Green swatch (you may need to scroll down in the list of swatches).

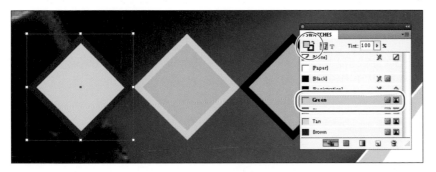

The diamond on the right requires the same Brown stroke and Green fill. You'll use the eyedropper to copy those stroke and fill attributes in one quick step.

9 Select the Eyedropper tool (✐), and click the diamond on the left. Notice that the eyedropper is now filled (↖), indicating that it picked up the attributes from that object.

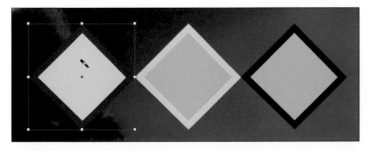

10 With the loaded eyedropper, click the gray background of the diamond on the right. That diamond now has the fill and stroke attributes of the diamond on the left.

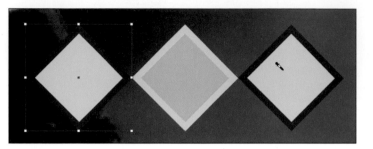

Now you'll change the fill color of the diamond in the center.

11 Choose Edit > Deselect All.

▶ **Tip:** [Paper] is a special color that simulates the paper color on which you're printing. Objects behind a paper-colored object won't print where the paper-colored object overlaps them. Instead, the color of the paper on which you print shows through.

12 Using the Selection tool (⬈), click the diamond in the center. Select the Fill box (⬚) in the Tools panel, and then click [Paper] in the Swatches panel.

13 Choose Edit > Deselect All, and then choose View > Fit Page In Window.

Now you'll stroke the six small diamonds and line at the bottom of the ad with brown.

14 Using the Selection tool (⬈), hold down the Shift key and select the six small diamonds on the bottom of the ad as well as the line behind them.

15 In the Swatches panel, select the Stroke box (⬚) and click the Brown swatch.

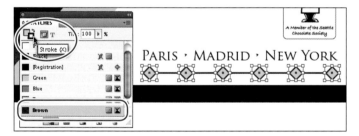

Creating dashed strokes

You'll now change the black line that borders the ad to a custom dashed line. Because you are using the custom dashed line on only one object, you will create it using the Stroke panel. If you need to save a stroke for repetitive use throughout a document, you can easily create a stroke style. For more information about saving Stroke styles, including dashes, dots, and stripes, see InDesign Help.

In this exercise, you will specify a dashed stroke for the frame on the ad, and then customize the dashes.

1 Deselect any selected objects. If necessary, choose View > Fit Page In Window.

2 Using the Selection tool (▸), select the black outline that borders the ad.

3 If the Stroke panel is not already visible, choose Window > Stroke.

4 Select Dashed from the bottom of the Type menu.

Six dash and gap boxes appear at the bottom of the Stroke panel. To create a dashed line, you specify the length of the dash and then the gap, or spacing, between the dashes.

5 Choose Brown from the Gap Color menu to fill the gaps with brown.

6 Type the following values in the Dash and Gap boxes: **12**, **4**, **2**, **4**, **2**, **4** (press Tab after you type each value to move to the next box).

7 Deselect the line and close the Stroke panel.

8 Then choose File > Save.

Working with gradients

A gradient is a graduated blend between two or more colors, or between tints of the same color. You can create either a linear or a radial gradient. In this exercise, you will create a linear gradient with the Swatches panel, apply it to several objects, and adjust the gradients with the Gradient tool.

A. Linear gradient   B. Radial gradient

Creating and applying a gradient swatch

Every InDesign CS4 gradient has at least two color stops. By editing the color mix of each stop and by adding additional color stops in the Gradient or Swatches panel, you can create your own custom gradients.

1 Make sure no objects are selected.

2 Choose New Gradient Swatch from the Swatches panel menu.

Gradients are defined by a series of color stops in the gradient ramp. A stop is the point at which each color is at full intensity between the transitions, and is identified by a square below the gradient ramp.

3 For Swatch Name, type **Brown/Tan Gradient**. Leave the Type set to Linear.

4 Click the left stop marker (🔒). For Stop Color, select Swatches, and then scroll down the list of color swatches and select Brown.

Notice that the left side of the gradient ramp is brown.

5 Click the right stop marker. For Stop Color, select Swatches, and then scroll down the list and select Tan.

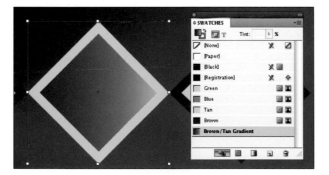

The gradient ramp shows a color blend between brown and tan.

6 Click OK.

Now you'll apply the gradient to the fill of the center diamond in the upper-right corner.

7 Zoom in on the upper-right corner, bringing the three diamond shapes into view.

8 Select the center diamond with the Selection tool (↖).

9 Select the Fill box (⬚) in the Tools panel, and then click Brown/Tan Gradient in the Swatches panel.

10 Choose File > Save.

Adjusting the direction of the gradient blend

Once you have filled an object with a gradient, you can modify the gradient by using the Gradient tool to "repaint" the fill along an imaginary line that you create. This tool lets you change the direction of a gradient and change the beginning point and end point of a gradient. You'll now change the direction of the gradient.

1 Make sure the center diamond is still selected, and then select the Gradient Swatch tool (▭) in the Tools panel.

Now you'll experiment with the Gradient tool to see how you can change the direction and intensity of the gradient.

2 To create a more gradual gradient effect, place the cursor outside of the selected diamond and drag as shown below.

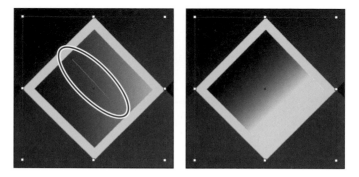

When you release the mouse button, you'll notice that the transition between brown and tan is more gradual than it was before you dragged with the Gradient tool.

3 To create a sharper gradient, drag a small line in the center of the diamond. Continue to experiment with the Gradient tool so that you understand how it works.

4 When you are finished experimenting, drag from the top to the bottom of the diamond. That's how you'll leave the gradient of the center diamond.

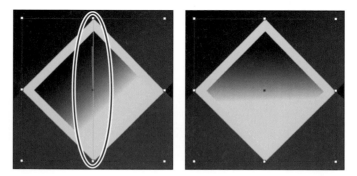

5 Choose File > Save.

Creating a tint

As well as adding colors, you can also add tints to the Swatches panel. A tint is a screened (lighter) version of a color. You'll now create a 30% tint of the brown swatch you saved earlier in this lesson.

1 Choose View > Fit Page In Window to center the page in your document window.

2 Deselect all objects.

3 Select Brown in the Swatches panel. Choose New Tint Swatch from the Swatches panel menu. For Tint percentage, type **30** and then click OK.

The new tint swatch appears at the bottom of the list of swatches. The top of the Swatches panel displays information about the selected swatch, with a Fill/Stroke box showing that the brown tint is currently the selected fill color and a Tint box showing that the color is 30% of the original Brown color.

4 Using the Selection tool ( ), click the word "¡Sí!" in the center of the page.

5 Make sure the Fill box ( ) is selected, and then click the Brown tint that you just created in the Swatches panel. Notice how the color changes.

6 Choose File > Save.

Tip: Tints are helpful because InDesign CS4 maintains the relationship between a tint and its parent color. For example, if you change the brown color swatch to a different color, the tint swatch you create in this exercise becomes a lighter version of the new color.

About spot and process colors

A spot color is a special premixed ink that is used instead of, or in addition to, CMYK process inks, and that requires its own printing plate on a printing press. Use spot color when few colors are specified and color accuracy is critical. Spot color inks can accurately reproduce colors that are outside the gamut of process colors. However, the exact appearance of the printed spot color is determined by the combination of the ink as mixed by the commercial printer and the paper it's printed on, not by color values you specify or by color management. When you specify spot color values, you're describing the simulated appearance of the color for your monitor and composite printer only (subject to the gamut limitations of those devices).

A process color is printed using a combination of the four standard process inks: cyan, magenta, yellow, and black (CMYK). Use process colors when a job requires so many colors that using individual spot inks would be expensive or impractical, as when printing color photographs.

- For best results in a high-quality printed document, specify process colors using CMYK values printed in process color reference charts, such as those available from a commercial printer.

- The final color values of a process color are its values in CMYK, so if you specify a process color using RGB (or LAB, in InDesign), those color values are converted to CMYK when you print color separations. These conversions differ based on your color-management settings and document profile.

- Don't specify a process color based on how it looks on your monitor, unless you are sure you have set up a color-management system properly, and you understand its limitations for previewing color.

- Avoid using process colors in documents intended for online viewing only, because CMYK has a smaller color gamut than that of a typical monitor.

Sometimes it's practical to use process and spot inks in the same job. For example, you might use one spot ink to print the exact color of a company logo on the same pages of an annual report where photographs are reproduced using process color. You can also use a spot color printing plate to apply a varnish over areas of a process color job. In both cases, your print job would use a total of five inks—four process inks and one spot ink or varnish.

—Condensed from InDesign Help

Creating a spot color

This ad will be printed by a commercial printer using the standard CMYK color model, which requires four separate plates for printing—one each for cyan, magenta, yellow, and black. However, the CMYK color model has a limited range of colors, which is where spot colors are useful. Because of this, spot colors are used to create additional colors beyond the range of CMYK or to create consistent, individual colors such as those used for company logos.

In this ad, the design calls for a spot ink not found in the CMYK color model. You'll now add a spot color from a color library.

1   Deselect all objects.

2   Choose New Color Swatch from the Swatches panel menu.

3   In the New Color Swatch dialog box, choose Spot from the Color Type menu.

4   Select PANTONE Solid Coated in the Color Mode list.

5   In the PANTONE C text box, type **567** to automatically scroll the list of Pantone swatches to the color you want for this project, which is PANTONE 567 C.

6   Click OK. The spot color is added to your Swatches panel. The icon (▣) next to the color name in the Swatches panel indicates that it is a spot color.

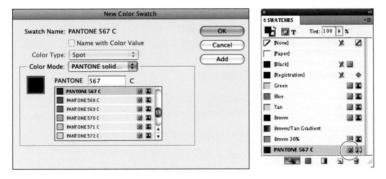

Applying color to text

As with images, you can apply a stroke or fill to text. You'll apply colors to the text on the top and bottom of the document.

1   With the Selection tool (▸), select the text frame containing the word "Indulgent?" and then hold down the Shift key and click the text frame containing the words "Paris · Madrid · New York."

2   In the Tools panel, click the Formatting Affects Text button (T) below the Fill box. Then, make sure the Fill box (▧) is selected.

3   In the Swatches panel, click PANTONE 567 C, and then click a blank area to deselect the text frames. The text now appears in the spot color.

4   Choose File > Save.

Applying colors to additional objects

Now you'll apply the same color used by the outlined text "Yes!" to color the outlined "Oui!" text. First you'll magnify the view of the outlined text "Yes!" to see which color is used.

1 In the Tools panel, select the Zoom tool (🔍), and then drag to place a marquee around the text in the middle of the page.

2 Select the Direct Selection tool (▷), and click the text "Yes!". Notice that the corresponding swatch in the Swatches panel becomes highlighted when you select the object to which the swatch is applied.

Now you'll apply this color to the "Oui!" text.

▶ **Tip:** If you applied the color to the wrong object, choose Edit > Undo Apply Attribute and try again.

3 Drag the Green fill swatch from the Swatches panel to the text "Oui!". Be sure to drop it inside the object and not on the object's stroke. The pointer changes to an arrow with a black box (▶■) when you drop the swatch onto the fill of the text. An arrow with a line to the right (▶⁄) appears if you drag the swatch onto the stroke of the text. Make sure that the Tint in the Swatches panel is 100%.

Dragging and dropping can be a more convenient way to apply color, because you don't have to select the object first.

Creating another tint

You'll now create a tint based on the Blue color. When you edit the Blue color, the tint that is based on the color also changes.

1 Deselect all objects.

2 Select Blue in the Swatches panel. Choose New Tint Swatch from the Swatches panel menu. Type **40** in the Tint box, and then click OK.

3 Select the text ";Si!" with the Selection tool (▶), and apply the Blue 40% fill.

Next you'll change the Blue color. Blue 40% is based on the Blue swatch, so the tint also changes.

4 Deselect all objects.

5 Double-click the Blue swatch (not the Blue tint swatch) to change the color. In the Swatch Name box, type **Violet Blue**. For the color percentages, type the following values:

   •   C = **59**, M = **80**, Y = **40**, K = **0**

6 Click OK.

As you can see, adding colors to the Swatches panel makes it easy to update colors.

7 Choose File > Save.

Using advanced gradient techniques

Earlier you created and applied a gradient and adjusted its direction using the Gradient tool. InDesign CS4 also lets you create gradients of multiple colors, and control the point at which the colors blend. In addition, you can apply a gradient to individual objects or to a collection of objects.

Creating a gradient swatch with multiple colors

Earlier in this lesson, you created a gradient with two colors—brown and tan. Now you'll create a gradient with three stops so that a yellow/green color on the outside fades to white in the middle. Make sure that no objects are selected before you begin.

1 Choose New Gradient Swatch from the Swatches panel menu, and then type **Green/White Gradient** in the Swatch Name box.

The colors from the previous blend appear in the dialog box.

2 Click the left stop marker (🔖), choose Swatches from the Stop Color menu, and select the Green swatch in the list box.

3 Click the right stop marker (🔖), choose Swatches from the Stop Color menu, and select the Green swatch in the list box.

● **Note:** If you press the Shift key while you adjust one color value, the other color values adjust in proportion automatically.

4 With the right stop marker still selected, choose CMYK from the Stop Color menu. While pressing the Shift key, drag the Yellow slider until the % value for Yellow is 40% and release. The gradient ramp is now made up of Green and light Green. Now you'll add a stop marker to the middle so that the color fades toward the center.

5 Click just below the center of the gradient bar to add a new stop. For Location, type **50** to make sure the stop is centered.

6 For Stop Color, select CMYK and then drag each of the four color sliders to 0 (zero) to create white. You could also select Swatches and choose the [Paper] color to create a white color stop.

7 Click OK, and then choose File > Save.

Applying the gradient to an object

Now you'll apply the new gradient fill you just created. First, change the view size so that you can see the entire page.

1 Choose View > Fit Page In Window or double-click the Hand tool (✋) in the Tools panel to achieve the same result.

2 With the Selection tool (▸), click the diagonal Green stripe on the right side of the chocolate bar picture to select it. (It may appear yellow/green.)

3 Select the Fill box (⬛) in the Tools panel, and then select Green/White Gradient in the Swatches panel.

4 To adjust the gradient transition, select the Gradient Swatch tool (▭) in the Tools panel and drag up and to the right of the object as shown. Resuls will vary according to where you start dragging.

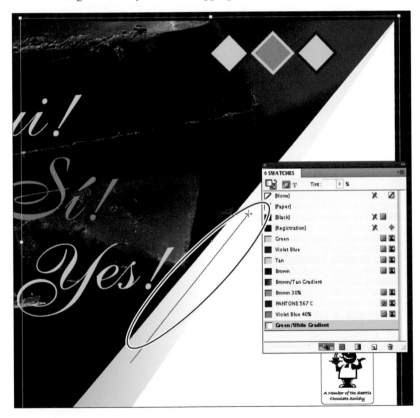

5 Choose Edit > Deselect All.

6 Choose File > Save.

Applying a gradient to multiple objects

Previously in this lesson, you used the Gradient tool to change the direction of a gradient, and to change the gradient's beginning point and end point. You'll now use the Gradient tool to apply a gradient across multiple objects in the three diamond shapes on the bottom of the page.

1 Double-click the Hand tool (🖐) to fit the page in your document window.

2 Using the Selection tool (▶), Shift+click the six diamond shapes below the "Paris · Madrid · New York" text, with the Selection tool.

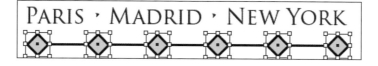

Now you'll apply the Green/White Gradient to the six different diamond objects.

3 Confirm that the Fill box (⬛) is selected in the Swatches panel. In the Tools panel, click the Gradient button to apply the last selected gradient.

Notice that the gradient affects each object on an individual basis. Now you'll use the Gradient tool to apply the gradient across the six selected objects as one.

4 With the six objects still selected, select the Gradient Swatch tool (⬛) in the Tools panel. Drag an imaginary line across the objects..

Now the gradient runs across all six selected objects.

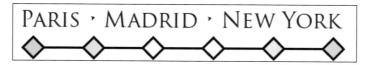

5 Choose File > Save.

Ensuring consistent color

Color management is important in environments where you must evaluate image color reliably in the context of your final output. Color correction is a different issue that involves images with tonal or color-balance problems, and is usually handled in the original graphics application, such as Photoshop.

Do you need color management?

Without a color management system, your color specifications are device-dependent. You might not need color management if your production process is tightly controlled for one medium only. For example, you or your print service provider can tailor CMYK images and specify color values for a known, specific set of printing conditions.

The value of color management increases when you have more variables in your production process. Color management is recommended if you anticipate reusing color graphics for print and online media, using various kinds of devices within a single medium (such as different printing presses), or if you manage multiple workstations.

You will benefit from a color management system if you need to accomplish any of the following:

- Get predictable and consistent color output on multiple output devices including color separations, your desktop printer, and your monitor. Color management is especially useful for adjusting color for devices with a relatively limited gamut, such as a four-color process printing press.

- Accurately soft-proof (preview) a color document on your monitor by making it simulate a specific output device. (Soft-proofing is subject to the limitations of monitor display, and other factors such as room lighting conditions.)

- Accurately evaluate and consistently incorporate color graphics from many different sources if they also use color management, and even in some cases if they don't.

- Send color documents to different output devices and media without having to manually adjust colors in documents or original graphics. This is valuable when creating images that will eventually be used both in print and online.

- Print color correctly to an unknown color output device; for example, you could store a document online for consistently reproducible on-demand color printing anywhere in the world.

—From InDesign Help

Note: Don't confuse color management with color correction. A color management system won't correct an image that was saved with tonal or color balance problems. It provides an environment where you can evaluate images reliably in the context of your final output.

Tip: If you decide to use color management, consult with your production partners— such as graphic artists and prepress service providers—to ensure that all aspects of your color management workflow integrate with theirs.

An overview of color management

Devices and graphics have different color gamuts. Although all color gamuts overlap, they don't match exactly, which is why some colors on your monitor can't be reproduced in print or online. The colors that can't be reproduced in print are called out-of-gamut colors because they are outside of the spectrum of printable colors. For example, you can create a large percentage of colors in the visible spectrum using programs such as InDesign CS4, Photoshop CS4, and Illustrator CS4, but you can reproduce only a subset of those colors on a desktop printer.

The printer has a smaller color space or gamut (the range of colors that can be displayed or printed) than the application that created the color.

Visible spectrum containing millions of colors (far left) compared with color gamuts of various devices and graphics.

To compensate for these differences and to ensure the closest match between on-screen colors and printed colors, applications use a color management system (CMS). Using a color management engine, the CMS translates colors from the color space of one device into a device-independent color space, such as CIE (Commission Internationale d'Éclairage) LAB. From the device-independent color space, the CMS fits that color information to another device's color space by a process called color mapping, or gamut mapping. The CMS makes any adjustments necessary to represent the color as consistently as possible among devices.

A CMS uses three components to map colors across devices:

- A device-independent (or reference) color space

- ICC profiles that define the color characteristics of different devices and images

- A color management engine that translates colors from one device's color space to another's color space

A. Scanners and software applications create color documents.
B. ICC source profiles describe document color spaces.
C. A color management engine uses ICC source profiles to map document colors to a device-independent color space through a supporting application such as InDesign.
D. The color management engine maps document colors from the device-independent color space to output-device color spaces using destination profiles.

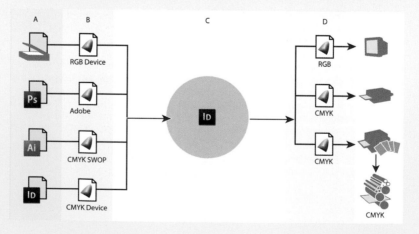

About the device-independent color space

To successfully compare gamuts and make adjustments, a color management system must use a reference color space—an objective way of defining color. Most CMSs use the CIE LAB color model, which exists independently of any device and is big enough to reproduce any color visible to the human eye. For this reason, CIE LAB is considered device-independent.

About ICC profiles

An ICC profile describes how a particular device or standard reproduces color using a cross-platform standard defined by the International Color Consortium (ICC).

ICC profiles ensure that images appear correctly in any ICC-compliant applications and on color devices. This is accomplished by embedding the profile information in the original file or assigning the profile in your application.

At a minimum, you must have one source profile for the device (such as a scanner or digital camera) or standard (such as SWOP or Adobe RGB) used to create the color, and one destination profile for the device (such as monitor or contract proofing) or standard (SWOP or TOYO, for example) that you will use to reproduce the color.

About color management engines

Sometimes called the color matching module (CMM), the color management engine interprets ICC profiles. Acting as a translator, the color management engine converts the out-of-gamut colors from the source device to the range of colors that can be produced by the destination device. The color management engine may be included with the CMS or may be a separate part of the operating system.

Translating to a gamut—particularly a smaller gamut—usually involves a compromise, so multiple translation methods are available. For example, a color-translation method that preserves correct relationships among colors in a photograph usually alters the colors in a logo. Color management engines provide a choice of translation methods, known as rendering intents, so that you can apply a method appropriate to the intended use of a color image. Examples of common rendering intents include Perceptual (images) for preserving color relationships the way the eye does, Saturation (images) for preserving vivid colors at the expense of color accuracy, and Relative and Absolute Colorimetric for preserving color accuracy at the expense of color relationships.

Components of a CMYK press-oriented workflow

In a CMYK workflow, you work with CMYK images prepared for a specific printing press or proofing device. You generate a source profile based on your press or contract-proofing standard and embed it into the CMYK images or assign the profile in InDesign CS4. The profile enables consistent CMYK printing at other color-managed sites, such as when printing a widely distributed magazine on presses in many different cities. Because you use color management, the reliability and consistency of the color display improves across all your workstations.

For final printed output, you select a printer profile in the Print dialog box that describes your contract-proofing standard or your printing press.

● **Note:** You can find additional information on color management on the Web and in print. Here are a few resources that are available as of the date of publication of this book: Adobe. com (search for color management), Apple.com (search for ColorSync), or the Peachpit book *Real World Color Management.*

Setting up color management in InDesign CS4

No monitor, film, printer, copier, or printing press can produce the full range of color visible to the human eye. Each device has a specific capability and makes different kinds of compromises in reproducing color images. The unique color-rendering abilities of a specific output device are known collectively as its gamut or color space.

InDesign CS4 and other graphics applications, such as Adobe Photoshop CS4 and Adobe Illustrator CS4, use color numbers to describe the color of each pixel in an image. The color numbers correspond to the color model, such as the familiar RGB values for red, green, and blue or the CMYK values for cyan, magenta, yellow, and black.

Color management is simply a consistent way of translating the color numbers for each pixel from the source (the document or image stored on your computer) to the output device (such as your monitor, color printer, or high-resolution printing press), each with its own specific gamut.

In an ICC workflow—that is, one that follows the conventions of the International Color Consortium—you specify a color management engine and a color profile. The color management engine is the software feature or module that does the work of reading and translating colors between different color spaces. A color profile is the description of how the color numbers map to the color space (capabilities) of output devices.

Adobe Creative Suite 4 components give you easy-to-use color management features and tools that help you achieve good, sellable color without needing to become a color management expert. With color management enabled out-of-the-box in CS4, you'll be able to view colors consistently across applications and platforms while ensuring more accurate color from edit to proof to final print.

A look at Adobe Bridge

The Adobe Bridge tool in Adobe Creative Suite 4 is a central location where users can select a color settings file (CSF) with preset color management policies and default profiles. Selecting a CSF in Adobe Bridge ensures that color is handled consistently and that color displays and prints the same way from all Adobe Creative Suite 4 components.

When users select a CSF, the file's preset values determine the color management behavior in all applications, such as how embedded profiles are handled, what the default RGB and CMYK working spaces are, and whether to display warning dialogs when embedded profiles don't match the default working space. Selecting the correct CSF depends on your workflow. For more information on the Adobe Bridge tool, search for "Adobe Bridge" in Help.

Specifying the Adobe ACE engine

Different companies have developed various ways to manage color. To provide you with a choice, you use a color management system to designate a color management engine that represents the approach you want to use. Remember that the color management engine translates colors from the source. InDesign CS4 offers the Adobe ACE engine as one of your choices. This engine uses the same architecture as in Photoshop and Illustrator, so that your color management choices are integrated across these Adobe applications.

1   Choose Edit > Color Settings.

The color management engine and other settings you choose in the Color Settings dialog box are saved with InDesign CS4 and apply to all InDesign CS4 documents you work on in the future.

By default, color management is enabled.

2   Choose the North America Prepress 2 from the Settings menu if it's not chosen already.

3   Select the Advanced Mode option.

4   Under Color Management Policies, choose Preserve Embedded Profiles from the CMYK menu.

5   Under Conversion Options in the lower part of the dialog box, select Adobe (ACE) in the Engine menu if it's not already chosen.

6   For Intent, choose Perceptual from the menu. Later in this lesson you'll explore the Intent options in more detail.

7   Leave the dialog box open so you can use it in the next section.

▶ **Tip:** Choose Adobe ACE unless your prepress service provider recommends another engine. Use the same engine throughout your CS4 workflow.

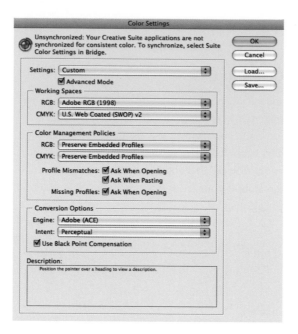

Setting up default working spaces

To complete the application-wide color management setup, you'll choose profiles for the devices used to reproduce the color, including your monitor, composite proofing device, and final separations standard. InDesign CS4 refers to these preset profiles as working spaces. These working spaces are also available in other Adobe graphics applications, including Illustrator CS4 and Photoshop CS4. Once you designate the same working space in all three applications, you've automatically set up consistent color for illustration, digital images, and document layouts.

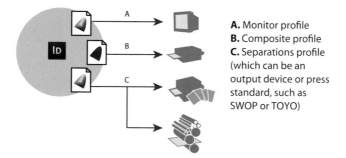

A. Monitor profile
B. Composite profile
C. Separations profile (which can be an output device or press standard, such as SWOP or TOYO)

First, you'll select a monitor profile. If the Color Settings dialog box is not open, reopen it.

1   Under Working Spaces, choose U.S. Web Coated (SWOP) v2 from the CMYK menu if it's not already chosen.

In a later section, you'll set the on-screen display of images to full resolution so that InDesign CS4 can color-manage all available image data.

2 Move the dialog box out of your way and study the colors in the ad.

Notice the heavy use of brown. You'll see a noticeable difference in the browns when you apply color management by closing the dialog box in the next step.

3 Click OK.

4 Choose View > Proof Colors. This shows soft-proof colors on your monitor. Depending on your viewing conditions, this can give you a more accurate preview of how your image will print.

Several colors change in the ad, but most noticeably the browns; they appear to have more detail. It's important to note that although the images look better than they did when you opened the document, the images themselves have not been altered—only the display of the images has changed. Specifically, what you see now represents the color characteristics of the following devices:

- The program or scanner that saved the image, using the source profile embedded in the image

- The final output device for the document, using the destination profile you set up earlier in the lesson

It's easy to see that the success of color management ultimately depends on the accuracy of your profiles.

Assigning source profiles

Source profiles describe the color space used when you create colors in InDesign CS4 and apply them to objects, or when you import an RGB, CMYK, or LAB color image that wasn't saved with an embedded profile. When you import an image with embedded profiles, InDesign CS4 color-manages the image using the embedded profiles rather than the profiles you choose here, unless you override the embedded profiles for an individual image.

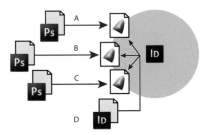

A. LAB profile **B.** RGB profile **C.** CMYK profile **D.** InDesign CS4 document applying a profile that matches the color model of each image that lacks a profile

1   Choose Edit > Assign Profiles.

2   In the RGB Profile area, select the Assign Current Working Space option, which should be set to Adobe RGB (1998).

3   In the CMYK Profile area, select the Assign Current Working Space option, which should be set to U.S. Web Coated (SWOP) v2.

Notice that the text following the words Working Space contains the same working-space information that you entered in the Color Settings dialog box. With these settings, the Adobe ACE engine won't unnecessarily convert colors for which you've already specified a profile.

4   Leave the dialog box open so you can use it in the next section.

Specifying the rendering intent

The rendering intent determines how the color management engine converts colors, based on the source and destination profiles you specify in InDesign CS4. You'll specify the color-translation method for the InDesign CS4 color management engine to apply to the images in the ad.

1   In the lower area of the Assign Profiles dialog box, leave Relative Colorimetric selected for the Solid Color Intent option. This option preserves individual colors at the expense of color relationships, so it's appropriate for business logos and other such images.

2   Make sure that Use Color Settings Intent is selected for both the Default Image Intent and After-Blending Intent options. These options are appropriate for this photo-intensive page spread.

3   Click OK to close the Assign Profiles dialog box.

4   Choose File > Save.

Using full-resolution display with color management

When you use image-display resolutions lower than high quality, the screen redraw is faster, but colors display less precisely. Image colors display most precisely when you view images at the highest resolution available (in addition to turning on color management). To see the difference:

1 Choose View > Display Performance > Fast Display. This display mode is ideal for quick text editing because images do not display.

2 Choose View > Display Performance > High Quality Display.

For the best output results, it's especially important to view color-managed images at high resolution when you work with duotones.

When color management is on, image display is set to full resolution, you use accurate profiles that are applied properly, and you see the best possible color representation that your monitor is capable of showing.

● **Note:** To save disk space, the sample files for this lesson are 150 pixels per inch (ppi), so the colors are not as precise as they would be using a higher resolution.

Color-managing imported images in InDesign CS4

When you import an image, you can control its color management in your document. If you know that an imported image contains an accurate embedded profile with an appropriate rendering intent, you just import it and continue working. InDesign CS4 reads and applies the embedded profile to the image, integrating it into the CMS for the document. If an imported bitmap image does not include an embedded profile, InDesign CS4 applies the default source profile (CMYK, RGB, or LAB) to the image.

InDesign CS4 also applies a default source profile to objects drawn in InDesign CS4. You can assign a different profile within InDesign CS4 (using Edit > Assign Profiles to open the Assign Profiles dialog box) or open the image in the original application and embed the profile there.

The ad already includes two images that were saved without embedded profiles. You'll integrate those images into the document CMS using two different methods: assigning a profile within InDesign CS4 and opening the original image so that you can embed the profile. Later in the lesson, you'll import two additional images and practice two methods of assigning a profile before you place them in the ad.

Assigning a profile after importing an image

When you import an image saved without an embedded profile into a layout, InDesign CS4 applies its default source profile to the image. If an imported image was not created in the default color space, you should assign the profile that describes the image's original color space.

 InDesign CS4 applies its default source profile to any bitmap image without embedded profiles.

You'll work with an image that was imported into InDesign CS4 before you turned on color management. First, you'll confirm the default profile InDesign CS4 is using to color-manage the image. Then, within InDesign CS4, you'll assign a new profile because the image's original color space is different from the default color space.

1   Using the Selection tool (⬆), select the plate of truffles on the left side of the ad.

2   Choose Object > Image Color Settings.

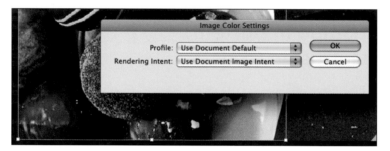

Notice that Use Document Default is selected for Profile. InDesign CS4 enables color management for each imported image and assigns the default source profile you set up earlier in this lesson. You can also assign a new profile here. Because you are assigning the profile within InDesign CS4, the change applies only to the selected image in this document.

3   For Profile, choose U.S. Sheetfed Coated v2 to match the image's original color space. This profile represents the color-lookup tables used by the scanner operator who originally scanned this as a CMYK image.

4   Leave the Rendering Intent set as Use Document Image Intent, and click OK. The colors deepen noticeably.

5   Choose File > Save.

InDesign CS4 color-manages the image using the newly assigned profile.

Embedding a profile in a Photoshop image

As a general rule, you should embed ICC profiles in files before importing the files into another document that uses color management. That way, images with embedded profiles more likely appear as intended in InDesign CS4 or other color-managed programs without requiring any additional work.

In this section, you'll work with a previously imported color bitmap image that does not contain an embedded profile.

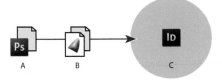

A. The working CMYK color space of the image
B. Image with embedded ICC profile
C. InDesign CS4 uses embedded profile

Setting up color management in Photoshop CS4

First, you'll define the working color spaces (used for viewing and editing) for the RGB and CMYK color modes of the image.

1 Start Photoshop, and choose Edit > Color Settings.

2 Choose North America Prepress 2 from the Settings menu. Click More Options at right to view all of the selections available.

3 For the CMYK option under Working Spaces, select U.S. Web Coated (SWOP) v2 if it is not already selected. This ensures that the embedded profile matches the default separations profile you specified in InDesign CS4.

● **Note:** If Photoshop isn't installed on your system, you can use the Photoshop files provided in the lesson folder. The steps indicate when to do so.

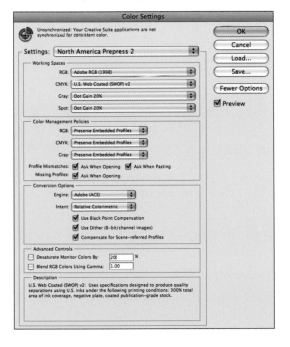

4 Leave the other settings as they are, and click OK.

Embedding the profile

Now that you have specified the working color spaces for the Photoshop image, you'll embed the specified profile.

1   From Photoshop, choose File > Open and select 07_d.psd in the Lesson_07 folder. Click Open to open the graphic file.

2   In Photoshop, if the Missing Profile dialog box appears, select Assign Working CMYK. Notice that it is already set to U.S. Web Coated (SWOP) v2, which is the profile you selected in the previous exercise, "Setting up color management in Photoshop." Click OK. If you do not receive a Missing Profile warning, choose Image > Mode > Convert To Profile and choose U.S. Web Coated (SWOP) v2 as the Destination Profile, and click OK.

3   To embed the profile, choose File > Save As. Select your Lesson_07 folder in your InDesignCIB folder, and then choose TIFF from the Format menu. Type **07_d_prof.tif** in the File Name box. Make sure that the ICC Profile: U.S. Web Coated (SWOP) v2 option (Windows) or the Embed Color Profile: U.S. Web Coated (SWOP) v2 option (Mac OS) is selected, and click Save.

4   In the TIFF Options dialog box, click OK to accept the default.

5   Choose File > Close to close the image.

6   Exit Photoshop, and return to InDesign CS4.

Updating the image within InDesign CS4

Now that you've embedded the ICC profile in the Photoshop file, you can update the image in InDesign CS4. InDesign CS4 color-manages the image using the embedded profile.

● **Note:** When relinking to a file using a different file format, choose All Files from the Files Of Type menu when browsing for the file on the Windows operating system.

1   In InDesign CS4, with the Selection tool (➤) double-click the large chocolate image.

2   Choose Window > Links. Using the Links panel, do one of the following:

•   If you used the Photoshop instructions in the previous sections, click the Relink button (🔗) at the bottom of the Links panel. Locate the 07_d_prof. tif file you just saved in the Lesson_07 folder, and double-click the file.

- If you don't have Photoshop, or skipped the previous two sections, click the Relink button(🔗) at the bottom of the Links panel. Locate the 07_d_prof. psd file in the Final folder, and double-click the file.

3 Choose Window > Info. Notice the ICC Profile listed for the image.

Now that you have fixed existing images in the document, you will finish the ad by importing two additional images and setting options as you import.

Assigning a profile while importing an image

If you know that a color-managed image uses a color space that is different from the color space described by the default source profile, you can assign a profile to it while you're importing the image into InDesign CS4. In this section, you'll import a legacy (archived) CMYK image scanned without a profile, and assign a profile before you place it in the ad.

You can assign a profile while you import an image.

1 In InDesign CS4, choose View > Show Frame Edges to show the outline of the frame for the image you're about to place—and the outlines for all the images frames in the ad.

2 If necessary, adjust your view so that you can see the frames in the lower-right area of the spread. Select the tallest of these three frames with the Selection tool (▶).

3 Choose File > Place to open the Place dialog box. Open the Lesson_07 folder in the InDesignCIB folder, and select the 07_e.psd file.

4 Select Show Import Options so that you'll have an opportunity to specify a profile. Click Open.

5 In the Image Import Options dialog box, select the color tab in the middle of the dialog box.

6 Select the following options, and then click OK.

• For Profile, select U.S. Sheetfed Coated v2 to match the image's original color space.

• For Rendering Intent, select Perceptual (Images).

Image Import Options (07_e.psd)

Image   Color   Layers

Profile: U.S. Sheetfed Coated v2

Rendering Intent: Perceptual (Images)

☑ Show Preview

Cancel   OK

The image appears in the selected frame. InDesign CS4 color-manages the image using the profile you assigned.

7 Choose Object > Fitting > Fit Content Proportionally.

Embedding a profile in an Illustrator image

In this lesson, you'll set up Illustrator (version 9 or later) so that its color-management settings match InDesign CS4. You'll then save a color-managed Illustrator image and place it in an InDesign CS4 document.

InDesign CS4 can color-manage vector images created in Illustrator 9 or later when you save them in formats that embed profiles, such as PDF or TIFF. In this lesson, you'll save a file as PDF and then place the image in InDesign CS4.

● **Note:** If Illustrator 9 or later isn't installed on your system, you can read the information in the next two sections, and then skip to step 2 in "Placing a color-managed Illustrator file into InDesign CS4" later in this lesson to use the Illustrator file provided in the Lesson_07 folder.

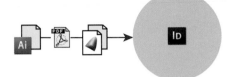

InDesign CS4 color-manages a PDF file using the profiles saved with the PDF version of the file.

Setting up color management in Illustrator CS4

Now you'll set up color management in Illustrator CS4 so that it matches the color management settings in InDesign CS4. This ensures that the colors are consistent from Illustrator to InDesign CS4 on-screen and in print. Setting up color management in Illustrator also enables you to embed an ICC profile in an exported version of the Illustrator file. When you place the exported Illustrator file in the InDesign CS4 layout, InDesign CS4 color-manages the logo using the embedded profile.

1 Start Adobe Illustrator CS4, and choose Edit > Color Settings.

2 Select Advanced Mode to expand the dialog box so that you see more options, and then in the Color Settings dialog box, select North America Prepress 2 if it is not already chosen.

3 Under Working Spaces, for RGB select sRGB IEC61966-2.1. Leave CMYK set for U.S. Web Coated (SWOP) v2.

4 Review the conversion options and make sure that the Adobe (ACE) engine and Relative Colorimetric Intent are selected.

5 Click OK.

You have finished setting up color management in Illustrator.

Embedding a profile in an image from Illustrator

You can embed an ICC profile in files that you create in Illustrator and export in PDF or bitmap (.bmp) formats. Then, InDesign CS4 can use the profile to color-manage the image. In this exercise, you'll export a file to PDF, and then place the image in an InDesign CS4 document.

1   In Illustrator, choose File > Open. Locate and double-click the 07_f.ai file in the Lesson_07 folder inside the InDesignCIB folder.

2   When the Missing Profile dialog box opens, select Assign Current Working Space: U.S. Web Coated (SWOP) v2, and click OK.

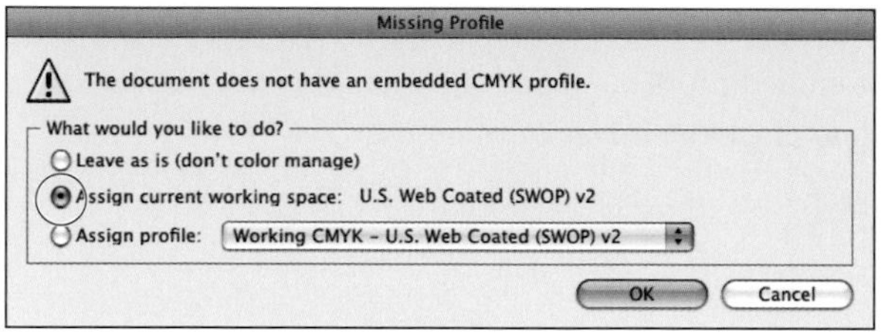

3   Choose File > Save As.

4   Name the file **07_Logo.pdf.**

5   Choose Adobe PDF from the Save As Type (Windows) or Format (Mac OS) menu.

6   Make sure that the Lesson_07 folder is selected, and then click Save to close the Save As dialog box. The Save Adobe PDF dialog box appears.

7   Make sure that the PDF compression options are appropriate for your final print production by clicking General on the left side of the dialog box.

8   Choose Acrobat 6 from the Compatibility menu, if it's not already selected. This ensures that the profile is saved with the PDF file. Match the settings shown below, and click Save PDF.

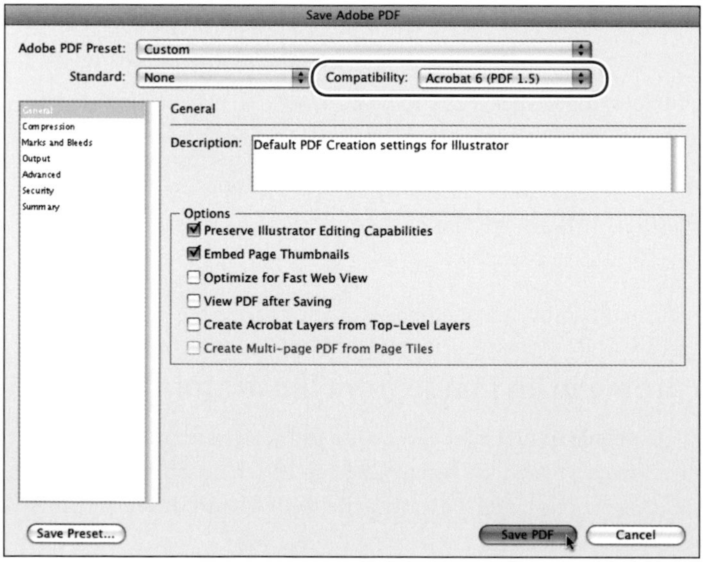

9   Close the file and quit Illustrator.

Placing a color-managed Illustrator file into InDesign CS4

Now that you have created a PDF file from the Illustrator document, you'll place it in InDesign CS4.

1 In InDesign CS4, select the remaining empty frame in the lower-right area of the ad.

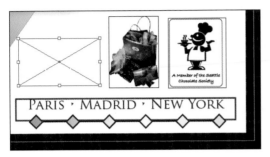

2 Do one of the following:

- If you used the Illustrator instructions in the previous steps, choose File > Place and select the 07_Logo.pdf file that you created. Make sure that Show Import Options is selected before you place the image.

- If you don't have Illustrator, or skipped the previous two exercises, choose File > Place and select the 07_Logo.pdf file in the Final folder in the Lesson_07 folder, located inside the Lessons folder within the InDesignCIB folder on your hard disk. Make sure that Show Import Options is selected before you click Open.

3 Choose Bounding Box from the Crop To menu in the Place PDF dialog box. This places only the logo's bounding box—the minimum area that encloses the logo.

4 Make sure that Transparent Background is selected so that you can see any text or images behind the bounding box, and click OK.

The logo appears in the selected frame. If necessary, click in the frame to place the graphic. InDesign CS4 color-manages the PDF file using the embedded profile.

5 Choose Object > Fitting > Fit Content Proportionally to fit the image in the frame.

● **Note:** To reset to the default color settings, choose Edit > Color Settings and choose North America General Purpose 2 from the Settings menu, and then click OK.

6 Choose File > Save.

In this lesson, you have learned how to set up color management across three Adobe applications—an admirable achievement. You have learned several methods for incorporating images so that they can be color-managed when placed in InDesign CS4 documents. Because you described your color environment to the other Adobe applications whose images you imported, you can expect predictable, consistent color for those images across the applications.

At this time, you could either hand off the native InDesign CS4 file with all of the linked files, or export the InDesign CS4 file as a PDF file, embedding the ICC profiles you assigned. If you create a PDF file, ideally the colors in the ad look the same across all publications that use the ad, regardless of the color-management settings used by the publication's layout application. Other users can preview and proof your color-managed files more accurately, and repurpose them for different print conditions when that is useful, or when it is a requirement of your project.

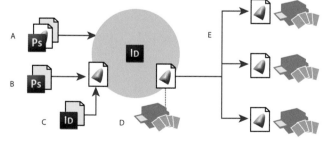

A. Image with embedded CMYK profile
B. Image with CMYK profile assigned in InDesign CS4
C. InDesign CS4 document using a CMYK profile based on a separation profile
D. Separation profile
E. Different separation profiles when targeting different presses

Exploring on your own

Follow these steps to learn more about importing colors and working with gradients:

1 To create a new document, choose File > New > Document, and click OK in the New Document dialog box.

2 If necessary, choose Window > Swatches to open the Swatches panel.

3 Choose New Color Swatch from the Swatches panel menu.

4 In the Color Mode menu, select Other Library and browse to find the Lesson_07 folder.

5 Double-click 07_End.indd. Notice that the colors you created earlier in this lesson appear in the New Color Swatch dialog box.

6 Select the Brown/Tan Gradient and click Add.

7 Continue selecting the swatches and clicking Add to load the colors into the new document.

8 Click Done when you're finished adding colors.

9 Using the lesson files or your own InDesign CS4 document, double-click the color swatch [Paper] and change its composition. For a more realistic preview, the color of the document changes to reflect the color of the paper on which the document will be reproduced.

Review questions

1 What is the advantage of applying colors in the Swatches panel instead of the Color panel?

2 What are the pros and cons of using spot colors versus process colors?

3 After you create a gradient and apply it to an object, how do you adjust the direction of the gradient blend?

4 What does a color management engine do?

5 What do source profiles describe?

6 What are three ways to use an ICC profile with an image so that InDesign CS4 can color-manage the image?

7 Why would you embed an ICC profile in an image?

8 Which file formats embed ICC profiles for use in both Windows and Mac OS?

Review answers

1 If you use the Swatches panel to apply a color to text and objects, and then decide you want to use a different color, you don't need to update each use of the color individually. Instead, change the color in the Swatches panel, and the color changes throughout the layout.

2 By using a spot color, you can ensure color accuracy. However, each spot color requires its own plate on the press, so using spot colors can be more costly. Use process colors when a job requires so many colors that using individual spot inks would be expensive or impractical, such as when printing color photographs.

3 To adjust the direction of the gradient blend, use the Gradient Swatch tool to repaint the fill along an imaginary line in the direction you want.

4 A color management engine translates colors from the color space of one device to another device's color space by a process called color mapping.

5 Source profiles selected in the Assign Profiles dialog box describe the color space InDesign CS4 assigns to objects you create using the drawing tools, or when you import an RGB, CMYK, or LAB color image that wasn't saved with an embedded profile.

6 You can embed the profile in the original file, assign a profile within InDesign CS4, or use the default profile you specified when you set up color management in InDesign CS4.

7 Embedding an ICC profile ensures that the image displays correctly in any application that uses ICC-compliant color management. The application that uses the image honors the embedded profile rather than applying a default one.

8 A growing number of formats can contain an embedded ICC profile, but the most widely supported formats to use with embedded ICC profiles at this time are bitmap image formats such as Photoshop (PSD), TIFF, and JPEG.

8 WORKING WITH STYLES

Lesson Overview

In this introduction to working with InDesign styles, you'll learn how to do the following:

- Create and apply paragraph styles.

- Create and apply character styles.

- Nest character styles inside paragraph styles.

- Create and apply object styles.

- Create and apply cell styles.

- Create and apply table styles.

- Globally update paragraph, character, object, cell, and table styles.

- Import and apply styles from other InDesign documents.

- Create style groups.

 This lesson will take approximately 60 minutes.

Expedition
TEA COMPANY

Extraordinary Adventures into the World of Tea

Premium Loose Leaf Teas, Teapots & Gift Collections

EXPEDITION TEA COMPANY™ carries an extensive array of teas from all the major tea growing regions and tea estates. Choose from our selection of teas, gift collections, teapots, or learn how to make your tea drinking experience more enjoyable from our STI Certified Tea Specialist, T. Elizabeth Atteberry.

LOOSE LEAF TEAS

We carry a wide selection of premium loose leaf teas including black, green, oolong, white, rooibos and chai. Many of these are from Ethical Tea Partnership (EPT) monitored estates, ensuring that the tea is produced in a socially responsible way.

TEA GIFT COLLECTIONS

Our gorgeous tea collections are packaged in golden tins within a keepsake wooden box with a leather handle and brass fittings. Give it as a gift to your favorite tea lover or to yourself!

TEAPOTS AND TEA ACCESSORIES

We carry a unique collection of modern and traditional teapots, chosen to satisfy many tastes including glass, ceramic, cast-iron, stainless, and silver. Our tea timers, tea bags, tea strainers, scoops and other tea things will make your tea time perfect.

EXPEDITION TEA COMPANY
www.expeditiontea.com • tea@expeditiontea.com
phone: (206) 463-9292 • fax: *(206) 299-9165*

With Adobe InDesign CS4, you can create styles—sets of formatting attributes—and apply them in one step to text, objects, tables, and more. Any changes to a style automatically affect all of the text or objects to which the style is applied. Styles offer a quick, consistent method for formatting documents.

Getting started

In this lesson, you'll work on a three-page product sheet for the Expedition Tea Company. Several items in the document, including text and graphics, have already been placed for you. Your objective is to create and apply styles, or grouped attributes that control formatting, to these items.

● **Note:** If you have not already copied the resource files for this lesson onto your hard disk from the Adobe InDesign CS4 Classroom in a Book CD, do so now. See "Copying the Classroom in a Book files" on page 2.

1 To ensure that the preferences and default settings of your Adobe InDesign CS4 program match those used in this lesson, move the InDesign Defaults file to a different folder following the procedure in "Saving and restoring the InDesign Defaults file" on page 2.

2 Start Adobe InDesign CS4. To ensure that the panels and menu commands match those used in this lesson, choose Window > Workspace > [Advanced], and then choose Window > Workspace > Reset Advanced.

To begin working, you'll open an existing InDesign document.

3 Choose File > Open, and open the 08_Start.indd file in the Lesson_08 folder, located inside the Lessons folder within the InDesignCIB folder on your hard disk.

4 If a message indicates missing or modified links to graphic files, click Don't Update Links. This lesson does not require the graphic files.

5 Choose File > Save As, rename the file **08_Working.indd**, and save it in the Lesson_08 folder.

6 If you want to see what the finished document will look like, open the 08_End.indd file in the same folder. You can leave this document open to act as a guide as you work. When you're ready to resume working on the lesson document, click its tab in the upper-left corner of the document window.

Creating and applying paragraph styles

Paragraph styles let you apply and globally update text formatting to speed up production and create a more consistent overall design. Paragraph styles incorporate all elements of text formatting, and can include character attributes such as font, size, style, and color, combined with paragraph attributes such as indents, alignment, tabs, and hyphenation. They differ from character styles because they are applied to entire paragraphs at once, not just to selected characters.

Creating a paragraph style

In this exercise you'll create and apply a paragraph style to selected paragraphs that have already been placed in the document. In this case, you'll format the text in the first part of the document locally (that is, not based on a style), and then have InDesign pick up this existing formatting and build it into a new paragraph style.

1   With 08Working.indd open, double-click page 1 in the Pages panel to center the page in the document window.

2   Using the Type tool (T), drag to select the "Loose Leaf Teas" headline, which follows the introductory paragraph in the first column of the document.

3   In the Control panel, click Character Formatting Controls (A), and specify the following:

- Font: Adobe Caslon Pro (you will find this alphabetized under "C").

- Style: Semibold.

- Size: 18 pt.

Leave all other settings at their defaults.

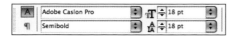

4   In the Control panel, click Paragraph Formatting Controls (¶), and increase the Space Before () to 0p3.

Now you'll create a paragraph style using this formatting so that you can use it to format the other headlines in the document.

> **Tip:** The easiest way to create a paragraph style is to format a sample paragraph using local (not style-based) formatting, and then create a new style based on that sample paragraph. Effectively, this lets you see the style before you build it. You can then efficiently use the new style in the rest of the document.

5 Make sure that the text insertion point is still in the text you just formatted. If it's not already visible, open the Paragraph Styles panel by choosing Type > Paragraph Styles.

The Paragraph Styles panel already has a few styles provided for you, including the default, [Basic Paragraph].

▶ **Tip:** If you change the Based On style—for example, by changing the font—the changes update all styles based on that style. Unique characteristics of styles based on other styles are maintained. Basing styles on other styles is helpful when creating a series of related styles such as Body Copy, Body Copy No Indent, Bulleted Copy, and so on.

6 In the Paragraph Styles panel, create a new paragraph style by choosing New Paragraph Style from the panel menu. The New Paragraph Style dialog box opens, displaying the formatting you just applied to the headline in the Style Settings section.

Notice that the new style is based on the Body Text style. Since Body Text was applied to the headline when you created the style, the new style is automatically based on Body Text. By using the Based On option in the General section of the New Paragraph Style dialog box, you can use an existing style as a starting point for a new style.

7 In the Style Name box at the top of the dialog box, type **Head2** to name this style as the second largest headline.

You can also have InDesign switch to another style automatically when you press Enter or Return after entering text.

8 Select Body Text from the Next Style menu, because this is the style used for the text following each Head2 headline.

You can also create a keyboard shortcut for easy application of this style.

● **Note:** If you are working on a laptop without a numeric keypad, you can skip this step.

9 Click in the Shortcut box, hold down Ctrl (Windows) or Command (Mac OS), and press 9 on the numeric keypad of your keyboard. (InDesign requires the use of a modifier key for style shortcuts.)

10 Select Apply Style To Selection to apply this new style to the text you just formatted.

If you don't select Apply Style To Selection, the new style appears in your Paragraph Styles panel, but is not automatically applied to the text you formatted and that text is not updated if you need to globally update the Head2 style.

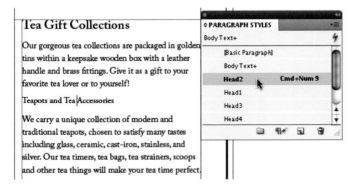

11 Click OK to close the New Paragraph Style dialog box. The new Head2 style appears in the Paragraph Styles panel.

12 Choose File > Save.

Applying a paragraph style

Now you'll apply your paragraph style to selected text in the other sections of the document.

1 In the Pages panel, double-click page 1 to center it in the document window.

2 Using the Type tool (T), click to place an insertion point in "Tea Gift Collections."

3 Click once on the Head2 style in the Paragraph Styles panel to apply the style to the text. You should see the text attributes change to reflect the paragraph style you've just created.

4 Repeat steps 2 and 3 to apply the Head2 style to "Teapots and Tea Accessories" in the second column.

5 Using the Pages panel to navigate between pages, repeat steps 2 and 3 to apply the Head2 style to:

- "Premium Loose Leaf Tea Selections" at the top of page 2.

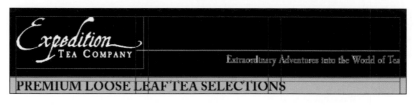

- "About Tea and Training" at the top of page 3.

6 Choose File > Save.

Creating and applying character styles

In the previous exercise, paragraph styles allowed you to apply character and paragraph formatting to text with a single click or a keypress. Similarly, character styles are a way to apply multiple attributes—such as size, font, and color—to text using a single action. Unlike paragraph styles, character styles apply formatting to ranges of text smaller than a paragraph (a character, a word, or a group of words).

Creating a character style

The text for the Expedition Tea Company document was written in a word processing application and imported into the lesson file for you. Now you will create and apply a character style sheet to selected text in the document. This demonstrates how character styles can make your work more efficient and consistent.

1 With 08Working.indd open, double-click page 1 in the Pages panel to center the page in your document window.

2   If it's not already visible, open the Character Styles panel by choosing Type >
Character Styles.

The only style listed in this panel is the default, [None].

As you did with the paragraph style in the previous section, you'll build a character
style based on existing text formatting. This approach lets you see the formatting
before you create the style. In this case, you'll format the Expedition Tea Company
name and build it into a character style, so that it can be reused efficiently throughout the document.

3   Using the Type tool (T), select the words "Expedition Tea Company™" in the
first column of page 1.

4   In the Control panel, click Character Formatting Controls (A) and select Small
Caps (Tr).

Now that the text is formatted, you'll create a new character style.

5   Choose New Character Style from the Character Styles panel menu. The New
Character Style dialog box opens, displaying the formatting you applied to the
text in the Style Settings section.

6 In the Style Name box at the top of the dialog box, type **Company** to define the purpose of the style.

7 In the General section of this dialog box, leave the Based On setting at the default, [None]. You're creating a new style, so you won't base it on a previously created style.

As you did for the paragraph style you created, now you'll create a keyboard shortcut for easy application of this style.

● **Note:** If you are working on a laptop without a numeric keypad, you can skip this step.

8 Click in the Shortcut box, hold down Ctrl (Windows) or Command (Mac OS), and press **8** on the numeric keypad of your keyboard.

9 Select Apply Style To Selection to apply this new style to the text you just formatted.

If you don't select Apply Style To Selection, the style appears in your Character Styles panel, but is not automatically applied to the text you formatted and the text is not updated if you need to globally update the Company style.

You have now created the character style.

10 Click OK to close the New Character Style dialog box. The new Company style appears in the Character Styles panel.

11 Choose File > Save.

Applying a character style

You're ready to apply your character style to selected text already placed in the document. As with paragraph styles, using character styles prevents you from having to manually and individually apply multiple type attributes to each instance of text.

1 If you aren't viewing page 1, double-click page 1 in the Pages panel to center the page in your document window.

At the bottom of the page, at the bottom of the second column, you'll see the words "Expedition Tea Company." To maintain a consistent look for the company name, you'll apply the Company character style.

2 Using the Type tool (T), select the words "Expedition Tea Company."

3 In the Character Styles panel, click once on the Company style to apply it to this text. You should see the font change to reflect the character style you created.

● **Note:** You can also use the keyboard shortcut you defined earlier (Ctrl+8 or Command+8) to apply the Company style.

4 Using either the Character Styles panel or the keyboard shortcut, apply the Company style to the words "Expedition Tea Company," which also appear twice near the bottom of page 3.

5 Choose File > Save.

Nesting character styles inside paragraph styles

To make the use of styles more convenient and powerful, InDesign lets you nest character styles within paragraph styles. These nested styles allow you to apply distinct character formatting to specific portions of a paragraph—such as the first character, the second word, or the third sentence—at the same time you apply a paragraph style. This makes nested styles ideal for creating run-in headings (where the first portion of a line or paragraph is styled differently from the rest of the line or paragraph), structured paragraphs, or formatted drop caps.

Creating character styles for nesting

▶ **Tip:** You can use the incredibly powerful nested styles feature to automatically apply different formatting within a paragraph according to a specific pattern. For example, in a table of contents, you can automatically apply bold to the text, change the tracking in the tab leader (the dots that lead to the page number), and change the font and color of the page number.

Using nested styles has two prerequisites: that you have created a character style, and that you have created a paragraph style in which to nest it. In this section, you'll create two characters styles and then nest them within the paragraph style Tea body, which already exists.

1   With 08Working.indd open, double-click page 2 in the Pages panel to center the page in the document window.

If the body copy is too small to view, zoom in to the first paragraph under the "Black Tea" heading, beginning with "Earl Grey." In this exercise, you'll create two nested styles to distinguish the tea name from the country where it was grown. Notice that a set of colons (::) separates the name and country, and a bullet (·) appears after the region. These characters will be important when creating your nested styles later in this section.

2   Using the Type tool (T), select the words "Earl Grey" in the first column.

3   In the Control panel, click Character Formatting Controls (A) and choose Bold from the Type Style menu. Leave all other settings at their defaults.

Formatting text by applying settings individually, rather than applying a style, is called local formatting. This locally formatted text is now ready to serve as the basis for a new character style.

4   If it's not already visible, open the Character Styles panel by choosing Type > Character Styles.

5   In the Character Styles panel, choose New Character Style from the panel menu. The New Character Style dialog box opens, displaying the formatting you applied.

6   In the Style Name box at the top of the dialog box, type **Tea Name** to define the text to which the style will be applied.

7   Select Apply Style To Selection so that when you finish creating this character style, it will be applied to the selected text.

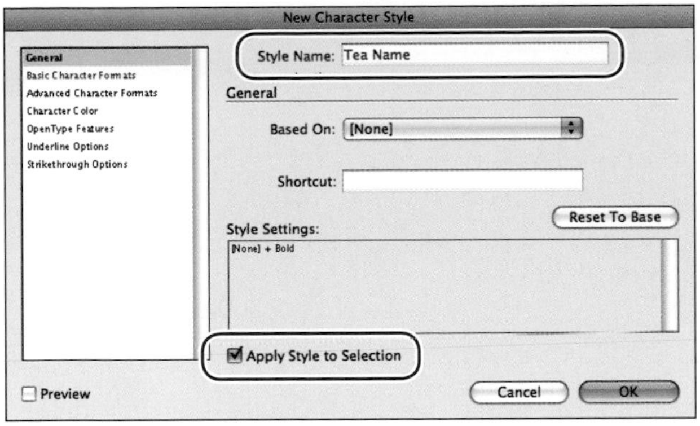

To make the tea name stand out a little more, you'll change the color from black to burgundy.

8 On the left side of the panel, click Character Color in the list.

9 In the Character Color settings that appear on the right side of the dialog box, select the burgundy color (C = 43, M = 100, Y = 100, K = 30).

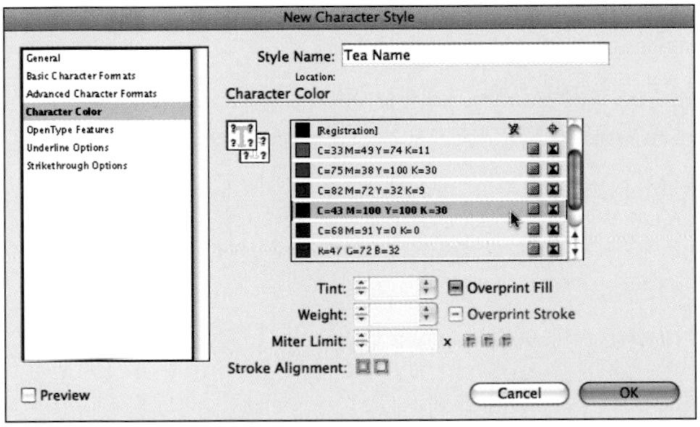

10 Click OK to close the New Character Style dialog box. You should see the new Tea Name style appear in the Character Styles panel.

Now you'll create a second character style for nesting.

11 To the right of the "Earl Grey" text you just formatted, select the text "Sri Lanka." Format this as Adobe Caslon Pro Italic.

12 Repeat steps 4 through 7 to create a new character style called Country. When finished, click OK to close the New Character Style dialog box. The new Country style appears in the Character Styles panel.

13 Choose File > Save.

You have successfully created two new character styles. Using these along with the existing Tea Body paragraph style, you are ready to create and apply your nested style.

Creating a nested style

▶ **Tip:** In addition to nested styles, InDesign provides nested line styles. These let you specify formatting for individual lines in a paragraph—such as a drop cap followed by small caps, which is common in the lead paragraphs of magazine articles. If the text or other formatting changes and the text reflows, InDesign adjusts the formatting to encompass only the specified lines. The controls for creating nested line styles are in the Drop Caps And Nested Styles panel of the Paragraph Style Options dialog box.

When you create a nested style within an existing paragraph style, you're essentially building a secondary set of rules for InDesign to follow while formatting a paragraph. In this exercise, you'll build a nested style into the Tea Body style using the two character styles you created in the previous exercise.

1 If it's not already centered on your screen, double-click page 2 in the Pages panel to center the page in the document window.

2 If the Paragraph Styles panel is not visible, choose Type > Paragraph Styles.

3 In the Paragraph Styles panel, double-click the Tea Body style to open the Paragraph Style Options dialog box.

4 From the categories on the left side of the dialog box, select Drop Caps And Nested Styles.

5 In the Nested Styles section, click the New Nested Style button to create a new nested style. The [None] style appears.

6 Click the [None] style to display a pop-up menu. Select Tea Name; this is the first nested style in the sequence.

7 Click the word "through" to reveal another pop-up menu. This menu contains only two choices: Through and Up To. You will set this style up to the first colon (:) after Earl Grey, so select Up To.

8 Click the number 1 next to Up To to open a text box into which you can type a number. The number defines how many elements the style applies through or up to. Although there are two colons, you only need to reference the first colon, so leave this as the default 1.

9 Click Words to reveal another text box and menu. Click the menu button to the right of the text box to open a menu containing many choices of elements to which the style will be applied, including sentences, characters, and spaces. In this case, you don't want any of the listed items. Instead, you want a colon (:). Click back in the text box to close the menu and type : (a colon) in the box.

10 If it is not already selected, select Preview and move the Paragraph Style Options dialog box so that you can see the columns of text. The name for each tea should be bold and burgundy up to (but not including) the colon. Click OK.

11 Choose File > Save.

Adding a second nested style

Now you'll add another nested style, but first you need to copy a bullet character from the page. Within the nested style you are creating, the formatting switch takes place up until a bullet character is encountered—but you cannot type a bullet within a dialog box, so you will need to paste it.

1 In the first column under "Black Tea," navigate to the bullet character after "Sri Lanka." Select it and choose Edit > Copy.

2 In the Paragraph Styles panel, double-click the Tea Body style. In the Drop Caps And Nested Styles section of the Paragraph Style Options dialog box, click the New Nested Style button to create another new nested style.

3 Repeat steps 6 through 10 of "Creating a nested style" to create your new nested style with the following formatting:

- First option: Choose Country.

- Second option: Choose Up To.

- Third option: Leave as the default 1.

- Fourth option: Enter the bullet character by pasting the bullet you copied (Edit > Paste).

4 Move the Paragraph Style Options dialog box as necessary so that you can see that each country name is italicized. However, the two semicolons between the tea name and country are also italicized.

To fix the italicized semicolons, you'll create another nested style that applies [None] to the colons.

5 Click the New Nested Style button to create another nested style.

6 Repeat steps 6 through 9 of "Creating a nested style" to create your new nested style with the following formatting:

- First option: Choose [None].

- Second option: Choose Through.

- Third option: Type 2.

- Fourth option: Type : [colon].

You now have a nested style, but it needs to be placed between the Name and Country nested styles to be in the proper position sequentially.

7 With the [None] nested style selected, click the Up Arrow button once to move the style between the other two.

8 Click OK to accept these changes. You have now finished creating a series of nested styles that apply the Tea Name and Country character styles to any paragraph styled with the Tea Body paragraph style.

GREEN TEA	CHAI TEA
Dragonwell (Lung Ching) :: *China* • Distinguished by its beautiful shape, emerald color, and sweet floral character. Full-bodied with a slight heady bouquet.	**Belgian Chocolate Chai** :: *Sri Lanka, India, Belgium* • For the chocolate lover! Chips of white chocolate drenched in luscious chai spices in rich Ceylon tea.
Genmaicha (Popcorn Tea) :: *Japan* • Green tea blended with fire-toasted rice with a natural sweetness. During the firing the rice may "pop" not unlike popcorn.	**Green Tea Chai** :: *Sri Lanka* • Green tea with strong Indian spices such as Cardamom, Cloves Coriander, Cumin Seed, Sweet cumin seeds, Curry leaves, Lemon

9 Choose File > Save.

Creating and applying object styles

Object styles let you apply and globally update formatting to graphics and frames. These formatting attributes, including fill, stroke, transparency, and text wrap options, create a more consistent overall design and speed up tedious production tasks.

Creating an object style

In this section, you will create and apply an object style to the black circles containing the etp symbols on page 2 of the product sheet. ("Etp" stands for Ethical Tea Partnership.) You'll base the new object style on the formatting of the black circle. So you'll start by beveling the black circle and changing its color; then you can define the new style.

1 Double-click page 2 in the Pages panel to center the page in the document window.

2 Select the Zoom tool (🔍) in the Tools panel and increase the magnification to better view the etp symbol near Earl Grey.

To format the symbol, you will fill it with a burgundy color and apply an Inner Bevel effect. To make this task easier, the type and circle for all the etp symbols have been placed on separate layers—the type on the layer called Etp Type and the circles on a layer called Etp Circle.

3 Choose Window > Layers to view the Layers panel. Click the empty box next to the Etp Type layer to display a lock icon (🔒). This locks the layer so you cannot accidentally change the text while editing the object.

4 With the Selection tool (↖), click the black etp symbol next to Earl Grey.

5 In the Swatches panel, change both the stroke and fill color to burgundy (C = 43, M = 100, Y = 100, K = 30).

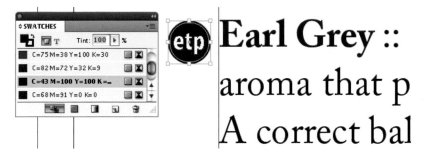

6 Choose Object > Effects > Bevel And Emboss. If it isn't already selected, in the Structure section, choose Inner Bevel from the Style pop-up menu. Make sure that the Preview option is selected, and then move the Effects dialog box to view the circle.

7 In the Size box, type **0p2** to change the shape of the bevel. Leave the other default settings as is.

> ▶ **Tip:** Just as with paragraph and character styles, you can base an object style on another object style. Changes made to the Based On style update all object styles based on that style. (Unique characteristics of styles based on other styles are maintained.) The controls for basing a style on another are in the General panel of the New Object Style dialog box.

8 Click OK. The symbol should now look embossed.

Now you're ready to create the object style.

9 Choose Window > Object Styles to open the Object Styles panel.

Keep the etp symbol selected to base the new object style's formatting on it.

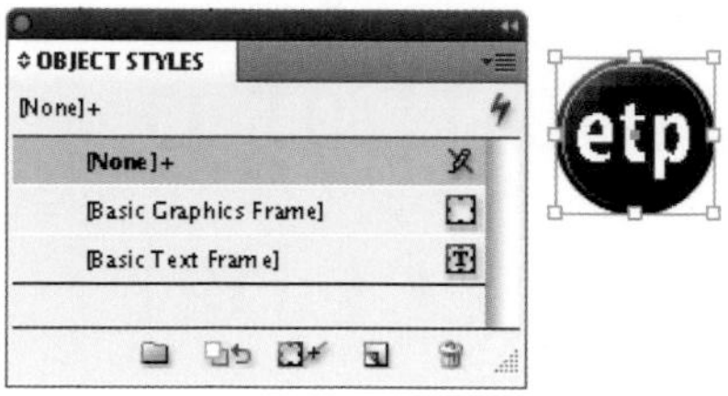

10 In the Object Styles panel, choose New Object Style from the panel menu. The New Object Style dialog box opens, offering you formatting options to be built into the style.

11 In the Style Name box at the top of the dialog box, type **ETP Symbol** to describe the purpose of the style.

12 Select Apply Style To Selection to apply this new object style to the circle you just formatted. If you don't select this option, the style appears in the Object Styles panel, but is not automatically applied to the circle you formatted and the circle is not updated if you need to globally update the ETP Symbol style.

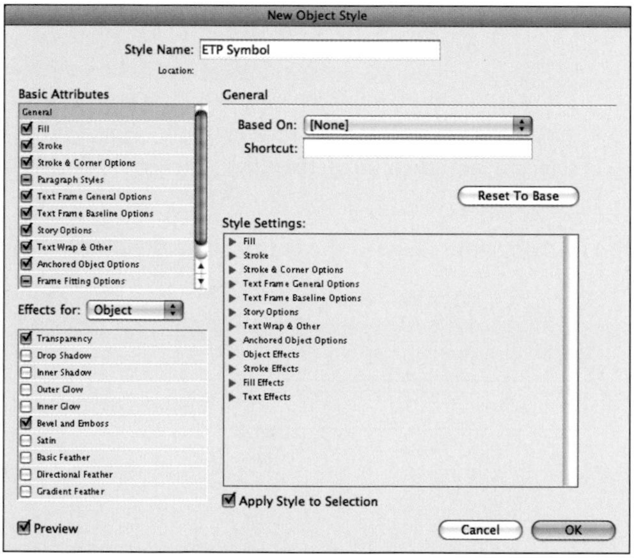

The check boxes on the left side of this dialog box show the attributes that will be applied when this style is used. Now you'll choose some of these attributes to modify the ETP Symbol style a bit more.

13 To add a drop shadow to the style, click the Drop Shadow attribute to select it and check its option. The Drop Shadow settings appear on the right side of the dialog box.

14 In the Drop Shadow settings, specify the following formatting:

- X Offset: 0p7

- Y Offset: 0p7

- Size: 0p4

- Make sure that the color swatch next to the Mode menu is black. This is the shadow color.

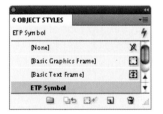

15 Click OK to close the New Object Style dialog box. The new ETP Symbol style should appear in the Object Styles panel.

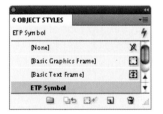

16 Choose File > Save.

Applying an object style

Now you'll apply your new object style to the other circles on page 2. Applying the object style changes the formatting of the circles automatically; you don't have to manually apply the color, shadow, and emboss effect to each circle individually.

1 In the Pages panel, double-click page 2 to center it in your document window.

▶ **Tip:** When you modify a style, the text, table, or objects to which the style is applied update automatically. If you have a specific instance of text, a table, or an object that you do not want to update, you can break its link to the style. Each styles panel (Paragraph Styles, Cell Styles, and so on) has a Break Link to Style command in the panel menu.

2 Using the Selection tool ( ), select the second circle, and then click the ETP Symbol style in the Object Styles panel. The circle will be formatted exactly like the first circle you formatted.

3 To speed up the process, press the Shift key and click to select all of the circles on page 2. Then apply the ETP Symbol style to the entire selection.

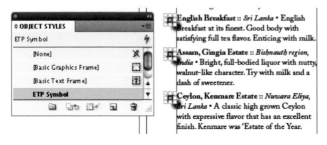

4 Choose File > Save.

Creating and applying table and cell styles

Table and cell styles let you format tables with the same convenience and consistency you get from styling text with paragraph and character styles. Table styles let you control the visual attributes of the table, including the table border, space before and after the table, row and column strokes, as well as alternating fill patterns. Cell styles let you control cell inset spacing, vertical justification, individual cell strokes and fills, as well as diagonal lines. You'll learn more about creating tables in Lesson 10, "Creating Tables."

In this exercise, you'll create and apply a table style and two cell styles to tables in the product sheet document, to help distinguish the different descriptions of tea.

Creating cell styles

You'll begin by creating cell styles for both the header row and body rows of the table at the bottom of page 2. Later, you'll nest these two styles inside the Table style, similar to how you nested character styles inside a paragraph style earlier in this lesson. You'll now create two cell styles.

1 If you aren't viewing page 2, double-click page 2 in the Pages panel to center the page in the window.

2 Using the Zoom tool ( ), drag around the table at the bottom of the page to make it easily visible.

3 Using the Type tool (T), select the first two cells in the header row containing the words "Tea" and "Finished Leaf."

Tea	Finished Leaf	Liquor	Caffeine
White	Soft, grayish white	Pale yellow or pinkish	15 mg
Green	Dull to brilliant green	Green or yellowish	20 mg
Oolong	Blackish or greenish	Green to brownish	30 mg
Black	Lustrous black	Rich red or brownish	40 mg

4 Choose Table > Cell Options > Strokes And Fills. For Cell Fill, select the pale yellow color (C = 4, M = 15, Y = 48, K = 0). Click OK.

5 With the cells still selected, open the Cell Styles panel by choosing Window > Type & Tables > Cell Styles.

6 Keep the table cells selected. From the Cell Styles panel menu, choose New Cell Style.

The cell formatting you applied is displayed in the Style Settings box. You'll also notice additional cell formatting options on the left side of the dialog box. In this exercise, however, you are only going to set the desired paragraph style to use for the text within the Header row.

7 In the Style Name box at the top of the New Cell Style dialog box, type **Table Head.**

8 From the Paragraph Style pop-up menu, choose Head4. This paragraph style was already created in the document. Click OK.

6 Choose the following Alternating options:

- For Color, select the pale yellow color (C = 4, M = 15, Y = 48, K = 0).
- For Tint, type **30**%.

7 Click OK. The new table style, Tea Table, appears in the Table Styles panel.

8 Choose File > Save.

Applying a table style

Now you'll apply the table style you just created to the two tables in the document.

1 With the table still easily visible onscreen, select the Type tool (T). Click to place an insertion point anywhere in the table.

2 In the Tables Styles panel, click the Tea Table style. The table is reformatted with the table and cell styles you created.

Tea	Finished Leaf	Liquor	Caffeine	...ure/Tin
White	Soft, grayish whi	Pale yellow or pinkish	15 mg	or mult
Green	Dull to brilliant green	Green or yellowish	20 mg	
Oolong	Blackish or greenish	Green to brownish	30 mg	or multi
Black	Lustrous black	Rich red or brownish	40 mg	

3 Now double-click page 3 in the Pages panel. Click to place an insertion point anywhere in the table.

4 In the Table Styles panel, click the Tea Table style. The table is reformatted with the table and cell styles you created.

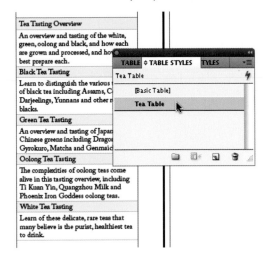

Notice that this table looks a little different than the first one. This table doesn't include a header row, so the reformatting ignored the Table Head cell style.

5 Choose File > Save.

Globally updating styles

There are two ways to update paragraph, character, object, table, and cell styles in InDesign. The first is simply to open a style itself and make changes to the formatting options, as you just did when you created cell and table styles. Because there's a parent-child relationship between the style and the text to which it's applied, all the text is updated to reflect any changes you make to the style.

The other way to update a style is to use local formatting to modify some text, and then redefine the style based on the updated text. In this exercise, you'll make a change to the Head3 style to include a rule below it.

1 With 08Working.indd open, double-click page 2 in the Pages panel to center the page in your document window. Then double-click the Zoom tool ( ) to increase the magnification to 100%.

2 Using the Type tool (T), click to place an insertion point in "Black Tea" in the first column.

▶ **Tip:** Once you have even a rough idea how you want text, objects, and tables to look, you can start creating styles and applying them. Then, as you experiment with design and make changes, you can simply update the style definitions—which automatically updates the formatting of anything to which the style is applied.

3 If it's not already visible, choose Type > Paragraph Styles to view the Paragraph Styles panel. Notice that the Head3 style is selected, indicating that it is applied to the selected text.

4 Choose Type > Paragraph to display the Paragraph panel. Choose Paragraph Rules from the panel menu.

5 In the Paragraph Rules dialog box, choose Rule Below from the pop-up menu at the top of the dialog box, and select Rule On. Make sure that Preview is selected, and move the dialog box so you can see "Black Tea" on your screen.

6 Format the rule using the following settings:

- Weight: 1 pt
- Color: C = 4, M = 15, Y = 48, K = 0
- Offset: 0p2

Leave all other settings at their defaults.

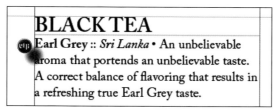

7 Click OK. A thin yellow line now appears below "Black Tea."

BLACK TEA
Earl Grey :: *Sri Lanka* • An unbelievable aroma that portends an unbelievable taste. A correct balance of flavoring that results in a refreshing true Earl Grey taste.

In the Paragraph Styles panel, notice that a plus sign (+) appears next to the Head3 style name. This indicates that the selected text has local formatting applied to it, which is overriding the applied style. Now you'll redefine the paragraph style so that the local change applies to all the headlines previously styled with the Head3 style.

8 In the Paragraph Styles panel menu, choose Redefine Style. The + should no longer appear next to the Head3 style name. All headlines in the document that have been styled with Head3 should globally update to reflect the changes you made.

Note: Redefining styles as shown here updates a style to match new formatting. You can, however, do the reverse and force formatting that has been changed to match a style. (If a selection does not precisely match its style, a plus sign appears next to the style name.) Each styles panel (Paragraph Styles, Object Styles, and so on) has a Clear Overrides control at the bottom indicated by an icon and a plus sign. Move your mouse over the icon to learn how to clear overrides in the selection.

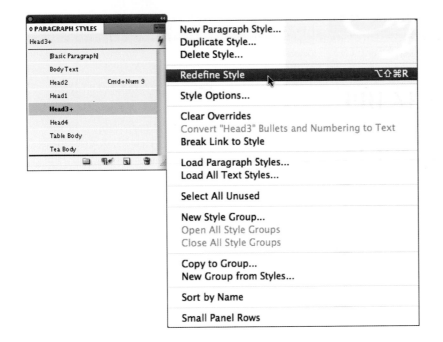

9 Choose File > Save.

● **Note:** You can use the same process in step 8 to redefine any type of style based on local formatting.

Loading styles from another document

Styles appear only in the document in which you create them. However, it's easy to share styles between InDesign documents by loading, or importing, styles from other InDesign documents. In this exercise, you'll import a paragraph style from the finished document 08End.indd and apply the style to the first body paragraph on page 3.

1 With 08Working.indd open, double-click page 3 in the Pages panel to center this page in the window.

2 If it's not already visible, choose Type > Paragraph Styles to view the Paragraph Styles panel.

3 Choose Load All Text Styles from the Paragraph Styles panel menu. You can choose from all the text styles in the 08_End.indd document.

4   In the Open A File dialog box, double-click 08_End.indd in the
    Lesson_08 folder. The Load Styles dialog box appears. Click Uncheck All
    to avoid overwriting existing styles on import.

5   Select the paragraph style Drop Cap Body. Scroll down to Drop Cap and make
    sure it is checked as well.

6   Click OK to import both styles.

7   Using the Type tool (T), place an insertion point in the first paragraph starting
    with "Tea, Tay" and select the new Drop Cap Body style in the Paragraph Styles
    panel. The initial "T" should become a burgundy drop cap.

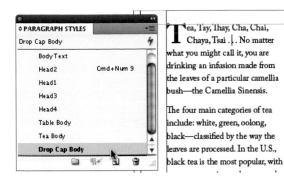

8 Choose File > Save.

Congratulations. You have finished the lesson.

Exploring on your own

In a long or complex document, you may create scores of styles. It's common, in fact, for a magazine or newspaper to have more than 100 styles. Each styles panel in InDesign provides a variety of options for organizing styles. With your lesson document still open, try organizing the paragraph styles.

1 Choose Type > Paragraph Styles to open the Paragraph Styles panel.

2 Click the Paragraph Styles panel menu and choose Sort by Name. This is the default and it sorts styles alphabetically.

3 Drag a style up or down in the list to see how you can arrange them.

4 Choose New Style Group from the Paragraph Styles panel menu.

5 In the Name box of the New Style Group dialog box, type a name such as Body Styles. Click OK.

6 Drag the Body Text, Drop Cap Body, and Tea Body styles into the new Body Styles group.

9 IMPORTING AND MODIFYING GRAPHICS

Lesson Overview

In this lesson, you'll learn how to do the following:

- Distinguish between vector and bitmap graphics.

- Place layered Adobe Photoshop and Adobe Illustrator graphics.

- Import clipping paths with graphics and create clipping paths.

- Manage placed files using the Links panel.

- Use and create libraries for objects.

- Import graphics using Adobe Bridge.

 This lesson will take approximately 60 minutes.

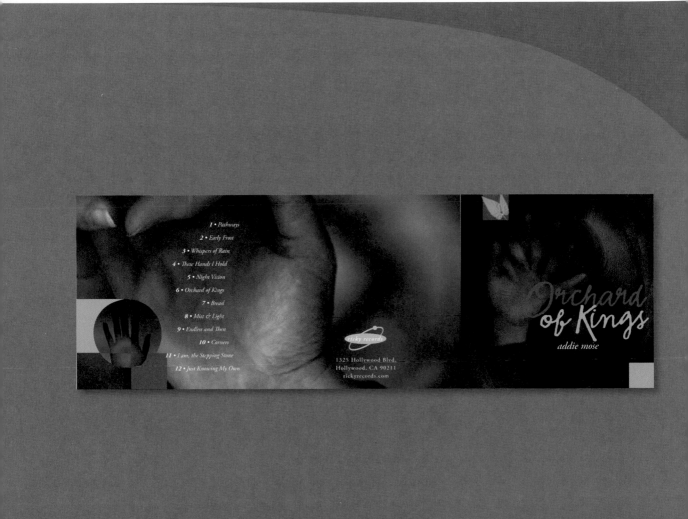

You can easily enhance your document with photographs and artwork imported from Adobe Photoshop, Adobe Illustrator, or other graphics applications. If these imported graphics change, InDesign can notify you that a newer version of a graphic is available. You can update or replace imported graphics at any time.

Getting started

In this lesson, you'll assemble a booklet for a compact disc (CD) by importing and managing graphics from Adobe Photoshop, Adobe Illustrator, and Adobe Acrobat. After printing and trimming, the insert will be folded so that it fits into a CD case.

This lesson includes steps that you can perform using Adobe Photoshop if you have it installed on your computer.

● **Note:** If you have not already copied the resource files for this lesson onto your hard disk from the Adobe InDesign CS4 Classroom in a Book CD, do so now. See "Copying the Classroom in a Book files" on page 2.

1 To ensure that the preference and default settings of your Adobe InDesign CS4 program match those used in this lesson, move the InDesign Defaults file to a different folder following the procedure in "Saving and restoring the InDesign Defaults file" on page 2.

2 Start Adobe InDesign CS4. To ensure that the panels and menu commands match those used in this lesson, choose Window > Workspace > [Advanced], and then choose Window > Workspace > Reset Advanced..

3 Choose File > Open, and open the 09_a_Start.indd file in the Lesson_09 folder, located inside the Lessons folder within the InDesignCIB folder on your hard disk. A message appears saying that the document contains links to sources that have been modified.

4 Click Don't Update Links. You will fix the modified links later in the lesson.

5 If necessary, close the Links panel so it doesn't obscure your view of the document. The Links panel opens automatically whenever you open an InDesign document that contains missing or modified links.

6 To see what the finished document looks like, open the 09_b_End.indd file in the same folder. If you prefer, you can leave the document open as you work to act as a guide. When you're ready to resume working on the lesson document, choose 09_a_Start.indd from the Window menu.

7 Choose File > Save As, rename the file **09_cdbook.indd**, and save it in the Lesson_09 folder.

● **Note:** As you work through the lesson, move panels around or change the magnification to a level that works best for you. For more information, see "Changing the magnification of a document" in Lesson 1, "Introducing the Workspace."

Adding graphics from other programs

InDesign supports many common graphics file formats. While this means that you can use graphics that were created using a wide range of graphics applications, InDesign works best with other Adobe professional graphics applications, such as Photoshop, Illustrator, and Acrobat.

By default, imported graphics are linked, which means that InDesign displays a preview of the graphics file in your layout without actually copying the entire graphics file into the InDesign document.

There are two major advantages to linking graphics files. First, it saves disk space, especially if you reuse the same graphic in many InDesign documents. Second, you can edit a linked graphic in the application you used to create it and then simply update the link in the InDesign Links panel. Updating a linked file maintains the current location and settings for the graphic file so you don't have to redo that work.

All linked graphics and text files are listed in the Links panel, which provides buttons and commands for managing links. When you create the final output using PostScript® or Portable Document Format (PDF), InDesign uses the links to produce the highest level of quality available from the original, externally stored versions of the placed graphics.

Comparing vector and bitmap graphics

The drawing tools of Adobe InDesign and Adobe Illustrator create vector graphics, which are made up of shapes based on mathematical expressions. Vector graphics consist of smooth lines that retain their clarity when scaled. They are appropriate for illustrations, type, and graphics, such as logos that are typically scaled to different sizes.

Bitmap images are based on a grid of pixels and are created by image-editing applications, such as Adobe Photoshop. In working with bitmap images, you edit pixels rather than objects or shapes. Because bitmap graphics can represent subtle gradations of shade and color, they are appropriate for continuous-tone images, such as photographs or artwork created in painting applications. A disadvantage of bitmap graphics is that they lose definition and appear "jagged" when enlarged. Additionally, bitmap images are typically larger in file size than a similar vector file.

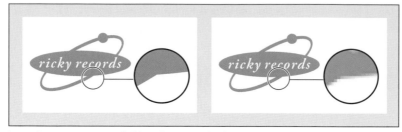

Logo drawn as vector art (left), and rasterized as bitmap art (right).

In general, use vector drawing tools to create art or type with clean lines that look good at any size, such as a logo used on a business card and also on a poster. You can create vector artwork using the InDesign drawing tools, or you might prefer to take advantage of the wider range of vector drawing tools available in Illustrator. You can use Photoshop to create bitmap images that have the soft lines of painted or photographic art and for applying special effects to line art.

Managing links to imported files

When you opened the lesson file, you saw an alert message about problems with the linked files. You'll resolve those issues using the Links panel, which provides complete information about the status of any linked text or graphics file in your document.

You can use the Links panel to manage placed graphics or text files in many other ways, such as updating or replacing text or graphics. All of the techniques you learn in this lesson about managing linked files apply equally to graphics files and text files that you place in your document.

Identifying imported images

To identify some of the images that have already been imported into the document, you'll use two different techniques involving the Links panel. Later in this lesson, you'll also use the Links panel to edit and update imported graphics.

1   Center page 4 in the document window by choosing it from the page box at the bottom of the document window.

2   If the Links panel is not visible, choose Window > Links.

3 Using the Selection tool (↖), select the Orchard of Kings logotype on page 4, the far right page of the first spread. Notice that the graphic's filename, 09_i.ai, becomes selected in the Links panel when you select the graphic on the layout.

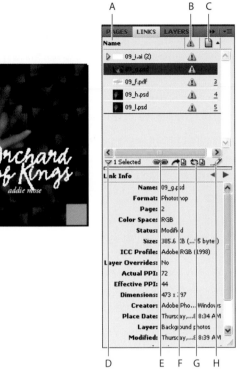

A. Filename column. B. Status column. C. Page column. D. Show/Hide Link Information button.
E. Relink button. F. Go To Link button. G. Update Link button. H. Edit Original button.

Now you'll use the Links panel to locate a graphic on the layout.

4 In the Links panel, select 09_g.psd, and then click the Go To Link button (⬅🖻). The graphic becomes selected and centered on the screen. This is a quick way to find a graphic when you know its filename.

These techniques for identifying and locating linked graphics are useful throughout this lesson and whenever you work with a large number of imported files.

Viewing information about linked files

The Links panel has been redesigned in Adobe InDesign CS 4 to make it easier to work with linked graphics and text files and to display more information about linked files.

1 If the Links panel is not visible, choose Window > Links to display it. If you cannot see the names of all the linked files without scrolling, drag the horizontal divider bar in the Links panel to enlarge the top half of the panel so that all the links are visible.

▶ **Tip:** You can detach the Links panel from its group of panels by dragging its tab onto an empty portion of the document window. Once you've detached the panel, you can resize it horizontally and vertically by dragging the lower-right corner of the panel.

2 Select the link 09_g.psd. The Link Info section at the bottom half of the panel displays information about the selected link.

3 Click the Select Next Link In The List triangle (▶) to view information about the following file in the Links panel list, 09_f.pdf. You can quickly examine all the links in the list this way. Currently, every link displays an alert icon (⚠) in the Status column. This icon indicates a linking problem, which you'll address later. After you've examined the link information, click the Show/Hide Link Information button (▽) above Link Info to hide the Link Info section.

By default, files are sorted in the Links panel with those that may need updating or relinking listed first. You can sort the file list in different ways.

Tip: You can rearrange the columns in the Links panel by dragging column headings.

4 Click the Name column heading in the Links panel. The panel now lists the links in alphabetical order. Each time you click a column heading, the list toggles between descending order and ascending order.

Showing files in Explorer (Windows) or Finder (Mac OS)

Although the Links panel gives you information about the attributes and location of a specific file, it does not give you access to the file itself. You can access a file directly from your hard drive with the Reveal In Explorer (Windows) or the Reveal In Finder (Mac OS) option.

1 Select 09_g.psd if it is not currently chosen. Right-click or Control-click (Mac OS) the graphic and choose Reveal In Explorer (Windows) or Reveal In Finder (Mac OS) from the context menu to open the folder where the linked file is currently stored. This feature is useful for locating documents on your hard drive and renaming them, if necessary.

2 Close the window and, if necessary, click the document to return to InDesign.

266 LESSON 9   importing and Modifying Graphics

Updating revised graphics

Even after you place text or graphics files in your InDesign document, you can still use other applications to modify those files. The Links panel indicates which files have been modified outside of InDesign and gives you the choice of updating your document with the latest versions of those files.

In the Links panel, the file 09_i.ai has an alert icon (⚠), indicating that the original has been modified. This is one of the files that caused the alert message to appear when you first opened this document. You'll update the link for this file so that the InDesign document uses the current version.

1   In the Links panel, click the disclosure triangle (▷) to the left of the file 09_i.ai to reveal two instances of the imported file. Select the file 09_i.ai that is on page 4, and click the Go To Link button (↗▤). You don't have to do this step to update a link, but it's a quick way to double-check which imported file you are about to update.

▶ **Tip:** You can click the page number to the right of a link name in the Links panel to go to the link and center it in the document window.

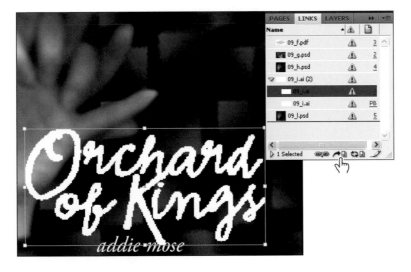

2   Click the Update Link button (🔄▤). The appearance of the image in the document changes to represent its newer version.

▶ **Tip:** All of the buttons at the bottom of the Links panel are also available as commands in the Links panel menu.

3 Select the other files that display an alert icon (⚠) and click the Update Link button. You can hold down the Shift key to select multiple consecutive files to be updated in a single step, or Ctrl-click (Windows) or Command-click (Mac OS) to select non-consecutive items in the Links panel.

Now you'll replace the image of the hands on the first spread (pages 2-4) with a modified image. You'll use the Relink button to reassign the link to another graphic.

4 Go to pages 2–4 (the first spread), and choose View > Fit Spread In Window.

5 Use the Selection tool (▶) to select the 09_h.psd image, which is the photograph of the interlocked hands that is on page 4. You can tell when you've selected the right image because the filename becomes selected in the Links panel.

6 Click the Relink button (⛓) in the Links panel.

7 Browse to find the 09_j.psd file in the Lesson_09 folder, and then click Open. The new version of the image (which has a different background) replaces the original image, and the Links panel is updated accordingly.

8 Click a blank area of the pasteboard to deselect all of the objects on the spread.

9 Choose File > Save to save your work.

▶ **Tip:** You can choose Panel Options from the Links panel menu and customize the columns and information shown in the panel. After adding columns, you can adjust their size and position.

Viewing link status in the Links panel

A linked graphic can appear in the Links panel in any of the following ways:

- An up-to-date graphic displays only the filename and its page in the document.

- A modified file displays a yellow triangle with an exclamation point (⚠). This alert icon means that the version of the file on disk is more recent than the version in your document. For example, this icon will appear if you import a Photoshop graphic into InDesign, and then another artist edits and saves the original graphic using Photoshop.

- A missing file displays a red hexagon with a question mark (●). The file isn't at the location from which it was originally imported, though the file may still exist somewhere. This can happen if someone moves an original file to a different folder or server after it's been imported into an InDesign document. You can't know whether a missing graphic is up to date until its original is located. If you print or export a document when this icon is displayed, the graphic may not print or export at full resolution.

—From InDesign Help

Adjusting view quality

Now that you've resolved all of the links, you're ready to start adding more graphics. But first, you will adjust the view quality of the Illustrator file 09_i.ai you updated earlier in this lesson.

When you place an image in a document, InDesign automatically creates a low-resolution (proxy) version of it, corresponding to the current settings in the Preferences dialog box. The images in this document are currently low-resolution proxies, which is why the image appears to have jagged edges. Reducing the onscreen quality of placed graphics displays pages faster and doesn't affect the quality of the final output. You can control the degree of detail InDesign uses to display placed graphics.

1 In the Links panel, select the 09_i.ai file you updated in the previous exercise (on page 4). Click the Go To Link button (⏎) to view the graphic in magnified view.

2 Right-click (Windows) or Control-click (Mac OS) the Orchard of Kings graphic, and then choose Display Performance > High Quality Display from the context menu that appears. The selected image appears at full resolution. Use this process to confirm the clarity, appearance, or position of an individually placed graphic in your InDesign layout.

Left: Onscreen display using Typical Display. Right: High Quality Display.

3 Choose View > Display Performance > High Quality Display. This setting changes the default display performance for the entire document. All graphics are displayed at the highest quality.

On older computers, or for designs with many imported graphics, this setting can sometimes result in slower screen redraw. In most cases, it is advisable to set your Display Performance to Typical Display and then change the display quality of individual graphics as needed.

4 Choose File > Save.

Working with clipping paths

You can remove unwanted backgrounds from images using InDesign. You'll get some experience doing this in the following exercise. In addition to removing the background in InDesign, you can also create paths or alpha channels in Photoshop, which can then be used to silhouette an image in an InDesign layout.

The image you will be placing has a solid rectangular background that blocks your view of the area behind it. You can hide unwanted parts of an image using a clipping path—a drawn vector outline that acts as a mask. InDesign can create clipping paths from many kinds of images:

* If you draw a path in Photoshop and save it with the image, InDesign can create a clipping path from it.

* If you paint an alpha channel in Photoshop and save it with the image, InDesign can create a clipping path from it. An alpha channel carries transparent and opaque areas and is commonly created with images used for photo or video compositing.

* If the image has a light or white background, InDesign can automatically detect its edges and create a clipping path.

The pear image you will be placing doesn't have a clipping path or an alpha channel, but it does have a solid white background that InDesign can remove.

Removing a white background using InDesign

Now you'll remove the white background from the pears in the image. You can use the Detect Edges option of the Clipping Path command to remove a solid white background from an image. The Detect Edges option hides areas of an image by changing the shape of the frame containing the image, adding anchor points as necessary.

1 Navigate to page 7 of your document by double-clicking page 7 in the Pages panel. Choose File > Place, and double-click the file 09_c.psd in the Lesson_09 folder.

2 In the Layers panel, make sure that the Photos layer is selected so that the image appears on that layer.

3 Position the loaded graphics icon ( ) outside the purple square—to the left and slightly below the top edge (make sure you are not placing the pointer in the square itself), and click to place an image of three pears on a white background. If you need to reposition the image, do so now.

4 Choose Object > Clipping Path > Options. Move the Clipping Path dialog box, if necessary, so that you can see the pear image.

5 Choose Detect Edges from the Type menu. If Preview is not selected, select it now. The white background is almost entirely eliminated from the image.

6 Drag the Threshold slider and watch the image on page 7 until the Threshold setting hides as much of the white background as possible without hiding parts of the subject (darker areas). This example uses a Threshold value of 20.

The Threshold option hides light areas of the image, starting with white. As you drag to the right to choose a higher value, increasingly darker tones are included within the range of tones that become hidden. Don't try to find a setting that matches the pear perfectly. You'll learn how to improve the clipping path later.

7 Drag the Tolerance slider slightly to the left until the Tolerance value is between 1 and 1.8.

● **Note:** If you can't find a setting that removes all of the background without affecting the subject, specify a value that leaves the entire subject visible along with small bits of the white background. You'll eliminate the remaining white background by fine-tuning the clipping path in the following steps.

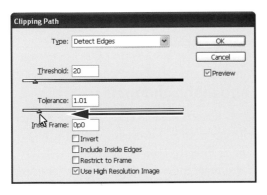

The Tolerance option determines how many points define the frame that's automatically generated. As you drag to the right, InDesign uses fewer points so that the clipping path fits the image more loosely (higher tolerance). Using fewer points on the path may speed up document printing, but may also be less accurate.

8 In the Inset Frame box, type a value that closes up any remaining background areas. This example uses 0p1 (zero picas, one point). This option shrinks the current shape of the clipping path uniformly, and is not affected by the lightness values in the image. Click OK to close the Clipping Path dialog box.

Before and after applying an inset of 1 point.

9   (Optional) You can refine the clipping path manually. With the Direct Selection tool (◥), select the pear image. You can now drag individual anchor points and use the drawing tools to edit the clipping path around the pears. With images that have complex edges, magnify the document to effectively work with the anchor points.

▶ **Tip:** You can also use Detect Edges to remove a solid black background. Just select the Invert option and specify a high threshold value.

10 Choose File > Save to save the file.

Working with alpha channels

When an image has a background that isn't solid white or black, Detect Edges may not be able to remove the background effectively. With such images, hiding the background's lightness values may also hide parts of the subject that use the same lightness values. Instead, you can use the advanced background-removal tools in Photoshop to mark transparent areas using paths or alpha channels, and let InDesign make a clipping path from those areas.

● **Note:** If you place a Photoshop (.psd) file that consists of an image placed on a transparent background, InDesign keeps the transparency without relying on clipping paths or alpha channels. A transparent background can be especially helpful when you place an image with a soft or feathered edge.

Importing a Photoshop file and alpha channels

You imported the previous image using the Place command. This time, use an alternate method: drag a Photoshop image directly onto an InDesign spread. InDesign can use Photoshop paths and alpha channels directly—you don't need to save the Photoshop file in a different file format. For more information, search for "drag and drop graphics" in InDesign Help.

1   In the Layers panel, make sure that the Photos layer is selected so that the image appears on that layer.

2   Navigate to page 2 of your document, and choose View > Fit Page In Window.

3   In Explorer (Windows) or the Finder (Mac OS), open the Lesson_09 folder, which contains the 09_d.psd file.

Resize and arrange your Explorer window (Windows) or Finder window (Mac OS) and your InDesign window, as needed, so that you can simultaneously see the list of files on the desktop and the InDesign document window. Make sure that the lower-left quarter of page 2 in your document is visible.

4   Drag the file 09_d.psd to page 2 in the InDesign document and place it on the pasteboard. Then use the Selection tool (⬆) to reposition the graphic so that it is in the lower-left corner of the page.

● **Note:** When you place the file, be careful to drop it on the pasteboard area to the left of page 2. If you drop it on a preexisting frame, it is placed inside the frame. If this happens, choose Edit > Undo, and try again.

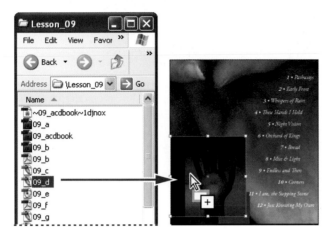

5   If necessary, maximize the InDesign window to its previous size. You've finished importing the file.

Examining Photoshop paths and alpha channels

In the Photoshop image that you just dragged into InDesign, the hand and the background share many of the same lightness values. Therefore, the background can't easily be isolated using the Detect Edges option in the Clipping Path dialog box.

Instead, you'll set up InDesign to use a path or alpha channel from Photoshop. First you'll use the Links panel to open the image directly in Photoshop to see what paths or alpha channels it already includes.

The procedure in this topic requires a full version of Photoshop 4.0 or later, and is easier if you have enough RAM available to leave both InDesign and Photoshop open as you work. If your configuration doesn't include these two conditions, you can still read these steps to help you understand what Photoshop alpha channels look like and do, and resume your work in the next section of this lesson.

1   With the Selection tool (⬆), select the 09_d.psd image in InDesign.

2   If the Links panel is not already open, choose Window > Links. The image filename appears selected in the Links panel.

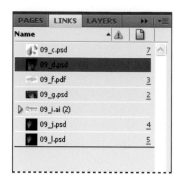

Note: The Edit Original button may open an image in an application other than Photoshop or the application in which it was created. When you install software, some installer utilities change your operating system's settings for associating files with applications. The Edit Original command uses these settings for associating files with applications. To change these settings, see the documentation for your operating system.

3 In the Links panel, click the Edit Original button (....✎....). This opens the image in an application that can view or edit it. This image was saved from Photoshop, so if Photoshop is installed on your computer, InDesign starts Photoshop with the selected file.

4 If an Embedded Profile Mismatch dialog box appears as the image opens in Photoshop, do one of the following:

- If you are not using color management, select Use The Embedded Profile (Instead Of The Working Space).

- If you've properly configured all Photoshop and InDesign color-management settings for your workflow using accurate ICC profiles, select Convert Document's Colors To The Working Space to reproduce the image properly in Photoshop.

5 In Photoshop, choose Window > Channels to display the Channels panel, or click the Channels panel tab.

6 Lengthen the Channels panel, if necessary, to view the three alpha channels (Alpha 1, Alpha 2, and Alpha 3) in addition to the standard RGB channels. These channels were drawn using the masking and painting tools in Photoshop.

Photoshop file saved with three alpha channels.

7 In the Channels panel in Photoshop, click Alpha 1 to see how it looks, and then click Alpha 2 and Alpha 3 to compare them.

8 In Photoshop, choose Window > Paths to open the Paths panel, or click the Paths panel tab.

The Paths panel contains two named paths, Shapes and Circle. These were drawn using the Pen tool (✎) and other path tools in Photoshop, although they could also be drawn in Illustrator and pasted into Photoshop.

9 In the Photoshop Paths panel, click Shapes to view that path, and then click Circle.

10 Quit Photoshop. You've finished using it for this lesson.

Using Photoshop alpha channels in InDesign

Now you'll return to InDesign and see how you can create different clipping paths from the Photoshop paths and alpha channels.

1 Switch to InDesign. Make sure that the 09_d.psd file is still selected on the page; if necessary, select it using the Selection tool (▶).

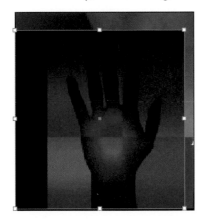

2 (Optional) Right-click (Windows) or Control-click (Mac OS) the hand image, and choose Display Performance > High Quality from the context menu that appears. This step isn't necessary, but it lets you precisely preview the following steps.

3 With the hand image still selected, choose Object > Clipping Path > Options to open the Clipping Path dialog box. If necessary, move the Clipping Path dialog box so that you can see the image as you work.

4 Make sure that Preview is selected, and then choose Alpha Channel from the Type menu. The Alpha menu becomes available, listing the three alpha channels you saw in Photoshop by the names used in that application.

5 In the Alpha menu, choose Alpha 1. InDesign creates a clipping path from the alpha channel. Then choose Alpha 2 from the same menu, and compare the results.

▶ **Tip:** You can fine-tune the clipping path that InDesign creates from an alpha channel by adjusting the Threshold and Tolerance options, as you did in "Removing a white background using InDesign" earlier in this lesson. For alpha channels, start with a low Threshold value, such as 1.

6 Choose Alpha 3 from the Alpha menu, and then select the Include Inside Edges option. Notice the changes in the image.

Selecting the Include Inside Edges option makes InDesign recognize a butterfly-shaped hole painted in the Alpha 3 channel, and adds it to the clipping path.

▶ **Tip:** You can see how the butterfly-shaped hole looks in Photoshop by viewing the Alpha 3 channel in the original Photoshop file.

7 Choose Photoshop Path from the Type menu, and then choose Shapes from the Path menu. InDesign reshapes the frame of the image to match the Photoshop path.

8 Choose Circle from the Path menu. Click OK.

Placing native files

InDesign allows you to import native Adobe files such as Photoshop, Illustrator, and Acrobat in unique ways and provides options for controlling how the file is displayed. For example, you can adjust the visibility of Photoshop layers in InDesign, as well as view different layer comps. Similarly, if you import a layered PDF created with Illustrator into an InDesign layout, you can vary the illustration by adjusting layer visibility.

Importing a Photoshop file with layers and layer comps

In the previous exercise, you worked with a Photoshop file with saved paths and alpha channels; however, the file had only a single background layer. When you work with a layered Photoshop file, you can adjust the visibility of the individual layers. Additionally, you can view different layer comps.

Created in Photoshop and saved as part of the file, layer comps are often used to make multiple compositions of an image to compare different styles or artwork. When the file is placed in InDesign, you can preview the different comps in relation to your entire layout. You'll view some layer comps now.

1   In the Links panel, click the link for 09_j.psd, and click the Go To Link button (⤴🖻) to select the file and center it in your document window. This file, which you relinked in a previous exercise, has four layers and three layer comps.

2   Choose Object > Object Layer Options to open the Object Layer Options dialog box. This dialog box allows you to turn layers off and on, and switch between layer comps.

3   Move the Object Layer Options dialog box to the bottom of your screen to see the selected image more clearly. Select the Preview option to allow you to view changes while keeping the dialog box open.

4   In the Object Layer Options dialog box, click the eye icon (👁) to the left of the Hands layer. This turns off the Hands layer, leaving only the Simple Background layer visible. Click the square next to the Hands layer to turn visibility back on.

5 Choose Green Glow from the Layer Comp menu. This layer comp has a different background. Now choose Purple Opacity from the Layer Comp menu. This layer comp has a different background, and the Hands layer is partially transparent. Click OK.

Layer comps are not merely an arrangement of different layers, but are able to save Photoshop layer effects, visibility, and position values. When the visibility of a layered file is modified, InDesign informs you in the Link Info section of the Links panel.

6 Click the Show/Hide Link Information button (▷) to show the Link Info section of the Links panel if it is not already showing. Locate the Layer Overrides listing. "Yes (2)" is displayed for Layer Overrides to let you know that two layers are overridden. "No" is displayed when there are no layer overrides.

7 Choose File > Save to save your work so far.

Placing inline graphics

Inline graphics flow with text. In this exercise you'll place the album logo in a text frame on page 6.

1 In the Pages panel, double-click the second spread and choose View > Fit Spread In Window. Scroll down if necessary. At the bottom of the pasteboard is the Orchard of Kings logo. You'll insert this graphic into a paragraph in the page above.

2 Using the Selection tool (▶), click the logo and choose Edit > Cut to place the graphic on the clipboard.

3   Select the Zoom tool (🔍) and click the text frame on page 6 to magnify the view. This exercise uses 150%.

4   Choose Type > Show Hidden Characters to view the spaces and paragraph returns in the text. This helps you locate where you want to paste the inline graphic.

5   Select the Type tool (**T**) and place an insertion point to the left of the second paragraph return below the word "streets." Choose Edit > Paste to place the graphic between the two paragraphs of text. Notice that the text after the graphic reflows when the image is placed.

Now you'll create space between the graphic and the surrounding text with the Space Before option.

6   Select the Paragraph Formatting Controls button (¶) in the Control panel. In the Space Before option (⁺≡), click the Up Arrow button to change the value to 0p4. As you increase the value, the inline graphic and text shift downward slightly.

● **Note:** Showing hidden characters is not a necessary step when placing inline graphics; it is used here to help identify the structure of the text.

7   Choose File > Save to save your work so far.

Adding text wrap to an inline graphic

You can easily add text wrap to an inline graphic. Text wrap allows you to experiment with different layouts and see the results immediately.

1 Using the Selection tool (➤), select the Orchard of Kings logo you placed in the previous exercise.

2 Press Shift+Ctrl (Windows) or Shift+Command (Mac OS) and drag the upper-right handle of the frame up and to the right, until you've scaled the graphic roughly 25% into the second column. The key combination lets you proportionally scale the graphic and the frame simultaneously.

3 Choose Window > Text Wrap to access the text wrap options. Even though the graphic is inline, it is placed beneath the existing text.

4 In the Text Wrap panel, select Wrap Around Object Shape (▣) to add text wrap to the graphic.

5 To increase space around the bounding box of the graphic, click the Up Arrow button in the Top Offset option (⬍) and change the value to 1p0.

Text can also wrap around a graphic's shape rather than the bounding box.

6 To see this more clearly, click the white pasteboard to deselect, and then click back on the Orchard of Kings logo. Press the Forward Slash key (/) to apply no fill color.

7 In the Text Wrap panel, choose Detect Edges from the Type menu. Because this image is a vector graphic, the text wrap honors the edges of the text. To view the document clearly, click the white pasteboard to deselect the graphic and choose Type > Hide Hidden Characters to hide the paragraph returns and space.

8 Using the Selection tool (▶), select the Orchard of "Kings" logo again.

9 In the Text Wrap panel, choose these options from the Wrap To menu in turn:

- Right Side. The type moves to the right side of the image, avoiding the area right below the image, even though there is space for it to display beneath the text wrap boundary.

- Both Right & Left Sides. The type moves into all available areas around the image. You'll notice that a small break in the type appears where the text wrap boundary drops into the type area.

- Largest Area. The text moves into the largest area to one side of the text wrap boundary.

10 (Optional) Select the Direct Selection tool (▷) and then click the graphic to view the anchor points used for the text wrap. When using the Detect Edges option, you can manually adjust the anchor points that define the text wrap, by clicking the anchor points and dragging them to a new position.

11 Close the Text Wrap panel.

12 Choose File > Save.

Importing an Illustrator file

InDesign takes full advantage of the smooth lines in EPS (Encapsulated PostScript) vector graphics such as those from Adobe Illustrator. When you use InDesign's high-quality screen display, EPS vector graphics and type appear with smooth edges at any size or magnification. Most EPS vector graphics don't require a clipping path because most applications save them with transparent backgrounds. In this section, you'll place an Illustrator graphic into your InDesign document.

1 In the Layers panel, select the Graphics layer. Choose Edit > Deselect All to make sure nothing is selected in your document.

2 Choose View > Fit Spread In Window to see the entire spread.

3 Then choose File > Place and select the Illustrator file 09_e.ai from the Lesson_09 folder. Make sure that Show Import Options is not selected. Click Open.

4 Click in the upper-left corner of page 5 with the loaded graphics icon to add the Illustrator file to the page. Position it as shown below. Graphics created in Illustrator are transparent in the areas where there is no artwork.

5 Choose File > Save to save your work.

Importing an Illustrator file with layers

You can import native Illustrator files with layers into an InDesign layout and control the visibility of the layers and reposition the graphic; however, you cannot edit the paths, objects, or text.

1 Deselect by clicking in the pasteboard of your document window.

2 Choose File > Place. In the lower-left corner of the Place dialog box, select Show Import Options. Select the file 09_n.ai and click Open. The Place PDF dialog box appears when Show Import Options is selected.

3 In the Place PDF dialog box, make sure that Show Preview is selected. In the Genre section, choose Bounding Box from the Crop To menu and make sure that Transparent Background is selected.

4 Click the Layers button to view the layers. This file has three layers: a background image of trees (Layer 3), a layer of text in English (English Title), and a layer of text in Spanish (Spanish Title).

Place PDF (09_n.ai)

Preview

General | Layers

Show Layers

☐ Spanish Title
◉ English Title
◉ Layer 3

Update Link Options

When Updating Link: Keep Layer Visibility Overrides ▾

◀ ◀ 1 ▶ ▶

Total pages: 1

☑ Show Preview

OK   Cancel

Although you can designate now which layers you would like to import, the small Preview area makes it difficult to see the results.

5 Click OK. You'll select the layers to import in the document itself.

6 With the loaded graphics icon (⬚), place the cursor to the left of the large blue box on page 5. Do not position the loaded graphics icon in the blue box because it inserts the graphic into that frame. Click once to place the graphic, and then use the Selection tool (▸) to position the graphic so that it is visually centered over the blue box.

7 Use the Zoom tool (🔍) to zoom in on the graphic.

8 With the graphic still selected, choose Object > Object Layer Options. Move the dialog box if necessary so that you can see the graphic in the document.

9 Select Preview and then click the eye icon (◉) next to the English Title layer to turn it off. Now click the empty box next to Spanish Title to turn on that layer. Click OK and deselect the graphic by clicking the white pasteboard.

Using layered Illustrator files allows you to re-purpose illustrations without having to create two separate documents.

10 Choose File > Save to save your work.

Using a library to manage objects

Object libraries let you store and organize graphics, text, and pages that you frequently use. You can also add ruler guides, grids, drawn shapes, and grouped images to a library. Each library appears as a separate panel that you can group with other panels any way you like. You can create as many libraries as you need—for example, different libraries for each of your projects or clients. In this section, you'll import a graphic currently stored in a library, and then you'll create your own library.

1   If you're not already on page 5, type **5** into the page box at the bottom of your document window to go to that page, and then press Enter or Return.

2   Choose View > Fit Page In Window to see the entire page.

3   Choose File > Open, select the file 09_k.indl in the Lesson_09 folder, and then click Open. Drag the lower-right corner of the panel to reveal all of the items it contains.

4   In the 09_k Library panel, select the Show Library Subset button (🔍). In the last box for the Parameters option, type **tree**, and click OK.

Show Subset
⊙ Search Entire Library   ◯ Search Currently Shown Items   [OK] [Cancel]
Parameters   [Item Name ▾] [Contains ▾] [tree]   [Back] [Forward]
[More Choices]   [Fewer Choices]

5   In the Layers panel, make sure the Graphics layer is targeted. Open the Links panel.

● **Note:** Your Links panel may display a missing link icon (❓) or a modified link icon (⚠) because you copied the Tree.psd file from its original location to your hard drive. To remove the warning, click the Update Link button in the Links panel or click the Relink button in the Links panel and navigate to the Lesson_09 folder to find Tree.psd.

6   Of the two objects visible in the 09_k Library panel, drag Tree.psd to page 5. The file is added to the page. Notice how the filename appears in the Links panel.

7   Using the Selection tool (▸), position the Tree.psd image as shown on the next page.

Creating a library

Now you'll create your own library. When adding a graphic to an InDesign library, the original file is not copied into the library; InDesign maintains a link to the original source file. Graphics stored in a library still require the original, high-resolution file for printing.

1   Choose File > New > Library. Type **CD Projects** as the library filename, navigate to the Lesson_09 folder, and click Save. The library appears as a floating panel, using the filename you specified.

2   Navigate to page 3. Using the Selection tool (↖), drag the Ricky Records logo to the library you just created. The logo is now saved in the library for use in other InDesign documents.

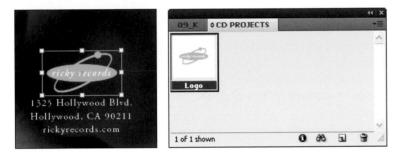

3   In the CD Projects library, double-click the Ricky Records logo. For Item Name, type **Logo**, and click OK.

4   Using the Selection tool (↖), drag the address text block to the CD Projects library.

5   In the CD Projects library, double-click the address text block. For Item Name, type **Address**, and click OK.

Now your library contains both text and graphics. As soon as you make changes to the library, InDesign saves the changes.

6   Close both libraries by clicking the close box in the upper-right corner of the library panel and choose File > Save.

Using snippets

A snippet is a file that holds objects and describes their location relative to one another on a page or page spread. Use snippets to conveniently reuse and position page objects. Create a snippet by saving objects in a snippet file, which has the .IDMS extension. (Previous InDesign versions use the .INDS extension.) When you place the snippet file in InDesign, you can determine whether the objects land in their original positions or where you click. You can store snippets in an Object library and Adobe Bridge as well as on your hard disk.

Snippets contents retain their layer associations when you place them. When a snippet contains resource definitions and these definitions are also present in the document to which it is copied, the snippet uses the resource definitions in the document.

Snippets you create in InDesign CS4 cannot be opened in previous versions of InDesign.

To create a snippet, do one of the following:

* Using a selection tool, select one or more objects, and then choose File > Export. From the Save As Type (Windows) or Format (Mac OS) menu, choose InDesign Snippet. Type a name for the file and click Save.

* Using a selection tool, select one or more objects, and then drag the selection to your desktop. A snippet file is created. Rename the file.

* Drag an item from Structure View to your desktop.

To add a snippet to a document:

1   Choose File > Place.

2   Select one or more snippet (.IDMS or .INDS) files.

3   Click the loaded snippet cursor where you want the upper-left corner of the snippet file to be.

    If you placed the insertion point in a text frame, the snippet is placed in the text as an anchored object.

    All objects remain selected after you place the snippet. By dragging, you can adjust the position of all objects.

4   If you loaded more than one snippet, scroll and click the loaded snippet cursor to place the others.

Rather than place snippet objects according to where you click on a page, you can place them in their original locations. For example, a text frame that appeared in the middle of a page when it was made part of a snippet can appear in the same location when you place it as a snippet.

* In File Handling preferences, choose Position At Original Location to preserve objects' original locations in snippets; choose Position At Cursor Location to place snippets according to where you click a page.

—From InDesign Help

Using Adobe Bridge to import graphics

Adobe Bridge is a separate tool that is installed with Adobe InDesign CS4. A cross-platform application, Adobe Bridge lets you browse your local and networked computers for images and then place them in InDesign—among many other features.

1 Choose File > Browse in Bridge to launch Adobe Bridge.

The Favorites and Folders panels in the upper-left corner of the Adobe Bridge window list various locations where you can browse for documents in Adobe Bridge.

2 Depending on where you placed the Lesson_09 folder, do one of the following:

- If you placed the Lesson_09 folder used for this lesson on your desktop, click Desktop in the Favorites panel, locate the folder in the Adobe Bridge window, and double-click to view its contents.

- If you placed the Lesson_09 folder in a different location, click My Computer (Windows) or Computer (Mac OS) in the Folders panel and then click the triangle to the left of each folder to navigate to the Lesson_09 folder. Click a folder icon to view its contents in the middle of the Adobe Bridge window.

Adobe Bridge lets you view the thumbnails of all of your images.

3 Adobe Bridge provides an easy way to locate and rename files. Click the graphic named Leaf.psd once; then click once on the filename to select the filename box. Rename the file **09_o.psd** and press Enter or Return to commit to the change.

4 To reduce the size of the Bridge window, click the Switch To Compact Mode button (■) in the upper-right corner of the window. Then drag the 09_o.psd file into the pasteboard area of your InDesign document.

5 Click the Switch To Compact Mode button again to enlarge the Bridge window, and then choose File > Return to Adobe InDesign to return to InDesign.

5 Position the leaf graphic in the upper left corner of page 4, on top of the purple box.

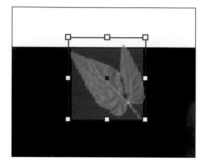

After importing graphics files into InDesign, you can easily locate and access the original files by taking advantage of the integration of Adobe Bridge and Adobe InDesign.

6 Select the 09_j.psd file in the Links panel. Then right-click (Windows) or Control-click (Mac OS) the link, and from the context menu, choose Reveal In Bridge.

This action switches you from InDesign to Adobe Bridge, and selects the 09_j.psd file.

7 Return to InDesign and save the file.

Congratulations! You've created a CD booklet by importing, updating, and managing graphics from many different graphics file formats.

Exploring on your own

Now that you've had some practice working with imported graphics, here are some exercises to try on your own.

1 Place different file formats with Show Import Options selected in the Place dialog box and see what options appear for each format. For a full description of all of the options available for each format, see InDesign Help.

2 Place a multiple-page PDF file with Show Import Options selected in the Place dialog box, and import different pages from it.

3 Create libraries of text and graphics for your work.

Review questions

1 How can you determine the filename of an imported graphic in your document?

2 What are the three options in the Clipping Path dialog box, and what must an imported graphic contain for each option to work?

3 What is the difference between updating a file's link and replacing the file?

4 When an updated version of a graphic becomes available, how do you make sure that it's up to date in your InDesign document?

Review answers

1 Select the graphic and then choose Window > Links to see if the graphic's filename is highlighted in the Links panel. The graphic appears in the Links panel if it takes up more than 48KB on the disk and was either placed or dragged.

2 The Clipping Path dialog box in InDesign lets you create a clipping path from an imported graphic by using:

   • The Detect Edges option when a graphic contains a solid white or solid black background.

   • The Photoshop Path option when a Photoshop file contains one or more paths.

   • The Alpha Channel option when a graphic contains one or more alpha channels.

3 Updating a file's link simply uses the Links panel to update the onscreen representation of a graphic so that it represents the most recent version of the original. Replacing a selected graphic uses the Place command to insert another graphic in place of the selected graphic. If you want to change any of a placed graphic's import options, you must replace the graphic.

4 In the Links panel, make sure that no alert icon is displayed for the file. If an alert icon appears, you can simply select the link and click the Update Link button. If the file has been moved, you can locate it again using the Relink button.

10 CREATING TABLES

Lesson Overview

In this lesson, you'll learn how to do the following:

- Import formatted tables from other applications, such as Microsoft Word and Microsoft Excel.

- Format tables with alternating row colors.

- Format cell and border strokes.

- Delete and resize columns.

- Set precise column dimensions.

- Create and apply cell styles.

- Place single or multiple graphics within a cell.

- Format text in tables by columns and by rows.

 This lesson will take approximately 60 minutes.

Tables are an efficient and effective way to communicate large amounts of information. With InDesign, you can easily create and modify visually rich tables. You can either create your own tables or import tables from other applications.

Getting started

In this lesson, you'll work on a fictional garden catalog spread that takes tables of information and brings them into the world of effective visual design. You'll format a large table using options in the Table menu and the Table panel, which both give you complete control over table features.

● **Note:** If you have not already copied the resource files for this lesson onto your hard disk from the Adobe InDesign CS4 Classroom in a Book CD, do so now. See "Copying the Classroom in a Book files" on page 2.

1 To ensure that the preferences and default settings of your Adobe InDesign CS4 program match those used in this lesson, move the InDesign Defaults file to a different folder following the procedure in "Saving and restoring the InDesign Defaults file" on page 2.

2 Start Adobe InDesign CS4. To ensure that the panels and menu commands match those used in this lesson, choose Window > Workspace > [Advanced], and then choose Window > Workspace > Reset Advanced.

3 Choose File > Open, and open the 10_a_Start.indd file in the Lesson_10 folder inside the Lessons folder located in the InDesignCIB folder on your hard disk. This layout contains specific information about a garden tour.

4 Choose File > Save As, name the file **10_Gardens.indd,** and save it in the Lesson_10 folder.

5 To see what the finished document will look like, open the 10_b_End.indd file in the same folder. You can leave this document open to act as a guide as you work. When you're ready to resume working on the lesson document, click the 10_Gardens.indd tab in the upper-left corner of the document window.

Creating a spread

In the Pages panel of your 10_Gardens.indd document, notice that page 1 and page 2 are on different spreads. You want those pages to face each other in a single spread, so you will number them pages 2 and 3.

Tip: Any time you need to start a facing-page document on a left-facing page, use the technique shown here—the key is to start the page numbering on an even number.

1 In the Pages panel, double-click page 1 to select it.

2 From the Pages panel menu, choose Numbering & Section Options.

3 In the Numbering & Section Options dialog box, select Start Page Numbering At and type **2**. Click OK.

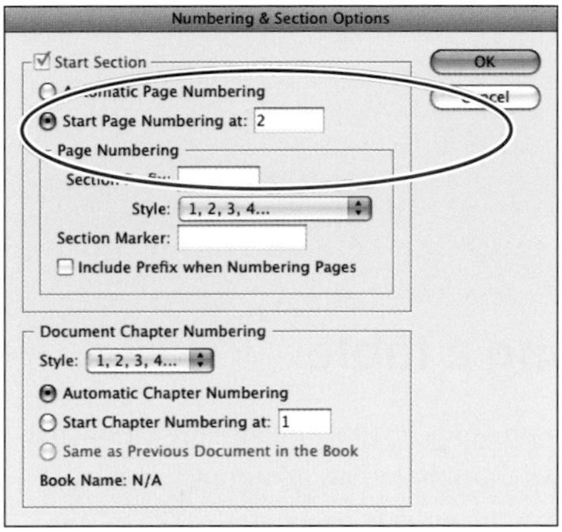

4 In the Pages panel menu, deselect Allow Selected Spread To Shuffle to keep this pair of pages together in case you add or remove pages.

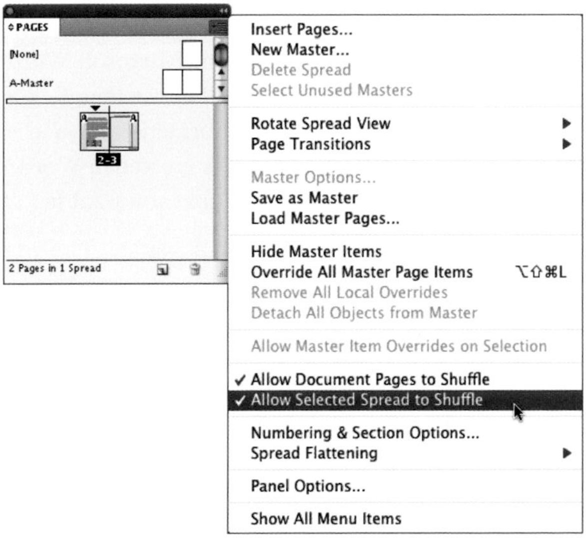

5 Choose File > Save.

Selecting the table's layer

In this document, the designer created separate layers for the text, background leaves, and table to prevent other objects from being accidentally selected and modified. To make it easier to work on the table, you will hide the Leaves layer, lock the Text layer, and then select the Table layer.

1 Choose Window > Layers.

2 Make sure the Text layer is locked (![lock]).

3 To select the Table layer so you can work on it, click its name.

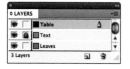

4 Choose File > Save.

Importing and formatting a table

Since you've worked with tables before in a previous lesson, you already know that tables are grids of individual cells set in rows (horizontal) and columns (vertical). The border of the table is a stroke that lies on the outside perimeter of the entire table. Cell strokes are lines within the table that set the individual cells apart from each other. Many tables include special header rows or columns that describe the category of information they contain. Typically, these are in the top row or the first column.

InDesign CS4 can import tables from other applications, including Microsoft Word and Microsoft Excel. You can even create a link to these external files so that if you update the Word or Excel file, you can easily update that information in your InDesign document. In this section, you'll import a table that was created in Word. This table contains all of the information about the garden tour that you want in your InDesign layout, organized in rows and columns.

Note: When you update linked tables, you will lose table and text formatting applied in InDesign.

Importing a Microsoft Word table

The table for this document already exists in a Microsoft Word file. In this exercise, you will change a preference to create a link to the Word file when you import it so that you can update the file later. Then you will import the table.

1 In the Pages panel, double-click page 3 to center it in the document window.

2 Choose View > Grids & Guides > Snap To Guides. Snap To Guides should be checked so objects are easy to align.

3 Choose Edit > Preferences > File Handling (Windows) or InDesign > Preferences > File Handling (Mac OS). In the Links section, select Create Links When Placing Text And Spreadsheet Files, and then click OK.

4 With the Type tool (T), click to place an insertion point in the burgundy-framed text frame on page 3. You will place the table in this frame.

5 Choose File > Place, and then navigate to the Lesson_10 folder. Make sure that Show Import Options is deselected, then double-click the 10_Table.doc file.

● **Note:** If a warning message about missing fonts appears, click OK.

The file flows into the text frame. Because it is a table, text wraps within the cells. You can edit text and select rows, columns, or the entire table.

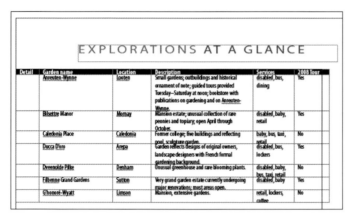

If a red dot appears in one of the columns, it indicates that the column is not wide enough to accommodate the text. Adjust the column by positioning the Type tool (T) over a column stroke. With the horizontal arrow icon, drag to make the column wider until the text fits.

● **Note:** If necessary, use the Selection tool to drag the bottom of the text frame down so the entire table fits.

You are now ready to begin formatting the table.

Formatting borders and alternating row colors

InDesign CS4 includes many easy-to-use formatting options for tables. You can use these to make tables attractive and easy for readers to get the information they want.

Now you'll add a black outline to each cell and then apply a color to alternating rows, to help better distinguish the information.

1 Using the Zoom tool (🔍), click the upper-left area of page 3 to increase the magnification to 200% or more. Center the page in the document window if necessary. Select the Type tool (T).

● **Note:** Increase the magnification if you have trouble getting the diagonal arrow to appear.

2 Move the pointer to the upper-left corner of the imported table, so that the pointer appears as a diagonal arrow. Click once to select the entire table.

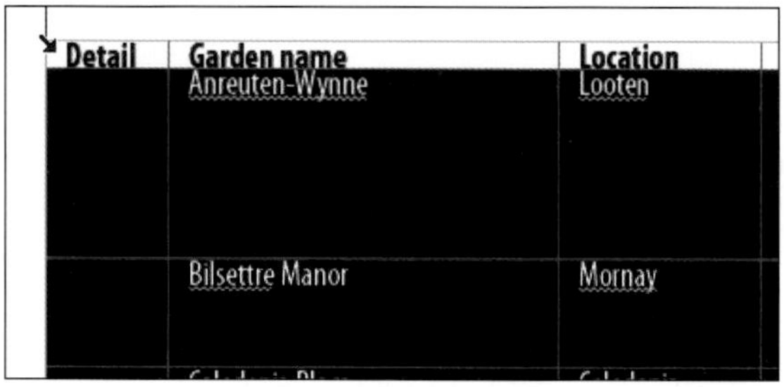

An alternate way to select an entire table is to click with the Type tool (T) anywhere in the table, and then choose Table > Select > Table. If the text insertion point is not in the table, this command is not available.

3 Choose Table > Table Options > Table Setup.

4 In the Table Setup tab, in the Table Border section, set the following options:

- Weight: 1 pt
- Color: [Black]
- Type: Solid
- Tint: 50%

5 Click the Fills tab and set the following options:

- From the Alternating Pattern menu, choose Every Other Row.

- From the Color menu on the left side of the dialog box, choose the khaki green color swatch named C = 43, M = 0, Y = 100, K = 56.

- Type **20%** in the Tint box.

- From the Color menu on the right side of the dialog box, choose [Paper].

- In the Skip First box, type **1** so that the alternating colors start on row 2 (the row below the headings).

6 Click OK. Choose Edit > Deselect All so that you can see the results.

7 Choose File > Save.

Every other row now has a pale green background.

Detail	Garden name	Location	Description	Services	2008 Tour
	Anreuten-Wynne	Looten	Small gardens; outbuildings and historical ornament of note; guided tours provided Tuesday–Saturday at noon; bookstore with publications on gardening and on Anreuten-Wynne.	disabled, bus, dining	Yes
	Bilsettre Manor	Mornay	Mansion estate; unusual collection of rare peonies and topiary; open April through October.	disabled, baby, retail	Yes
	Caledonia Place	Caledonia	Former college; five buildings and reflecting pool, sculpture garden.	baby, bus, taxi, retail	No
	Ducca D'oro	Arepa	Garden reflects designs of original owners, landscape designers with French formal gardening background.	disabled, bus, lockers	Yes
	Dveenolde Pilke	Denham	Unusual greenhouse and rare blooming plants.	disabled, baby, bus, taxi, retail	No
	Filbenne Grand Gardens	Sutton	Very grand garden estate currently undergoing major renovations; most areas open.	disabled, baby	Yes
	G'honoré-Wyatt	Limson	Mansion, extensive gardens.	retail, lockers, coffee	No

Editing cell strokes

Cell strokes are the lines around individual cells. You may want to edit the default black strokes, or remove the strokes altogether. In this section, you will alter the cell strokes so that they match the new table border.

1 Using the Type tool (T), move the pointer to the upper-left corner of the table until it turns into a diagonal arrow (↘), and then click to select the entire table.

2 Choose Table > Cell Options > Strokes And Fills, or choose the same command from the Table panel menu.

3 In the Cell Stroke section of the dialog box, set the following options:

- Weight: 1 pt
- Color: [Black]
- Type: Solid
- Tint: 50%

4 Click OK, and then choose Edit > Deselect All to see the results of your formatting.

5 Choose File > Save.

Formatting the header cells

Another element that makes reading a table easier is setting the categories apart from the table data. If you make the categories visually distinctive, readers are more likely to comprehend the table information. In this exercise, you'll create insets so that the text doesn't run into the strokes on each cell, and then give the heading row a unique color fill.

1 Using the Type tool (T), move the pointer over the left edge of the first row until it appears as a horizontal pointer (→). Then click to select the entire first row.

Note: When you select the header row, which has white text on a black background, the selection appears white.

2 Choose Table > Cell Options > Text.

3 In the Text tab, set the following options:

- Under Cell Insets, type **0p3.6** for Top, and then click the Make All Settings The Same icon (🔳) to set the Bottom, Left, and Right values to match.

- Under Vertical Justification, choose Align Center from the Align menu.

- For First Baseline, make sure that the Offset is set as Ascent. Leave the dialog box open.

4 Click the Strokes And Fills tab. In the Cell Fill section, choose the khaki green color swatch named C = 43, M = 0, Y = 100, K = 56.

5 Type **40%** in the Tint box and leave the dialog box open.

6 Select the Rows And Columns tab. For Row Height, choose Exactly from the menu, and then type **2p0** in the box to the right of the menu.

7 Click OK to close the dialog box. Choose Edit > Deselect All.

8 Choose File > Save.

The header row of the table now appears formatted with white type against a green background.

Detail	Garden name	Location	Description	Services	2008 Tour
	Anreuten-Wynne	Looten	Small gardens; outbuildings and historical ornament of note; guided tours provided Tuesday–Saturday at noon; bookstore with publications on gardening and on Anreuten-Wynne.	disabled, bus, dining	Yes
	Bilsettre Manor	Mornay	Mansion estate; unusual collection of rare peonies and topiary; open April through October.	disabled, baby, retail	Yes
	Caledonia Place	Caledonia	Former college; five buildings and reflecting pool, sculpture garden.	baby, bus, taxi, retail	No
	Ducca D'oro	Arepa	Garden reflects designs of original owners, landscape designers with French formal gardening background.	disabled, bus, lockers	Yes
	Dveenolde Pilke	Denham	Unusual greenhouse and rare blooming plants.	disabled, baby, bus, taxi, retail	No
	Filbenne Grand Gardens	Sutton	Very grand garden estate currently undergoing major renovations; most areas open.	disabled, baby	Yes
	G'honoré-Wyatt	Limson	Mansion, extensive gardens.	retail, lockers, coffee	No

Deleting a column

After you create or import a table, you can add or delete entire rows or columns to or from your table structure. Sometimes, you'll want to delete just the contents of a cell, row, or column. Other times, you'll want to delete the entire cell, row, or column, including its contents.

The information about the 2009 Tour in the column on the far right side of this table is unnecessary, so you'll delete the entire column.

1 Using the Type tool (T), move the pointer to the top edge of column 6 (the last column on the right) until the pointer turns into a downward-pointing arrow (↓). Then click to select the entire column.

2 Choose Table > Delete > Column. The entire column disappears.

3 Choose File > Save.

● **Note:** The suggested zoom levels are appropriate for a larger monitor. If you have a smaller monitor, zoom to comfortable levels while working on the table.

● **Note:** To delete only the contents of a column, you can select the column and press the Delete key.

Using graphics within tables

You can use InDesign to create effective tables that combine text, photographs, and illustrations. The techniques involved are as easy as working with text. In this section, you'll adjust your table formatting so that the cells are the correct sizes for the garden images and icons that you'll place in them. Then you'll anchor (place) the graphics into the cells.

Setting fixed column and row dimensions

You can define the sizes of cells, columns, or rows to fit precise measurements. In this exercise, you will adjust the size of the first column so that the 1-inch images fit nicely within the cells.

1 Using the Type tool (T), select the first column, either by dragging from top to bottom or by clicking the top edge of the column when the downward-pointing arrow (↓) appears. Or, you can click in any cell of the column and select Table > Select > Column.

2 Choose Window > Type & Tables > Table to show the Table panel, if it is not already visible.

3 In the Column Width box (▤), type **6p10.8**, and press Enter or Return. Click anywhere in the table to deselect the column.

4 Using the Type tool, drag down from the second cell in the first column. Select all of the cells except the top cell in the column.

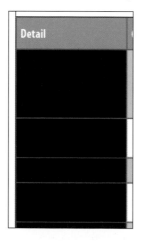

5 In the Table panel, select Exactly for the Row Height option (▤), and then type **6p10.8** in the box to the right of the menu. Press Enter or Return.

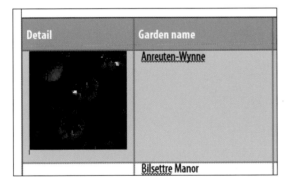

6 If necessary, use the Selection tool (▸) to resize the text frame so the table fits.

7 Choose File > Save.

Placing graphics in table cells

The images you will add to the table are all stored in a library. You can drag the them out of the library and onto the document page or pasteboard. The images are then anchored into the table cells.

To begin, you'll import one image that is not yet part of the InDesign file.

1 Using the Type tool (T), click to place the insertion point in the first cell in the second row (just below the "Detail" cell).

2 Choose File > Place, and locate the 10_c.tif file in your Lesson_10 folder. Make sure that Show Import Options is deselected, and then double-click to open the file. The image of flowers appears in the first cell.

● **Note:** If a red plus sign (+) appears in the out port of the table frame, choose Object > Fitting > Fit Frame To Content.

● **Note:** You must use the Type tool to place or paste content into table cells. You cannot drag items into table cells. Dragging only positions the item above or below the table in the layout stacking order; it does not place the item within a cell.

3 Double-click page 3 in the Pages panel to center it in the document window.

4 Choose File > Open, and locate the 10_GraphicsLibrary.indl file in your Lesson_10 folder. The .indl extension indicates a library file. Double-click to open the library.

5 Choose Large Thumbnail View from the Library panel menu so you can see the images and their names. If necessary, resize the library to see all the images.

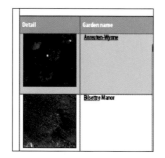

Bilsettre M... | Caledonia... | Ducca D'oro | Dveenolde... | Filbenne Gr... | G'honoré-...

Disability P... | Baby Chan... | Bus Service | Taxi Service | Retail Store | Locker Stor...

Coffee Shop | Dining Serv...

14 of 14 shown

▶ **Tip:** You can quickly switch from the Type tool to the Selection tool by pressing the Ctrl (Windows) or Command (Mac OS) key.

6 Using the Selection tool (↖), drag all the images—garden photos and icons—from the library onto the pasteboard to the right of page 3. Leave the library open for reference.

7 Using the Selection tool, click the Bilsettre Manor image on the pasteboard. (If you're not sure which image it is, look at the names in the library.) Choose Edit > Cut.

8 Double-click to place an insertion point in the third row of the first column, just below the image you placed in the previous step. Choose Edit > Paste.

9 Continue cutting and pasting to place each of the remaining five images into the empty cells in column 1.

10 Choose Window > Layers to open the Layers panel. To show the Leaves layer, click in the blank box to the far left of its name. The eye icon (👁) appears.

11 Choose File > Save.

Placing multiple graphics in a cell

The graphics you place or paste into table cells are anchored to the text within the cells. Because of this, you can add as many graphics to a single cell as you need. You are limited only by the size of the cell.

Now you'll place icons indicating the services available at the various gardens.

1 Select the Zoom tool (🔍), and then click and drag to isolate the upper-right corner of page 3, along with the icons you dragged to the pasteboard.

2 Using the Selection tool (↖), select the wheelchair icon on the pasteboard.

3 Choose Edit > Cut.

4 Switch to the Type tool (T), and look in column 5, labeled Services, for the first instance of "disabled." Drag to select the entire word, the comma, and the space after it.

5 Choose Edit > Paste. Press the spacebar to add a space after the icon.

● **Note:** To reveal the graphics on the pasteboard of the document, drag any open panels out of the way, minimize them, or close them.

6 Find the other instances of the word "disabled" in the remaining cells of that column, select them, and replace the text with the wheelchair icon.

7 Repeat this process for each of the remaining words and icons: "Baby," "Bus," "Taxi," "Retail," "Lockers," "Coffee," and "Dining." (If you're not sure which icon it is, look at the names in the library.)

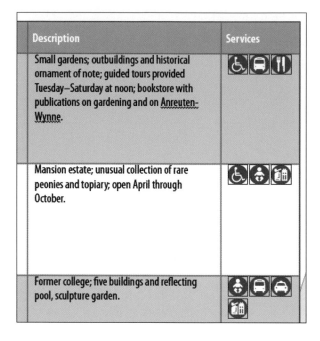

Because you haven't yet adjusted the column widths, your icons may overlap each other vertically at this phase of your work. You'll fix that in the next section.

8 In the Pages panel, double-click page 3 to center it in the document window.

9 Choose File > Save. Click the library's close button to close it.

Formatting text within a table

All that remains in your table project is to make some final adjustments so that the spacing of the text, graphics, and table fit the rest of the spread.

Editing imported paragraph styles in a table

If you are already comfortable formatting text in text frames, formatting text in tables is an easy and natural extension of your InDesign skills. In this exercise, you will change the formatting of the header and body text and then redefine the paragraph styles.

1 Select the Zoom tool (🔍) and click to zoom to 200% if necessary.

2 Choose Type > Paragraph Styles to open the Paragraph Styles panel.

3 Choose Type > Character to open the Character panel.

4 Using the Type tool (T), select the word "Detail" in the first row of the table. Notice in the Paragraph Styles panel that this text already has the paragraph style "header" applied to it.

This style was imported with the Word document, where the table was originally formatted. You will specify new formatting and update the style to reflect the new formatting.

5 In the Character panel, set the following attributes:

- Font: Myriad Pro

- Style: Regular

- Size: 10 pt

- Leading: 14 pt

- Tracking: 150

- Horizontal Scale: 125%

6 Choose All Caps from the Character panel menu.

7 Choose Window > Swatches. Click Black for the selected text.

In the Paragraph Styles panel, a plus sign (+) now appears next to the header style.

8 Choose Redefine Style from the Paragraph Styles panel menu.

9 In the third column, select the word "Looten."

Notice in the Paragraph Styles panel that this text already has the paragraph style "bodytable" applied to it. This style was imported with the Word document, where the table was originally formatted. You will specify new formatting and then update the style to reflect it.

10 In the Character panel, set the following attributes:

- Font: Myriad Pro

- Style: Regular

- Size: 8 pt

- Leading: 10 pt

● **Note:** If some of the text no longer fits into the cells, you will have a chance to fix it later in this lesson. Overset text inside of cells is represented by a red dot inside the cell.

In the Paragraph Styles panel, a plus sign (+) now appears next to the bodytable style.

11 Choose Redefine Style from the Paragraph Styles panel menu.

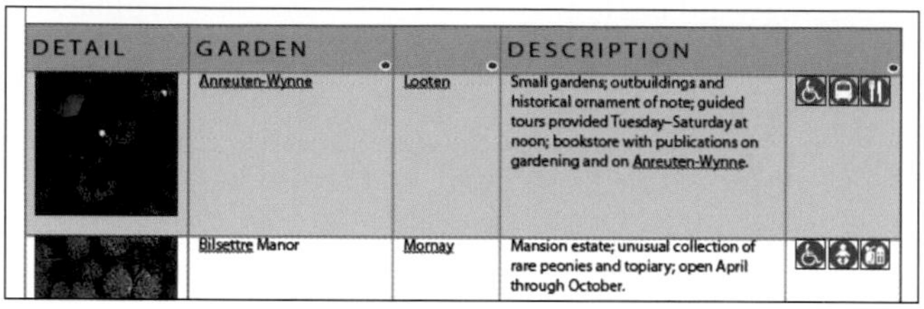

Creating a new cell style

Now you'll create a new cell style, as you did in Lesson 8, that contains the paragraph style that you just edited, as well as cell formatting. You'll vertically align the text in these cells in the center.

1 Select the Type tool (T), and click to place an insertion point in the word "Looten."

2 Choose Window > Type & Tables > Cell Styles. In the Cell Styles panel menu, choose New Cell Style.

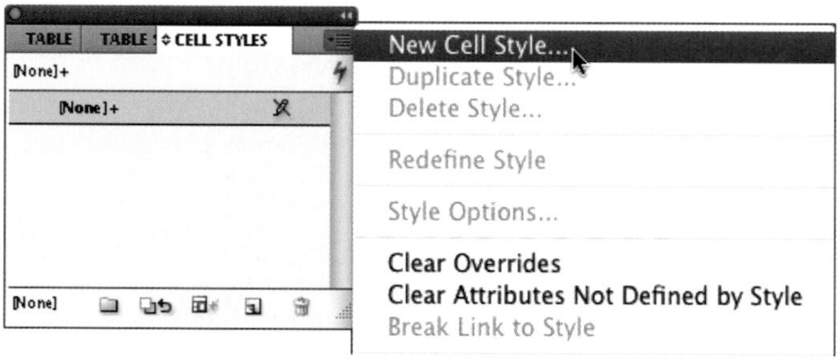

3 Name the style **Table Body** in the Style Name box.

4 In the Paragraph Style menu, choose bodytable. This ensures that the style is part of the cell formatting.

5 Select Text on the left side of the dialog box. In the Cell Insets section, type **0p5** in the Top box, and click the Make All Settings The Same icon (⬛) to fill in the same values for Bottom, Left, and Right.

6 In the Vertical Justification section of the dialog box, choose Align Center from the Align menu.

7 Click OK. The new Table Body cell style appears in the Cell Styles panel.

8 With the Type tool (T), drag to select all rows and columns (excluding the header row) and click Table Body to apply the new style to all of the selected cells.

● **Note:** If the text does not change and you still see a plus sign (+) next to the style, press the Alt (Windows) or Option (Mac OS) key as you click the style. This overrides any existing formatting in the text.

Even though there is no text in the first and last columns, applying the cell style centers the anchored graphics within the cells.

Duplicating a cell style

The leading in the last column is too narrow to accommodate the icons. To fix this, you will increase the leading and then create a new paragraph style. Finally, you will create a new cell style that uses the new paragraph style.

1 With the Type tool (T), select the three icons that slightly overlap. They are in the second body cell in the last column. To select anchored objects such as these, drag as if you were selecting text.

2 In the Character panel, increase the leading to 24 pt. Keep the icons selected.

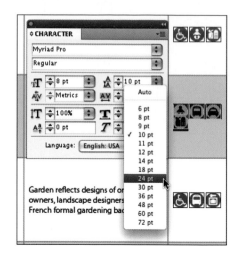

3 From the Paragraph Styles panel menu, choose New Paragraph Style. Your new leading displays in the Style Settings box.

4 Type **Table Icons** in the Style Name box to assign a name to this style. Click OK.

5 Choose Window > Type & Tables > Cell Styles and click the Table Body style.

6 Choose Duplicate Style from the Cell Styles panel menu. The Duplicate Cell Style dialog box displays all of the same attributes as the original Table Body style.

7 Type **Table Icons** in the Style Name box.

8 In the Paragraph Styles section of the dialog box, choose Table Icons from the Paragraph Style menu.

9 Click OK. The Table Icons style now appears in the Cell Styles panel.

10 With the Type tool (T), select all of the cells with green icons, except the header row.

11 Click Table Icons in the Cell Styles panel to apply the new style to these cells.

12 Choose File > Save.

All the icons in the last column should now be spaced properly and, if necessary, you only need to adjust the column widths to accommodate the text and graphics.

Dragging to adjust column size

In tables, text or graphics that don't fit into a cell are considered overset, which is indicated by a small red dot in the lower-right corner of the cell. Table cells do not support linking. If the content does not fit in a cell, it must be made smaller, or the cell must be made larger.

For this garden catalog table, you'll resize the columns so that everything fits into the table.

1 Choose View > Fit Page In Window to see the entire table.

2 Position the Type tool (T) over the vertical line separating the "Region" and "Description" columns until the pointer becomes a double arrow (↔), and then drag the column edge to the right to make it wider until the contents of each cell in the column are visible.

3 Moving from left to right, resize each of the columns so that the contents fit inside.

4 If necessary, use the Selection tool (▶) to resize the text frame horizontally and vertically so the entire table fits.

5 Deselect all, choose View > Fit Spread In Window, and choose File > Save.

Finishing up

As a final step, you'll preview your completed garden catalog.

1   In the Tools panel, click Preview.

2   Press Tab to hide all of the panels and review the results of your work.

Congratulations! You have now completed this lesson.

Exploring on your own

Now that you're skilled in the basics of working with tables in InDesign, you can experiment with other techniques for building tables.

1   To create a new table, scroll beyond the spread to the pasteboard, and drag the Type tool (T) to create a new text frame. Then choose Table > Insert Table and enter the number of rows and columns you want in your table.

2   To enter information in your table, make sure that the insertion point is in the first cell and then type. To move forward to the next cell in the row, press Tab. To move to the cell below in the column, press the Down Arrow key.

3   To add a column by dragging, move the Type tool (T) over the right edge of one of the columns in your table so that the pointer becomes a double arrow (↔) and begin dragging to the right. Hold down Alt (Windows) or Option (Mac OS) and drag a short distance to the right, perhaps half an inch or so. When you release the mouse button, a new column appears, having the same width as the distance you dragged.

4   To combine several cells into one cell, drag with the Type tool (T) to select two or more cells, and then choose Table > Merge Cells.

5   To convert the table to text, choose Table > Convert Table To Text. Tabs can separate what were previously columns, and paragraph breaks can separate rows. You can also modify these options. Similarly, you can convert tabbed text to a table by selecting the text and choosing Table > Convert Text To Table.

6   To create rotated text, click with the Type tool to place an insertion point in the merged cell you just created. Choose Window > Type & Tables > Table. In the Table panel, select the Rotate Text 270° (⇥) option. Then type the text you want in this cell.

Review questions

1 What are the advantages of using tables rather than just typing text and using tabs to separate the columns?

2 When might you get an overset cell?

3 What tool is used most frequently when you work with tables?

Review answers

1 Tables give you much more flexibility and are far easier to format. In a table, text can wrap within a cell, so you don't have to add extra lines to accommodate cells that contain a lot of text. Also, you can assign styles to individual rows, columns, and cells—including character styles and even paragraph styles—because each cell is considered a separate paragraph.

2 Overset cells occur when the contents don't fit inside the cell's current dimensions. This overset occurs if you have defined the exact width and height of the cell (or its row and column). Otherwise, when you place text in the cell, the text wraps within the cell, which then expands vertically to accommodate the text. When you place a graphic in a cell that does not have defined size limits, the cell expands vertically but not horizontally, so the column keeps its original width.

3 The Type tool must be selected to work with a table. You can use other tools to work with the graphics within table cells, but to work with the table itself, such as selecting rows or columns, inserting text or graphic content, adjusting table dimensions, and so forth, you use the Type tool.

11 WORKING WITH TRANSPARENCY

Lesson Overview

In this lesson, you'll learn how to do the following:

- Colorize an imported grayscale image.

- Change the opacity of objects drawn in InDesign.

- Apply transparency settings to imported graphics.

- Apply transparency settings to text.

- Apply blending modes to overlapping objects.

- Apply feathering effects to objects.

- Apply multiple effects to an object.

- Edit and remove effects.

 This lesson will take approximately 45 minutes.

InDesign CS4 offers an array of transparency features to feed your imagination and creativity. These include controls over opacity, effects, and color blends. You can also import files that use transparency and apply additional transparency effects.

Getting started

● **Note:** If you have not already copied the resource files for this lesson onto your hard disk from the Adobe InDesign CS4 Classroom in a Book CD, do so now. See "Copying the Classroom in a Book files" on page 2.

The project for this lesson is a menu for a fictional restaurant, Bistro Nouveau. By applying transparency effects using a series of layers, you'll create a visually rich design.

1   To ensure that the preference and default settings of your Adobe InDesign CS4 program match those used in this lesson, move the InDesign Defaults file to a different folder following the procedure in "Saving and restoring the InDesign Defaults file" on page 2.

2   Start Adobe InDesign CS4. To ensure that the panels and menu commands match those used in this lesson, choose Window > Workspace > [Advanced], and then choose Window > Workspace > Reset Advanced.

To begin working, you'll open an InDesign document that is already partially completed.

3   Choose File > Open, and open the 11_a_Start.indd file in the Lesson_11 folder, which is located within the Lessons folder in the InDesignCIB folder on your hard disk.

4   Choose File > Save As, name the file **11_Menu.indd**, and save it in the Lesson_11 folder.

The menu appears as a long, blank page because all of the layers are currently hidden. You'll reveal these layers one by one as you need them, so it will be easy to focus on the specific objects and tasks in this lesson.

5   To see what the finished project looks like, open the 11_b_End.indd file in the Lesson_11 folder.

6 When you are ready to start working, either close the 11_b_End.indd file or leave it open for your reference. Then return to your lesson document by choosing 11_Menu.indd from the Window menu or clicking the 11_Menu.indd tab at the top of the document window.

Importing and colorizing a grayscale image

You'll begin by working with the Background layer for the restaurant menu. This layer serves as a textured background that is visible through the objects layered above it that have transparency effects. By applying transparency effects, you can create see-through objects that reveal any objects underneath.

Because nothing is below the Background layer in the layer stack, you won't apply any transparency effects to objects on this layer.

1 Choose Window > Layers to display the Layers panel.

2 In the Layers panel, select the layer labeled Background, scrolling as necessary to find it at the bottom of the layer stack. You'll place the image you import on this layer.

3 Make sure that the two boxes to the left of the layer name show that the layer is visible (the eye icon (👁) appears) and unlocked (the layer lock icon (🔒) does not appear). The pen icon (✒) to the right of the layer name indicates that this is the layer on which the imported objects will be placed and new frames will be created.

4 Choose View > Grids & Guides > Show Guides. You'll use the guides on the page to align the background image that you import.

5 Choose File > Place, and then open the 11_c.tif file in your Lesson_11 folder. This file is a grayscale TIF.

6 Move the loaded graphics icon (⬛) slightly outside the upper-left corner of the page; then click the corner where the red bleed guides meet so that the placed image fills the entire page, including the margins and bleed area. Keep the graphics frame selected.

7 Choose Window > Swatches. You'll use the Swatches panel to colorize the image, first adjusting the tint of the swatch that you'll use.

8 In the Swatches panel, select the Fill box (⬛). Scroll down the list of swatches to find the Light Green swatch and select it. Click the Tint menu at the top of the panel and drag the slider to 76%.

The white areas of the image are now a 76% tint of the green color, but the gray areas remain unchanged.

9 Choose Edit > Deselect All to deselect the image.

10 In the Tools panel, select the Direct Selection tool (↖), click the image to select it, and then select Light Green in the Swatches panel. Light Green replaces gray in the image, leaving the Light Green 76% areas as they were.

● **Note:** Remember that the Direct Selection tool appears as a hand (✍) when it is over a frame, but it still selects the contents of an image frame when you click.

When you click within a graphics frame with the Direct Selection tool, you select the graphic instead of the frame. If you then apply a fill color, the color is applied to the gray portions of the image rather than the background of the frame as it would if you clicked within the frame with the Selection tool (▶).

11 In the Layers panel, click the empty box to the left of the Background layer name to lock the layer. Leave the Background layer visible so that you can see the results of the transparency work you will be doing above this layer.

12 Choose File > Save to save your work.

You've just learned a quick method for colorizing a grayscale image. While this method is effective for creating composites, you may find the color controls available in Adobe Photoshop CS4 more effective for creating your final artwork.

Applying transparency settings

InDesign CS4 has extensive transparency controls. For example, by lowering the opacity of objects, text, and even imported graphics, you can reveal underlying objects that would otherwise not be visible. Additional transparency features such as blending modes, drop shadows, feathered and glowing edges, and bevel and emboss effects provide a wide range of options for creating special visual effects; you'll learn about these additional features later in the lesson.

In this part of the project, you'll practice using various transparency options on each layer in the restaurant menu artwork.

About the Effects panel

You use the Effects panel (Window > Effects) to specify the opacity and blending mode of objects and groups, isolate blending to a particular group, knock out objects inside a group, or apply a transparency effect.

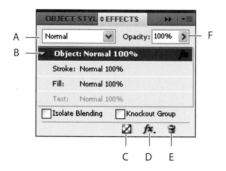

A. Blending mode B. Levels C. Clear effects D. FX button E. Delete F. Opacity

Effects panel overview

Blending Mode—Lets you vary the ways in which the colors of overlapping objects blend.

Opacity—As you lower the opacity value of an object, the object becomes increasingly translucent and underlying objects become increasingly visible.

Level—Tells you the Object, Stroke, Fill, and Text opacity settings of the selected object, as well as whether transparency effects have been applied. Click the triangle to the left of the word Object (or Group or Graphic) to alternately hide and display these level settings. The FX icon appears on a level after you apply transparency settings there, and you can double-click the FX icon to edit the settings.

Isolate Blending—Applies a blending mode to a selected group of objects but does not affect underlying objects that are not part of the group.

Knockout Group—Makes the opacity and blending attributes of every object in a group knock out, or block out, underlying objects in the group.

Clear All button—Clears effects—stroke, fill, or text—from an object, sets the blending mode to Normal, and changes the Opacity setting to 100% throughout the object.

FX button—Displays a list of transparency effects.

Changing the opacity of solid-color objects

With the background graphic complete, you can start applying transparency effects to objects on layers stacked above it. You'll start with a series of simple shapes that were drawn using InDesign CS4.

1 In the Layers panel, select the Art1 layer so that it becomes the active layer, and click the lock icon to the left of the layer name to unlock the layer. Click the empty box on the far left of the Art1 layer name so that the eye icon (👁) appears, indicating that the layer is visible.

● **Note:** If the
Swatches panel is not
still open from the
previous exercise,
choose Window >
Swatches to open it.
The shapes mentioned
are named by the color
swatch applied to the
fill of the object.

2 Using the Selection tool (⬉), click the circle filled with the Yellow/Green swatch on the right side of the page. This ellipse frame with a solid fill was drawn in InDesign.

3 Choose Window > Effects to display the panel.

4 In the Effects panel, click the arrow on the right side of the Opacity percentage. An Opacity slider adjustment appears. Drag the slider to 70%. Alternatively, enter **70%** in the Opacity box and press Enter or Return.

After you change the opacity of the Yellow/Green Circle, the vertical purple bar is partially visible with the change of color.

5 In the document window, select the Light Green-filled semicircle in the upper-left corner of the page; then go to the Effects panel and set the Opacity value to 50%. The semicircle now appears as a subtle variation in color against the background.

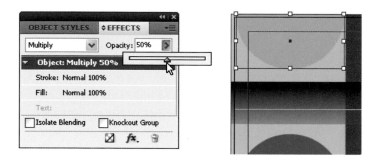

6 Repeat step 5 for the remaining circles on the Art1 layer, using the following settings to change the opacity of each circle:

- Left side, middle circle filled with the Medium Green swatch, Opacity = 60%

- Left side, bottom circle filled with the Light Purple swatch, Opacity = 70%

- Right side, circle filled with the Light Purple swatch and a black stroke, Opacity = 60%

- Right side, bottom semicircle filled with the Light Green swatch, Opacity = 50%

7 Choose File > Save to save your work.

Applying a blending mode

Changing the opacity creates a color that combines the color values of the object with the objects below it. Using blending modes is another way to create color interactions between layered objects.

In this procedure, you'll apply the Multiply blending mode to one of the circles whose opacity you changed earlier in the lesson.

1 Using the Selection tool (↖), select the Yellow/Green-filled circle on the right side of the page.

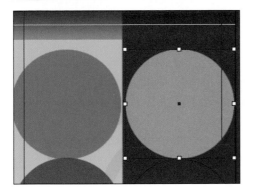

2 In the Effects panel, choose Overlay from the Blending Mode menu. Notice how the appearance of the colors changes.

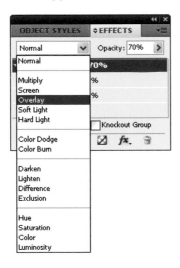

3 Select the Light Green-filled semicircle in the lower-right section of the page, and then hold down the Shift key and select the semicircle in the upper-left section of the page.

4 In the Effects panel, choose Multiply from the Blending Mode menu.

5 Choose File > Save.

For more information on the different blending modes, see "Specify how colors blend" in InDesign Help.

Adjusting transparency settings for EPS images

You have applied various transparency settings to objects drawn using InDesign. You can also change the opacity values and blending mode for graphics imported from other applications such as Adobe Illustrator.

1 In the Layers panel, unlock and make the Art2 layer visible.

2 In the Tools panel, make sure that the Selection tool (⬆) is selected.

3 On the left side of the page, click the black spiral image, which is on top of the Medium Green-colored circle. With the black spiral still selected, hold down the Shift key and click to select the spiral that is above the Light Purple circle on the right side of the page. Both spiral objects should now be selected.

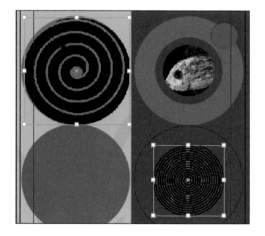

4 In the Effects panel, choose Color Dodge from the Blending Mode menu and set the Opacity to 30%.

Next you will apply a blending mode to the stroke on the fish image.

5 With the Selection tool (⬆), click the fish image on the right side of the page.

6 In the Effects panel, click the Stroke level beneath Object. Selecting the Stroke level applies any opacity or blending mode changes you make to the stroke of the selected object.

A level indicates the Object, Stroke, Fill, and Text opacity settings of the object and the applied blending mode, as well as whether transparency effects have been applied. You can hide or display these level settings by clicking the triangle to the left of the word Object (or Group or Graphic).

7 From the Blending Mode menu, choose Hard Light.

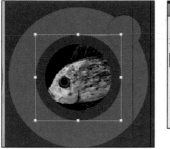 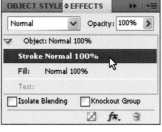 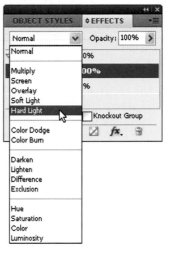

Select the image (left); then select the Stroke level (center); and choose Hard Light (right).

8 Choose File > Save to save your work.

Adjusting transparency to images

Next you'll apply transparency to an imported Photoshop file. Although this example uses a monochromatic image, you can also apply InDesign transparency settings to complex multicolor photographs. The process is the same as applying transparency to any other InDesign object.

1 In the Layers panel, select the Art3 layer. Click to unlock this layer and to make it visible. You can hide either the Art1 layer or the Art2 layer to make it easier to work. Be sure to keep at least one underlying layer visible so that you can see the results of the transparency interactions.

2 Using the Selection tool (✱), click the black starburst image on the right side of the page.

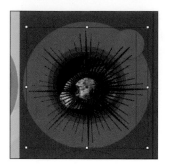

3 In the Effects panel, enter **70%** as the Opacity value.

4 Switch to the Direct Selection tool (⤷), move the pointer over the starburst image so that it changes to a hand (✋), and then click the image once.

5 In the Swatches panel, click the Fill box (■), and then select the Red color swatch so that the red color replaces the black areas of the image.

If other layers are visible below the Art3 layer, you can see the starburst as a muted orange color. If no other layers are visible, the starburst is red.

6 If the starburst image is not still selected, reselect it with the Direct Selection tool.

7 In the Effects panel, choose Screen from the Blending Mode menu and leave the Opacity value at 100%. The starburst changes colors based on the layers that are visible beneath it.

8 Choose File > Save to save your work.

Importing and adjusting Illustrator files that use transparency

When you import Adobe Illustrator files into your InDesign layout, InDesign CS4 recognizes and preserves any transparency settings that were applied in Illustrator. You can also apply additional transparency settings in InDesign, adjusting the opacity, blending modes, and feathering of the entire image.

Now you will place an image of some drinking glasses, and then adjust its transparency.

1 In the Layers panel, make sure that the Art3 layer is the active layer and the Art3, Art2, Art1, and Background layers are visible.

2 Lock the Art2, Art1, and Background layers to prevent them from being modified.

3 Select the Selection tool (➤) in the Tools panel, and then choose Edit > Deselect All so that the image you import is not placed into an existing object.

4 Choose View > Fit Page In Window.

5 Choose File > Place. Select Show Import Options at the bottom of the Place dialog box.

6 Locate the 11_d.ai file in your Lesson_11 folder, and double-click to place it.

7 In the Place PDF dialog box, make sure that Bounding Box is selected in the Crop To menu.

8 Click OK. The dialog box closes and the pointer becomes a loaded graphics icon.

9 Position the loaded graphics icon (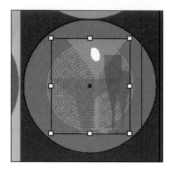) over the light purple circle on the right side of the page. Click to place the image. If necessary, drag the image to center it within the purple circle.

10 In the Layers panel, click to hide the Art2, Art1, and Background layers so that only the Art3 layer is visible, and you can view the placed image on its own and see the transparent color interactions within the image.

11 Then click to redisplay the Art2, Art1, and Background layers. Notice that the white "olive" shape is completely opaque while the other shapes of the drinking glasses are partly transparent.

12 With the glasses image still selected, change the Opacity setting in the Effects panel to 80%. Keep the image selected. You can now see the spiral behind the white olive and that the glasses are more subdued in color.

13 In the Effects panel, choose Color Burn from the Blending Mode menu. Now the colors and interactions of the image take on a completely different character.

14 Choose File > Save.

Applying transparency settings to text

Changing the opacity of text is as easy as applying transparency settings to graphic objects in your layout. You'll try out the technique now as you also change the color of the text.

1 In the Layers panel, click to lock the Art3 layer, and then click to unlock and make the Type layer visible.

2 In the Tools panel, select the Selection tool (▶), and then click the text frame "I THINK, THEREFORE I DINE." If necessary, zoom in so that you can read the text easily.

To apply transparency settings to text or to a text frame and its contents, you must select the frame with the Selection tool. You cannot specify transparency settings when the text is selected with the Type tool.

3 In the Effects panel, select the Text row so that any opacity or blending mode changes you make will apply to the text only.

4 Choose Overlay from the Blending Mode menu and change the Opacity to 70%.

5 Choose Edit > Deselect All.

Now you'll change the opacity of a text frame fill.

6 In the Tools panel, make sure the Selection tool (➤) is selected, and then click the text frame at the bottom of the page that contains, "Boston | Chicago | Denver | Houston | Minneapolis." If necessary, zoom in so that you can read the text easily.

7 Select the Fill row in the Effects panel and change the Opacity to 70%.

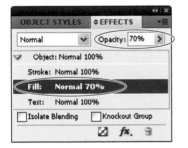

8 Choose Edit > Deselect All, and then choose File > Save.

Working with effects

So far in this lesson, you've learned how to apply transparency by changing blending modes and the opacity of objects drawn in InDesign, imported graphics, and text. Another way to apply transparency is by using the nine transparency effects in InDesign. Many of the settings and options for creating these effects are similar.

You'll try out some of these effects now, as you fine-tune the menu's artwork.

Transparency effects

Drop Shadow—Adds a shadow that falls behind the object, stroke, fill, or text.

Inner Shadow—Adds a shadow that falls just inside the edges of the object, stroke, fill, or text, giving it a recessed appearance.

Outer Glow and Inner Glow—Add glows that emanate from the outside or inside edges of the object, stroke, fill, or text.

Bevel and Emboss—Adds various combinations of highlights and shadows to give text and images a three-dimensional appearance.

Satin—Adds interior shading that makes a satiny finish.

Basic Feather, Directional Feather, and Gradient Feather—Soften the edges of an object by fading them to transparent.

—From InDesign Help

Applying basic feathering to the edges of an image

Feathering is another way to apply transparency to an object. Feathering creates a subtle transition between an object and any underlying images. InDesign CS4 features three types of feathering;

- Basic Feather softens or fades the edges of an object over a distance that you specify.

- Directional Feather softens the edges of an object by fading the edges to transparent from directions that you specify.

- Gradient Feather softens the areas of an object by fading them to transparent.

First, you'll apply a Basic Feather, and then move onto the Gradient Feather.

1 On the Layers panel unlock the Art 1 layer if it's locked.

2 Select the Selection tool (↖), and then select the Light Purple filled circle on the left side of the page.

3 Choose Object > Effects > Basic Feather. The Effects dialog box appears, displaying options for the various transparency effects.

4 In the Options section of the Effects dialog box, set these options:

- In the Feather Width box, type **0.375 in**.

- Change both the Choke value and Noise value to **10%**.

- Leave the Corners option set at Diffused.

5　Make sure that Preview is selected and, if necessary, move the dialog box to view the effects of your changes. Notice how the edges of the purple circle are now blurred.

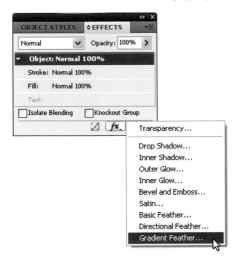

6　Click OK to apply the settings and close the Effects dialog box.

7　Choose File > Save.

Applying a gradient feather

You can use the Gradient Feather effect to soften the areas of an object by fading them to transparent.

1　On the right side of the page, use the Selection tool (➤) to click the Light Purple-filled vertical bar.

2　At the bottom of the Effects panel, click the FX button (*fx.*) and choose Gradient Feather from the pop-up menu.

● **Note:** When you export your InDesign document as an Adobe PDF file, transparency is preserved if you create the file using Adobe Acrobat 5.0 or later as the compatibility option.

The Effects dialog box appears, displaying Gradient Feather options.

● Note: The Effects dialog box shows you which effects are applied to a selected object (indicated by a check mark on the left side of the box), and allows you to apply multiple effects to a single object.

3 In the Gradient Stops section of the Effects dialog box, click the Reverse Gradient button (⬚) to reverse the solid and transparent colors.

Effects

Settings for: Object

Transparency
☐ Drop Shadow
☐ Inner Shadow
☐ Outer Glow
☐ Inner Glow
☐ Bevel and Emboss
☐ Satin
☐ Basic Feather
☐ Directional Feather
☑ Gradient Feather

Gradient Feather

Gradient Stops

Opacity: ⬚ › Location: ⬚ ›

Options

Type: Linear

Angle: ⟲ 0°

OBJECT: Normal 100%; Gradient Feather
STROKE: Normal 100%; (no effects)
FILL: Normal 100%; (no effects)

☑ Preview

OK   Cancel

4 Click OK. The purple rectangle should fade to transparent from right to left.

Now you will adjust the direction of the fade.

5 In the Tools panel, select the Gradient Feather tool (▦). Press the Shift key, and drag the pointer from the bottom to the top of the purple rectangle to change the gradient direction. You can edit the gradient as many times as you like.

6 Choose Edit > Deselect All, and then File > Save.

Next you will apply multiple effects to a single object and then edit them.

Adding a drop shadow to text

When you add a drop shadow to an object, the result is a 3D effect that makes the object appear to float above the page and cast a shadow on the page and objects below. You can add a drop shadow to any object, and you have the option to assign a shadow independently to an object's stroke or fill or to the text within a text frame.

Now you'll try this technique by adding a drop shadow to the "bistro" text.

1   Using the Selection tool (▶), select the text frame that contains the word "bistro." Use the Zoom tool (🔍) to magnify the frame so that you can see it clearly.

2   At the bottom of the Effects panel, click the FX button (*fx.*), and choose Drop Shadow from the menu.

3   In the Effects dialog box in the Options section, enter **0.125** in for Size and **20%** for Spread. Make sure that Preview is selected so that you can see the effects on your page.

4   Click OK to apply the drop shadow to the text.

5   Choose File > Save to save your work.

Applying multiple effects to an object

You can apply several different types of transparency effects to an object. For example, you can create the impression that an object is embossed and that it has a glow around it by applying two transparency effects.

In this exercise, you'll apply an embossed effect and an outer glow effect to the two semicircles on the page.

1   Choose View > Fit Page In Window.

2   Using the Selection tool (➤), select the Light Green-filled semicircle in the upper-left corner of the page.

3   At the bottom of the Effects panel, click the FX button (*fx.*), and choose Bevel And Emboss from the menu.

4   In the Effects dialog box, make sure that Preview is selected so that you can view the effects on the page. Then specify these settings in the Structure section:

- Size: **0.3125 in**

- Soften: **0.3125 in**

- Depth: **30%**

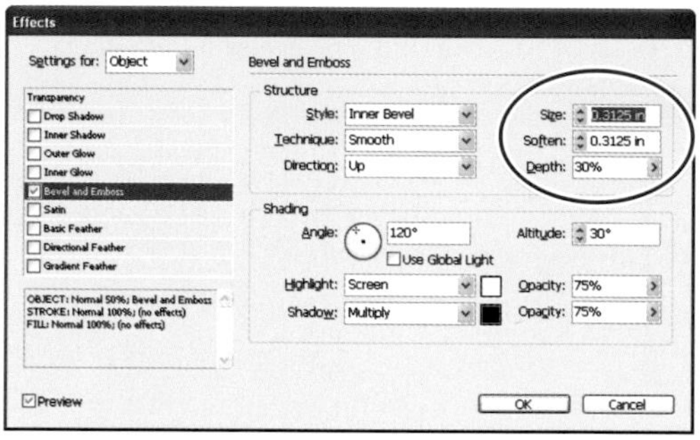

5   Leave the rest of the settings as is and keep the Effects dialog box open.

6   On the left side of the dialog box, click the check box to the left of Outer Glow to add an outer glow effect to the semicircle.

7   Click the words Outer Glow to edit the effect, and specify these settings:

- Mode: **Multiply**

- Opacity: **80%**

- Size: **0.25 in**

- Spread: **10%**

8 Click OK to apply the settings for the multiple effects.

Next you will apply the same effects to the other semicircle on the page, simply by dragging the FX icon from the Effects panel to the semicircle.

9 Double-click the Hand tool (✋) to fit the page in the window.

10 In the Tools panel, select the Selection tool (▶). If the green semicircle in the upper-left corner of the page is still not selected, select it now.

● **Note:** If you miss the semicircle, choose Edit > Undo Move Object Effects and try again.

11 With the Effects panel open, drag the FX icon on the right side of the Object level to the page and directly on top of the green semicircle in the lower-right corner.

Dragging the FX icon onto the semicircle (left and center); result (right).

Now you will apply the same effects to the small gray circle on the page.

12 In the Layers panel, click the eye icon (👁) to turn off the visibility for the Art3 layer and unlock the Art2 layer.

13 Make sure the green semicircle is still selected. In the Effects panel, click and drag the FX icon onto the gray circle above and to the right of the fish image.

14 Choose File > Save.

Editing and removing effects

Effects that are applied can easily be edited or removed. You can also quickly check whether any effects have been applied to an object.

First you'll edit the gradient fill behind the restaurant title, and then you'll remove the effects applied to one of the circles.

1 In the Layers panel, make sure that the Art1 layer is unlocked and that it is visible.

2 With the Selection tool (▶), click the frame with the gradient fill that's behind the text "bistro Nouveau."

3 With the Effects panel open, click the FX button (*fx.*) at the bottom of the panel. In the menu that appears, the Gradient Feather effect has a check mark next to it. Choose the Gradient Feather option from the menu.

4 In the Effects dialog box, under Gradient Stops, click the color stop at the right end of the gradient ramp. Change Opacity to 30%, and change Angle to 90°.

5 Click OK to update the gradient options.

Now you will remove all of the effects applied to an object.

6 With the Selection tool (▶), click the small gray circle to the right and above the fish image on the right side of the page.

7 At the bottom of the Effects panel, click the Clear Effects button (◨) to remove all of the effects applied to the circle.

● **Note:** The Clear Effects button also removes any transparency changes such as opacity from the object.

8 In the Layers panel, turn on the visibility for all the layers.

9 Choose File > Save.

Congratulations! You have completed the lesson.

Exploring on your own

Try some of the following ways of working with InDesign transparency options:

1 Scroll to a blank area of the pasteboard and create some shapes (using the drawing tools or by importing new copies of some of the image files used in this lesson) on a new layer. Position your shapes so that they overlap each other, at least partially. Then:

- Select the uppermost object in your arrangement of shapes. Using the controls in the Effects panel, experiment with other blending modes, such as Luminosity, Hard Light, and Difference. Then select a different object and choose the same blending modes in the Effects panel to compare the results. When you have a sense of what the various modes do, select all of your objects, and choose Normal as the blending mode.

- In the Effects panel, change the Opacity value of some of the objects but not others. Then select different objects in your arrangement and use the Object > Arrange > Send Backward and Object > Arrange > Bring Forward commands to observe different results.

- Experiment with combinations of different opacities and different blending modes applied to an object. Do the same with other objects that partially overlap the first object, to explore the variety of effects you can create.

2 In the Pages panel, double-click page 1 to center it in the document window. In the Layers panel, click the eye icons for the different Art layers one at a time to see the differences this creates in the overall effect of the layout.

3 In the Layers panel, make sure that all the layers are unlocked. In the layout, click the image of the glasses to select it. Use the Effects panel to apply a drop shadow.

Review questions

1 How do you change the color of the white areas of a grayscale image? How do you change the gray areas?

2 How can you change transparency effects without changing the Opacity value of an object?

3 What is the importance of the stacking order of layers and of objects within layers when you work with transparency?

4 If you've applied transparency effects to an object, what is the easiest way to apply the same effects to a different object?

Review answers

1 To change the white areas, select the object with the Selection tool and then select a color in the Swatches panel. To change the gray areas, select the object with the Direct Selection tool and then select the color you want to use in the Swatches panel.

2 Besides selecting the object and changing the Opacity value in the Effects panel, you can also create transparency effects by changing the blending mode; feathering an object several ways; adding drop shadows, bevel and emboss effects; and more. Blending modes determine how the base color and the blend color combine to produce a resulting color.

3 The transparency of an object affects the view of objects below (behind) it in the stacking order. For example, objects below a semitransparent object can be seen behind it—like objects behind a colored plastic film. An opaque object blocks the view of the area behind it in the stacking order, regardless of whether the objects behind it have reduced opacity values, feathering, blending modes, or other effects.

4 Select the object to which you've applied transparency effects and then drag the FX icon displayed on the right side of the Effects panel to another object.

12 WORKING WITH LONG DOCUMENTS

In this lesson, you'll learn how to do the following:

- Combine multiple InDesign documents into a book file.
- Control page numbering across documents in a book.
- Create text variables for running headers or footers.
- Add footnotes.
- Create cross-references.
- Specify a source document for defining a book's styles.
- Create a table of contents for a book.
- Create index references.
- Generate an index file and sort entries.
- Edit index references.

 This lesson will take approximately 45 minutes.

#3: Customizing Keyboard Shortcuts

InDesign provides hundreds of keyboard shortcuts to streamline your work. The shortcuts do you little good, however, if you can't remember them. Fortunately, you can change the keyboard shortcuts to better suit the type of work you do and your manual dexterity. For example, if you frequently use the Change Case commands or the Fill with Placeholder Text command in the Type menu, you can create keyboard shortcuts for those commands. Or, if a command you use frequently has a finger-contorting shortcut, you can replace it with an easier one.

InDesign stores keyboard shortcuts in sets. You can create your own sets of keyboard shortcuts and select a different set at any time while you're working.

Selecting a Shortcut Set

To specify a shortcut set for use with InDesign, choose Edit > Keyboard Shortcuts. Choose an option from the Set menu. If you're familiar with QuarkXPress 4 or PageMaker 7, you can use that program's keyboard shortcuts for similar features. The selected shortcut set is in use for your copy of InDesign—it is *not* saved with the active document.

Editing Shortcut Sets

You can edit the shortcuts for any command in any set—even the Default, QuarkXPress 4, and PageMaker 7 sets. However, it's a good idea to keep these default sets intact. Instead of editing them, create a new set based on one of them, and then edit it. To edit shortcut sets:

1. Choose Edit > Keyboard Shortcuts.

2. Click New Set. Enter a name for the set and choose an option from the Based on Set menu to specify a source for the initial list of keyboard shortcuts. You can also choose an existing set to edit from the Set menu.

3. To locate the command whose shortcut you want to edit, choose an option from the Product Area menu. For example, if the command is in the Type menu, choose Type Menu.

4. Scroll through the Commands list to locate the individual command and select it. For example, if you want to edit the Show Hidden Characters shortcut, select it (**Figure 3**).

Longer publications, such as books and magazines, generally consist of one document per chapter or article. InDesign's book features allow you to combine the documents so you can track page numbers across chapters; create tables of contents, indexes, cross-references, and footnotes; globally update styles; and output the book as one file.

Getting started

● **Note:** If you have not already copied the resource files for this lesson onto your hard disk from the Adobe InDesign CS4 Classroom in a Book CD, do so now. See "Copying the Classroom in a Book files" on page 2.

In this lesson, you'll combine several documents into an InDesign book file. A book file allows you to perform many functions across all the documents—such as creating a table of contents or updating styles—while retaining the ability to open and edit each document individually. The four sample documents you'll work with consist of the table of contents, first chapter, second chapter, and index from an 11-chapter book. The skills you learn in this lesson apply to book files consisting of any number of documents.

1   To ensure that the preferences and default settings of your Adobe InDesign CS4 program match those used in this lesson, move the InDesign Defaults file to a different folder following the procedure in "Saving and restoring the InDesign Defaults file" on page 2.

2   Start Adobe InDesign CS4. To ensure that the panels and menu commands match those used in this lesson, choose Window > Workspace > [Advanced], and then choose Window > Workspace > Reset Advanced.

Starting a book

In InDesign, a book is a special type of file that displays as a panel, much like a library. The Book panel displays the documents you add to the book and provides quick access to most book-related functions. In this section, you will create a book file, add documents (chapters), and specify the page numbering for the chapters.

Creating a book file

Before starting a book, it's a good idea to collect all of the InDesign documents for the book into a single folder for the project. This folder is also a good place to store all the fonts, graphic files, libraries, preflight profiles, color profiles, and other files required for completing the publication.

In this exercise, the InDesign documents are already stored in the lesson folder. You will create a new book file and store it in the lesson folder.

▶ **Tip:** You open and close book files the same way you open and close libraries. Use File > Open to open the book, and click the panel's close button to close a book.

1   Choose File > New > Book.

2   In the New Book dialog box, type **HowTos.indb** in the Save As box. Click Save to store the file in the Lesson_12 folder. The new Book panel appears.

3   Position the Book panel in the center of your screen.

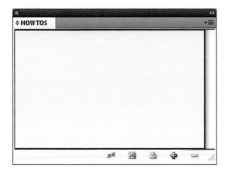

Adding documents to a book file

The Book panel displays a link to each document in the book—it does not literally contain the documents. You can add documents one at a time, as they become available, or all at once. If you start with a few documents and add more documents later, you can always change the order of the documents and update the page numbering, styles, table of contents, and more as necessary. In this exercise, you will add all four book chapters at once.

1 Choose Add Document from the Book panel menu.

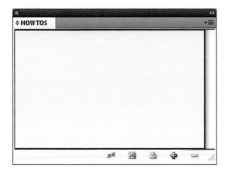

▶ **Tip:** You can also click the Add Documents button at the bottom of the Book panel to add documents to a book.

2 In the Add Documents dialog box, select all four InDesign files in the Lesson_12 folder. You can select a range of continuous files by Shift-clicking the first file and the last file.

3 Click Open to display the documents in the Book panel. If the Save As dialog box displays for each document, click Save.

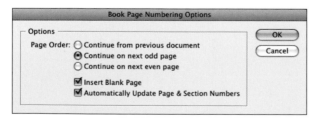

4 Choose Save Book from the Book panel menu.

Specifying page numbering across the book

A challenging aspect of working with multi-document publications is tracking page numbers across individual files. InDesign's book feature can automate this for you, numbering pages in a book from start to finish across multiple documents. You can override the page numbering as necessary by changing the numbering options for a document or creating a new section within a document.

In this part of the lesson, you will specify page numbering options to ensure continuous, up-to-date page numbers as chapters are added or rearranged.

1 Notice the page numbering shown next to each chapter in the Book panel.

2 Choose Book Page Numbering Options from the Book panel menu.

3 In the Book Page Numbering Options dialog box, select Continue On Next Odd Page in the Page Order section.

4 Select Insert Blank Page to ensure that each chapter ends on a left-facing page. If a chapter ends on a right-facing page, a blank page is automatically added.

5 If necessary, select Automatically Update Page & Section Numbers to keep page numbers updated across the book.

6 Click OK. Choose Save Book from the Book panel menu.

Customizing page numbering

At this point, page numbering is set from the first page in the first chapter of the book to the last chapter. The first chapter in the book, containing the table of contents, should use Roman numerals. The second chapter in the book, containing the Getting Started chapter, should start on page 1.

1 In the Book panel, click to select the first chapter: 12_00_ID_HowTos_TOC.

2 Choose Document Numbering Options from the Book panel menu.

This opens the chapter and displays the Document Numbering Options dialog box.

3 Under Page Numbering, choose the lowercase Roman numerals (i, ii, iii, iv) from the Style menu.

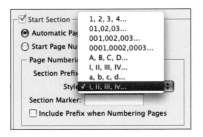

Typically, front-matter pages, such as the table of contents, are numbered with Roman numerals.

4 Click OK.

5 Choose File > Save and close the document.

6 In the Book panel, click to select the second chapter: 12_01_ID_HowTos_GettingStarted.

7 Choose Document Numbering Options from the Book panel menu.

8 In the Document Numbering Options dialog box, select Start Page Numbering At, and then type **1** in the text box.

9 Make sure that Arabic numerals (1, 2, 3, 4) are selected in the Style menu.

10 Click OK.

11 Choose File > Save and close the document.

Tip: As you add, edit, and rearrange chapters, you can also force page numbering to update by choosing one of the Update Numbering commands from the Book panel menu.

12 Review the book page numbering now. The first document, containing the table of contents, is now numbered i–iv with the remaining documents starting on page 1 and continuing to page 43. Try dragging the last two chapters up and down in the list to see how the page numbering changes when you rearrange documents in a book file. When you have finished, put the chapters back in the correct order.

◇ HOWTOS		
12_00_ID_HowTos_TOC	i–iv	
12_01_ID_HowTos_GettingStarted	1–17	
12_02_ID_HowTos_Documents	19–40	
12_03_ID_HowTos_Index	41–43	

Creating a running footer

Tip: Running headers and footers are just one use for the Text Variables feature. You might use a text variable to insert and update the date in a document, for example.

A running header or footer is text that repeats on chapter pages—such as the chapter number in the header and the chapter title in the footer. InDesign can automatically fill in the text for a running footer according to a chapter's title. To do this, you create a text variable for the source text, in this case the chapter title. You then place the text variable on the master page in the footer (or wherever you want it to appear in the document).

The advantage to using a text variable rather than simply typing the chapter title on the master page is that if the chapter title changes (or you're starting a new chapter from a template), the footer is automatically updated. Because you can place the text variables wherever you want, the steps for creating running headers and running footers are the same.

In this part of the lesson, you will create a text variable for the chapter title in the second chapter, place it on the master page, and see how it updates on all the pages of the chapter.

Defining a text variable

First, you'll create a text variable for the chapter title.

1 In the Book panel, double-click the second chapter: 12_01_ID_HowTos_ GettingStarted. If necessary, double-click the page 1 icon in the Pages panel to center it in the document window.

2 Choose Type > Paragraph Styles to open the Paragraph Styles panel.

3 Using the Type tool (T), click in the chapter title "Getting Started with InDesign" to see the paragraph style applied to it: Chapter Title.

You will use this information to create the text variable, which will specify that whatever text is using the Chapter Title paragraph style will be placed in the footer.

4 Close the Paragraph Styles panel.

5 Choose Type > Text Variables > Define.

6 In the Text Variables dialog box, click New.

7 Type **Chapter Title for Footer** in the Name box.

Now you will specify that you want text formatted with a specific paragraph style to be used for a running header (or in this case, a running footer).

8 Choose Running Header (Paragraph Style) from the Type menu. The Style menu lists all the paragraph styles in the document.

You will choose the paragraph style that is applied to the chapter title.

9 Choose Chapter Title from the Style menu.

10 Leave all the other settings at the defaults, and click OK. The new text variable appears in the list of variables. Click Done to close the Text Variables dialog box.

Inserting a text variable

Now that you've created the text variable, you can insert it on the master page (or anywhere in the document).

1 Click the page number menu in the lower-left of the document window. Scroll down to the master pages, and choose T-Text.

2 Choose Type > Show Hidden Characters, if necessary, so that you can see where to place the text variable.

3 Zoom in on the lower-left corner of the left-facing master page.

4 Using the Type tool, click to place the text insertion point after the tab character (>>). This is where you will place the variable.

5 Choose Type > Text Variables > Insert Variable > Chapter Title for Footer.

6 From the page number menu in the lower-left document window, choose 2.

On page 2, notice how the chapter title is now placed in the running footer.

7 Choose View > Fit Spread In Window and scroll through the pages to see how the running footer is updated everywhere.

8 Choose File > Save. Leave the document open for the next part of the lesson.

Each chapter in the book can use the same text variable but have a different running footer according to its chapter title.

> ▶ **Tip:** Changing the source text—in this case, the first instance of text formatted with the Chapter Title paragraph style—automatically changes the running footer on every page.

Adding a footnote

With InDesign, you can create footnotes or import them from text imported as a Microsoft Word document or as a rich-text format (RTF) file. In the latter case, InDesign automatically creates and places the footnotes, which you can then fine-tune in the Document Footnote Options dialog box. If you're working with a book file, you can specify whether footnote numbering restarts with each document or continues from document to document.

In this exercise, you will add a footnote and customize its formatting.

1 With the 12_01_ID_HowTos_GettingStarted chapter open, choose page 11 from the page menu in the lower left of the document window.

2 Zoom as necessary to see the main body paragraph, starting with "To reduce the size."

3 Using the Type tool (T), select the second to last sentence in the paragraph, starting with "For example."

4 Choose Edit > Cut. This text will be used in a footnote rather than in the body of the text.

> To·reduce·the·size·and·complexity·of·the·Control·panel,·you·can·cus⁼
> tomize·it·to·display·only·the·controls·you·need.·Choose·Customize·from
> the·Control·panel·menu·to·open·the·Customize·Control·Panel·dialog·box
> (**Figure·5d**).·Click·the·arrow·next·to·a·category·of·controls·(such·as·Charac⁼
> ter)·to·see·all·the·options·(such·as·Fonts,·Kerning,·Style,·etc.)·and·uncheck
> any·options·you·want·to·hide.·For example, if you're not using Adobe
> Bridge, you can uncheck it to remove that button from the Control panel.
> When·you're·finished,·click·OK.¶

5 Position the text insertion point just after "hide."

6 Choose Type > Insert Footnote.

A footnote reference number appears in the text. In addition, a footnote text frame and placeholder appear at the bottom of the page, along with the blinking text insertion point to the right of the footnote number.

7 Choose Edit > Paste.

> 1 » For·example,·if·you're·not·using·Adobe·Bridge,·you·can·uncheck
> it·to·remove·that·button·from·the·Control·panel.#
>
>   #5:⁻Using·the·Control·Panel

8 Choose Type > Document Footnote Options.

Notice all the options for customizing the footnote numbering and formatting. Here you can control the numbering style and appearance of the footnote reference numbers and footnote text throughout a document.

9 In the Footnote Options dialog box under Footnote Formatting, choose Tip/ Note Text from the Paragraph Style menu. Click Preview to see the change to the footnote text formatting.

10 Click the Layout tab to view all the options for customizing the placement and formatting of footnotes throughout a document. Leave all settings at the defaults.

11 Click OK to format the footnote.

12 Choose File > Save. Leave the chapter open for the next part of the lesson.

Adding a cross-reference

Cross-references, common in technical books, point you to another section of a book for more information. Keeping cross-references up-to-date as chapters in a book are edited and revised can be difficult and time-consuming. InDesign CS4 lets you insert automatic cross-references that update across the documents in a book file. You can control the text used in the cross-references as well as their appearance.

In this exercise, you will add a cross-reference that refers the reader to a section in another chapter of the book.

1   With 12_01_ID_HowTos_GettingStarted open, choose page 3 from the page menu in the lower left of the document window.

2   Zoom as necessary to see the text under "Creating new files."

3   Using the Type tool (T), select the "#9" text.

You will replace this manually created cross-reference with an automatic cross-reference that updates if the text in the chapter reflows.

> ● » **Document:** This lets you set up the page size and other details for a new document (see #9 for more information).¶
>
> ● » **Book:** This lets you create a book file for managing all the documents that make up a single publication (see #85 for more information).¶

4   Choose Type > Hyperlinks & Cross-References > Insert Cross-Reference.

5   In the New Cross-Reference dialog box, leave the Link To setting as Paragraph.

You will link the cross-reference to text that is formatted with a specific paragraph style.

6   Under Destination, choose Browse from the Document menu. Select 12_02_ID_HowTos_Documents.indd in the Lesson_12 folder and click Open.

7   In the scroll list at left, select Head 1 to specify the paragraph style of the referenced text. The cross-reference you're creating is to a section name in another document that is formatted with the Head 1 style.

All the text formatted with Head 1 appears in the scroll list at right. In this case, you know that section #9, to which you are cross-referencing, is titled "Creating New Documents." When creating cross-references across documents, you may need to look at the referenced document first to determine how the referenced text is formatted.

8 In the scroll list at right, select #9: Creating New Documents. Drag the New Cross-Reference dialog box out of the way so that you can see the text inserted in place of #9.

Now you'll format the text of the cross-reference.

9 Under Cross-Reference Format, choose Page Number from the Format menu.

10 Click the Create Or Edit Cross-Reference Formats button (✐) to the right of the Format menu.

11 In the Cross-Reference Formats dialog box, select Character Style for Cross-Reference. Choose Body Bold-P from the menu to specify the character formatting of the cross-reference text.

12 Click OK to apply the change and return to the New Cross-Reference dialog box.

13 Under Appearance, choose Invisible Rectangle from the Type menu to remove the box around the cross-reference text.

14 Click OK to create the cross-reference and close the dialog box.

15 Choose File > Save. Leave the document open for the next exercise.

> ● » **Document:** This lets you set up the page size and other details for a new document (see page 20 for more information).¶
>
> ● » **Book:** This lets you create a book file for managing all the documents that make up a single publication (see #85 for more information).¶

Synchronizing a book

● **Note:** Synchronizing documents compares all the styles in a document to the source document. The process adds any missing styles and updates any variations from the source chapter, but does not change any additional styles not included in the source document.

To maintain consistency across the documents in a book file, InDesign allows you to specify a source document for specifications such as paragraph styles, color swatches, object styles, text variables, and master pages. You can then synchronize selected documents with the source document.

In this exercise, you will add a color swatch to a chapter, use the new color in a paragraph style, and then synchronize the book so that the color is used consistently.

1 With 12_01_ID_HowTos_GettingStarted open, choose View > Fit Page in Window. It does not matter which page is displayed.

2 Choose Window > Swatches to open the Swatches panel.

3 Choose New Color Swatch from the Swatches panel menu.

4 From the Color Mode menu, choose Pantone Process Coated.

5 Type **73-1C** in the Pantone DS box (or scroll to locate and select the color).

6 Click OK to add the color and close the New Color Swatch dialog box.

7 Choose Type > Paragraph Styles to open the Paragraph Styles panel. Click the pasteboard to make sure nothing is selected.

8 Double-click Head 1 to edit the style. From the categories on the left side of the Paragraph Style Options dialog box, select Character Color.

9 To the right under Character Color, click the new PANTONE DS 73-1 C swatch. Leave the Tint set at 70%.

10 Click OK to update the paragraph style.

11 Choose File > Save to save the change with the document.

You now need to specify that the current chapter, Getting Started, is the source document in the book.

12 In the Book panel to the left of the 12_01_ID_HowTos_GettingStarted chapter name, click in the blank box.

Tip: InDesign allows you to synchronize master pages in a book. For example, if you add a block of color to a master page used for chapter openers, you can synchronize master pages to have the change affect all the chapters.

13 Choose Synchronize Options from the Book panel menu. Review the options available in the Synchronize Options dialog box; then click Cancel.

Now you will select the chapters you want to synchronize—in this case, all of them.

14 Shift-click the first chapter and last chapter in the Book panel to select all the chapters in the book.

You can choose to synchronize only selected chapters—for example, you can omit selecting the cover if the book has a cover that you don't want to change.

15 Choose Synchronize Book from the Book panel menu.

16 At the alert indicating the process has completed, click OK.

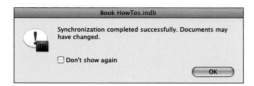

Synchronization completed successfully. Documents may have changed.

☐ Don't show again

OK

17 Choose Save Book from the Book panel menu. Double-click another chapter to open it. Notice the new swatches in the Swatches panel; this color is now applied to text that is formatted with the Head 1 style.

You will notice that the subheads changed color as well. That's because, in the template for this book, Head 2 is based on Head 1, so it adopts any changes made to the common formatting in Head 1.

Generating a table of contents

With InDesign, you can generate a fully formatted table of contents with accurate page numbers for a single document or all the documents in a book file. The table of contents consists of text that you can place anywhere—at the beginning of a document or in its own document within a book file. The feature works by copying text formatted with specific paragraph styles, compiling the text in order, and then reformatting the text with new paragraph styles. The veracity of the table of contents, therefore, depends on correctly applied paragraph styles.

In this exercise, you will generate a table of contents for the book.

Preparing to generate the table of contents

To generate a table of contents, you need to know what paragraph styles are applied to the text that will go in the table of contents. You also need to create paragraph styles to format the text in the table of contents. Now you will open a chapter to study its paragraph styles and open the table of contents chapter to see how it is formatted.

1 In the Book panel, double-click 12_01_ID_HowTos_GettingStarted to open the chapter.

2 Choose Type > Paragraph Styles to open the Paragraph Styles panel.

3 On page 1 of the Getting Started chapter, click in the chapter title. In the Paragraph Styles panel, notice the Chapter Title paragraph style is applied.

4 On page 2 of the chapter, click in the numbered section name. In the Paragraph Styles panel, notice the Head 1 paragraph style is applied.

> **Tip:** Although the feature is called Table of Contents, you can use it to create any type of list based on text that is formatted with specific paragraph styles. The list does not need to contain page numbers and can be alphabetical. If you were working on a cookbook, for example, you can use the Table of Contents feature to compile an alphabetical list of the recipe names in the book.

5 Close the Getting Started chapter; then double-click 12_00_ID_HowTos_TOC in the Book panel to open it.

▶ **Tip:** To see how the TOC Section Name style is created, double-click it in the Paragraph Styles panel. In the Paragraph Style Options dialog box, select Drop Caps And Nested Styles at left. You will see a character style applied until a colon is encountered in the text. Both paragraph styles for the table of contents also specify a Right-Justified tab with a dot leader for the page number.

6 With the Paragraph Styles panel open, use the Type tool (T) to click in the three different types of formatting you see on the page:

- TOC Chapter Title is applied to the first-level heads, the chapter names.

- TOC Section Name is applied to the second-level heads, the numbered section names.

7 Choose Edit > Select All. Then press Backspace or Delete to delete the table of contents.

You are going to generate your own table of contents in the next two exercises.

8 Choose File > Save.

Setting up the table of contents

Now that you are familiar with all the paragraph styles that will be used to generate the table of contents, you will "map" them in the Table of Contents dialog box. In this exercise, you will specify the title, what paragraph styles to include, and how to format the final table of contents.

1 Choose Layout > Table of Contents.

2 In the Table Of Contents dialog box, type **Contents** in the Title box. This is the title that will appear above the table of contents.

3 To specify how the title is formatted, choose Chapter Title from the Style menu.

4 Under Styles In Table Of Contents, scroll through the Other Styles list box to locate Chapter Title. Select it and click Add.

5 Repeat step 4 to locate and select Head 1. Click Add. Leave the dialog box open.

Now that you have specified what text needs to go in the table of contents—text formatted with Chapter Title followed by Head 1—you will specify how it should look in the table of contents.

6 On the left side of the Table of Contents dialog box in the Include Paragraph Styles list box, select Chapter Title. Under Style: Chapter Title, choose TOC Chapter Title from the Entry Style menu.

7 In the Include Paragraph Styles list box, select Head 1. Under Style: Head 1, select TOC Section Name from the Entry Style menu.

8 Select Include Book Documents to generate a table of contents for all the chapters in the book file.

▶ **Tip:** In the Table of Contents dialog box, click More Options to see controls for suppressing page numbers, alphabetizing the list, and applying more sophisticated formatting. If you have more than one list in a document—for example, a table of contents and a figures list—you can click Save Style to save the settings for each type.

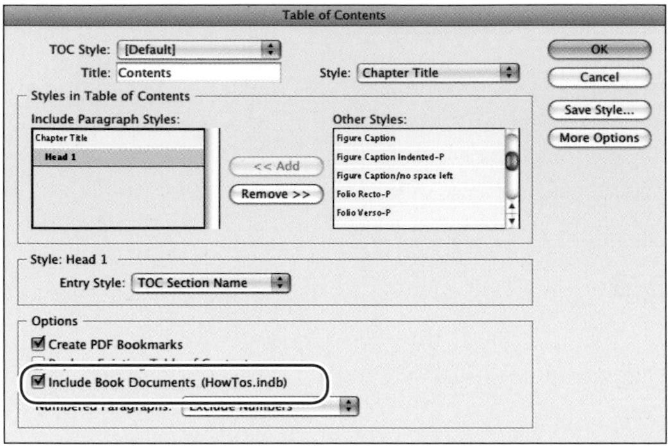

9 Click OK. This loads the pointer with the table of contents text.

Flowing the table of contents

▶ **Tip:** As chapters
are added to the book,
edited, and reflowed,
you can update the
table of contents by
choosing Layout >
Update Table Of
Contents.

You flow the table of contents text the same way you flow other imported text. You can either click in an existing text frame or drag to create a new text frame.

1 Click in the frame that held the sample table of contents. The table of contents flows into the text frame.

2 Choose File > Save and close the document.

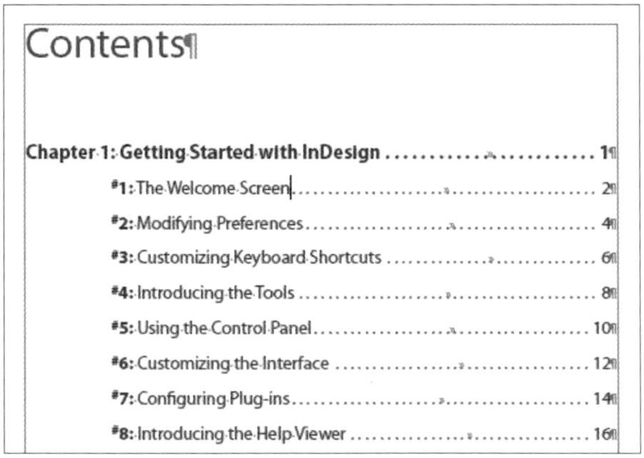

3 From the Book panel menu, choose Save Book. This saves all changes made to the book file.

Indexing a book

To create an index in InDesign, you apply nonprinting tags to text. The tags indicate the index topic—the text that shows up in the index. The tags also indicate the reference—the range of pages or cross-reference that shows up in the index. You can create up to a four-level index with cross-references for an individual document or for a book file. When you generate the index, InDesign applies paragraph and character styles, and inserts punctuation. While indexing is an editorial skill that requires special training, designers can create simple indexes and generate an index from tagged text.

In this exercise, you will add a few index topics and references, and then generate a partial index for the book.

Adding index topics and references

An index reference is what an index entry refers you to—a page-number reference or another entry, such as a "see also" reference. The first time you add an index reference, the index entry is added as well.

Now you will view existing index entries in a chapter and add two topics with references.

Tip: InDesign lets you import a list of index topics from another InDesign document. You can also create a list of topics independent of index references. Once you have the list of topics, you can start adding references.

1   In the Book panel, double-click 12_01_ID_HowTos_GettingStarted to open the chapter. Zoom in on the first paragraph of the first page.

2   Choose Window > Type & Tables > Index to open the Index panel.

3   Note the index markers ⌃ in the text, and the topics listed in the Index panel. Click the arrows in the Index panel to see the topics.

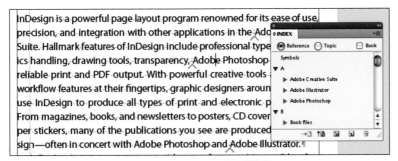

4   Navigate to page 5 of the document and zoom as necessary to see the bulleted list at the top of the page.

5   Using the Type tool (T), select the words "Type pane" in the first bullet.

6   Make sure Reference is selected in the Index panel, then choose New Page Reference from the Index panel menu.

through the panes in the Preferences dialog box to see if there's anything
you'd like to change. Prefe... change include:

- **Type pane:** If you're a... rather than character-... Paragraphs while adjus...

- **Units & Increments p...** default measurement s...

- **Spelling pane:** If InDesign is your primary word p... prefer to have possible misspellings flagged as yo... Enable Dynamic Spelling.

- **Display Performance pane:** By default, InDesign...

(Index panel and menu screenshot showing: INDEX, Reference, Topic, Book, Symbols, A, Adobe Creative Suite, Adobe Illustrator, Adobe Photoshop, B; menu items: New Page Reference... ⌘7, Duplicate..., Delete, Import Topics..., Remove Unused Topics, Go to Selected Marker, Options..., Capitalize..., Sort Options..., Update Preview, Generate Index..., Show Find Field, Show Unused Topics)

7   In the New Page Reference dialog box under Type, make sure that Current Page
is selected in the menu.

The options in the Type menu indicate what text this reference to the index topic
covers—and therefore, what page numbers to list. A common choice to indicate that
the topic changes with the next subhead is To Next Style Change.

(New Page Reference dialog box screenshot showing: Topic Levels: 1 Type pane, 2, 3, 4; Sort By; OK, Cancel, Add, Add All; Type menu: ✓ Current Page, To Next Style Change, To Next Use of Style, To End of Story, To End of Document, To End of Section, For Next # of Paragraphs, For Next # of Pages, Suppress Page Range, See [also], See, See also, See herein, See also herein, [Custom Cross-reference])

8   Click OK to add the index topic and a reference to the current page. In the Index
panel, scroll down to the T section. Click the arrow next to T to see the page
reference.

The second index topic you add will be a subtopic under the existing "Preferences"
topic.

9   Using the Type tool, select the words "Units & Increments pane" in the second
bullet.

10 Choose New Page Reference from the Index panel menu.

11 Click the down arrow next to "Units & Increments pane" in the 1 Topic Levels
box. This moves the index entry down to a second-level index topic.

12 In the list box at the bottom of the dialog box, locate the "P" heading and click the arrow next to it. Double-click Preferences to make it the first-level index topic.

13 Click OK to add the second-level topic and the reference.

14 Choose File > Save.

Creating an index cross-reference

In an index, a cross-reference such as "see" or "see also," is just another way of specifying an index topic's reference. Rather than listing page numbers, however, you are sending the reader to a different part of the index to find the page number.

In this exercise, you will add an index topic and a "see also" reference.

1 With the 12_01_ID_HowTos_GettingStarted chapter still open, navigate to page 9. Zoom as necessary to see the sidebar at right.

2 Using the Type tool (T), select the words "Tool Preferences" in the sidebar head.

3 Choose New Page Reference from the Index panel menu.

4 In the New Page Reference dialog box, choose See [Also] from the Type menu.

5   In the list box at the bottom of the dialog box, locate the "P" heading and click the arrow next to it. Drag the Preferences entry to place it in the Referenced box.

6   Click OK to add the cross-reference and close the dialog box.

7   In the Index panel, scroll to the "T" heading and click the arrow next to it to see the topics. Click the arrow next to "Tool Preferences" to view "See [also] Preferences."

8   Choose File > Save. Close the Getting Started chapter.

Generating an index

As with a table of contents, when you generate an index you need to specify paragraph styles. You can also fine-tune the index with character styles and custom punctuation. InDesign provides default styles for the index, but you will generally use styles set up for a book's template.

In this exercise, you will review the styles in a sample index, view the index for a book, and generate the formatted index.

1   In the Book panel, double-click 12_03_ID_HowTos_Index to open the index chapter.

2   In the Index panel, click Book in the upper-right corner to display the index for all chapters in the book.

3 Choose Type > Paragraph Styles. Using the Type tool (T), click in the four different types of formatting you see:

- Chapter Title is applied to the heading "Index" at the top of the page.

- Index Letter-P is applied to the letter headings: A, B, C, and so on.

- Index 1-P is applied to the first-level topics.

- Index 2-P is applied to the second-level topics.

4 Using the Type tool (T), click in the text frame containing the sample index.

You'll delete the sample index so that you can generate an updated one.

5 Choose Edit > Select All, and then press Backspace or Delete. Leave the text insertion point in the text frame.

6 In the Index panel, choose Generate Index from the panel menu.

7 In the Generate Index dialog box, delete the highlighted word "Index" in the Title box. The title is already placed on the page in a different text frame.

8 Click More Options to see all the index controls.

9 At the top of the dialog box, select Include Book Documents to compile the index from all the chapters.

10 Select Include Index Section Headings to add letter headings: A, B, C, and so on.

11 On the right side of the dialog box under Index Style, choose Index Letter-P from the Section Heading menu. This specifies the formatting of the letter headings.

12 Under Level Style, choose Index1-P for Level 1 and Index2-P for Level 2 to specify the paragraph styles applied to the various levels of entries in the index.

13 At the bottom of the dialog box under Entry Separators, type a comma and a space in the Following Topic box. This specifies the punctuation inserted after an index topic and the first reference.

Now you'll flow the index into the text frame.

14 Click OK to automatically flow the index into the selected text frame. If the text frame is not selected, click the loaded pointer in the main text frame to flow the index.

Index

A
Adobe Creative Suite, 5
Adobe Illustrator, 5
Adobe Photoshop, 5

B
Book files, 7

15 Choose File > Save and close the document.

Congratulations. You have completed the lesson.

Exploring on your own

To experiment more with long-document features, try the following:

• Add and delete pages from one of the documents in a book file to see how the page numbers in the Book panel automatically update.

• Change an object on a master page in the source document. Then choose Synchronize Options from the Book panel menu and check Master Pages in the Synchronize Options dialog box. Synchronize the book to see how all pages based on that master page update.

• Add a new footnote and experiment with the layout and formatting controls.

• Create different cross-references in the book to reference a chapter name or section name rather than page number.

• Generate a list other than a table of contents. For example, you can compile a list of tips in the book from the text formatted with the Sidebar Head paragraph style.

• Add more index topics and references at various levels.

Review questions

1   What are the advantages of using the book feature?

2   Describe the process and results of moving a chapter file in a book.

3   Why go to the trouble of creating an automatic table of contents or index?

4   How do you create running headers and footers?

Review answers

1   The book feature allows you to combine multiple documents into a single publication with the appropriate page numbering and a complete table of contents and index. You can also output multiple files in one step.

2   To move a file in a book, select it in the Book panel and drag it up or down. The book repaginates as necessary.

3   The automatic table of contents and index features require some thought and setup, but are automatically formatted, accurate, and easy to update.

4   Use the Running Header text variable on a master page to create a running header or footer. The text on each document page updates according to the text variable's definition.

13 OUTPUT AND EXPORTING

Lesson Overview

In this lesson, you'll learn how to do the following:

- Confirm that an InDesign file and all of its elements are ready for printing.

- Assemble all necessary files for printing or delivery to a service provider or printer.

- Generate an Adobe PDF file for proofing.

- Preview a document before printing.

- Print a document that contains process and spot colors.

- Select appropriate print settings for fonts and graphics.

- Create a Print preset to automate the printing process.

 This lesson will take approximately 45 minutes.

REFINE DESIGN '09
www.refinedesignconference.com

WHEN
June 19-20, 9:00am – 5:00pm
(registration begins at 8:30am)

WHERE
Seattle Central Library
(1000 Fourth Ave., 4th Floor)

Keynote Speaker:
Coming Soon!

Session Speakers:
Brian Wood,
VP/Director of Training, eVolve
evolveseattle.com
Gary Affonso, greywether.com
Liz Atteberry, Expedition Tea
and more to come...

Refine Design

Hone your skills and learn new time-saving tricks in Adobe's **Lightroom**, **Creative Suite 4**, and others. Whether you're looking to learn **CSS**, delve deeper into **Flash** or sharpen your **InDesign** and **Photoshop** skills, this is one event you won't want to miss!

Sessions include:

» **Dreamweaver**: Tables to XHTML + CSS

» **InDesign** High Voltage: Work smarter not harder

» **Photoshop** & **Flash** Integration: Optimizing Pixels and Workflow

» Interactive Portfolio: **PDF** like you've never seen

» A new era in Digital Asset Management: **Adobe Lightroom**

» Adobe **Illustrator** CS4: Taming complex illustrations

» Rescuing, Retouching and Restoring with **Photoshop**

» **Flash ActionScript** workshop **and much more...**

Sign up before May 15th for the early bird rate!

www.refinedesignconference.com/

Hosted by:

evolve
Computer Graphics Training Inc.

Adobe InDesign CS4 provides advanced printing and print preparation controls to manage your print settings, regardless of your output device. You can easily output your work to a laser or inkjet printer, high-resolution film, or a computer-to-plate imaging device.

Getting started

In this lesson, you'll work on a single-page product-marketing brochure that contains full-color images and also uses a spot color. The document will be printed on a color inkjet or laser printer for proofing and also on a high-resolution imaging device, such as a computer-to-plate or film imagesetter. Prior to printing, the document will be sent for review as a PDF file, which you will export from Adobe InDesign CS4.

● **Note:** If you have not already copied the resource files for this lesson onto your hard disk from the Adobe InDesign CS4 Classroom in a Book CD, do so now. See "Copying the Classroom in a Book files" on page 2.

● **Note:** If you don't have a printer or you only have access to a black-and-white printer, you can still follow the steps in this lesson. You will use some default print settings that help you better understand the controls and capabilities that InDesign CS4 offers for printing and imaging.

▶ **Tip:** A new preference option in InDesign CS4 lets you control whether an alert is displayed when you open a document with missing or modified links. To disable the alert, uncheck the Check Links Before Opening Document option in the File Handling pane of the Preferences dialog box.

1. To ensure that the preference and default settings of your Adobe InDesign CS4 program match those used in this lesson, move the InDesign Defaults file to a different folder following the procedure in "Saving and restoring the InDesign Defaults file" on page 2.

2. Start Adobe InDesign CS4. To ensure that the panels and menu commands match those used in this lesson, choose Window > Workspace > [Advanced], and then choose Window > Workspace > Reset Advanced.

3. Choose File > Open and open the 13_Start.indd file in the Lesson_13 folder, located inside the Lessons folder within the InDesignCIB folder on your hard disk.

4. An alert message informs you that the document contains missing or modified links. Click OK to close the alert window; you will correct this problem later in this lesson.

When you print or generate a PDF file, InDesign CS4 must access the original artwork that was placed in the layout. If the original artwork has been moved, its name changed, or the location where the files are stored is no longer available, InDesign CS4 alerts you that the original artwork cannot be located. This alert appears when a document is opened, printed, exported, or checked for printing using the Preflight command. InDesign CS4 shows the status of all files necessary for printing in the Links panel.

5. Choose File > Save As, rename the file **13_Brochure.indd**, and save it in the Lesson_13 folder.

Preflighting files

Adobe InDesign CS4 provides integrated controls for performing a quality check on a document prior to printing or handing off the document to a service provider. *Preflight* is the standard industry term for this process. In "Preflighting as you work" in Lesson 2 on page 19, you learned how you can take advantage of the live preflight capabilities that are new in InDesign CS4 and specify a preflight profile in the early stages of creating a document. This lets you monitor a document as you create it to prevent potential printing problems from occurring.

You can use the Preflight panel to confirm that all graphics and fonts used in the file are available for printing and that there are no instances of overset text. Here, you'll use the Preflight panel to identify a missing graphic in the sample layout.

1   Choose Window > Output > Preflight.

2   In the Preflight panel, make sure that On is checked and confirm that "[Basic] (Working)" is selected in the Profile menu. Notice that one Error is listed.

Notice that no TEXT errors appear in the Error section, which confirms that the document has no missing fonts and no overset text.

3   Click the triangle to the left of LINKS; then click the triangle to the left of Missing Link to display the name of the missing graphic file. Double-click the rdlogo_red.ai link name; this centers the graphic in the document window and selects the graphics frame.

4   At the bottom of the Preflight panel, click the triangle to the left of Info to display information about the missing file.

In this case, the problem is a missing graphic file and the fix is to use the Links panel to find the linked file. Now you'll replace the RDlogo_red.ai graphic with a revised version that includes a color change.

5   Choose Window > Links. Make sure that the RDlogo_red file is selected in the Links panel, and then choose Relink from the panel menu. Browse to the Links folder inside the Lesson_13 folder. Double-click the RDlogo_red_new.ai file. The new file is now linked, instead of the original file.

6   Choose File > Save to save the changes you've made to the document.

Creating a preflight profile

You can create your own preflight profiles or load them from your print output provider or other source. When you turn on the live preflight feature (check On in the Preflight panel), the default preflight profile is [Basic] (Working) preflight. This profile checks for three conditions: missing or modified graphics files, overset text, and missing fonts.

If you want to check for additional conditions, you can configure custom preflight profiles that define which conditions are detected. Here's how to create a profile that alerts you when non-CMYK colors are used in a layout:

1 Choose Window > Output > Preflight, and then choose Define Profiles from the Preflight panel menu.

2 Click the New Preflight Profile button (⊞) on the lower-left side of the Preflight Profiles dialog box to create a new preflight profile. In the Profile Name box, enter **CMYK Colors Only**.

3 Click the triangle to the left of Color to display color-related options, check to select Color Spaces And Modes Not Allowed, and then check to select all color modes except CMYK (RGB, Gray, Lab, and Spot Color).

4 Leave existing preflight criteria for Links, Images And Objects, Text, and Document as is. Click Save, and then click OK.

5 Choose CMYK Colors Only from the Profile menu. Notice the additional errors in the Preflight pane.

6 Click the arrow next to Color to expand the display, and then click the arrow next to Color Space Not Allowed to see a list of objects that do not use the CMYK color model. Click various objects to view information about the problem and how to fix it.

7 Choose [Basic] (Working) from the Profile menu to return to the default profile used for this lesson.

Packaging files

You can use the Package command to assemble a copy of your InDesign document and all linked items, including graphics, into a convenient folder. InDesign also copies the fonts needed for printing. Now you'll package the files for the marketing brochure in preparation for sending them to your print provider. This ensures that all project components required for output are provided.

1 Choose File > Package. The Summary pane notifies you of two more printing issues, in addition to the missing link that was listed in the Preflight panel:

- Because the document contains an RGB graphic, InDesign CS4 alerts you to its presence. You'll convert this image to CMYK later in this lesson.

- The document also contains two duplicate spot colors. You'll use the Ink Manager feature later in the lesson to manage this situation.

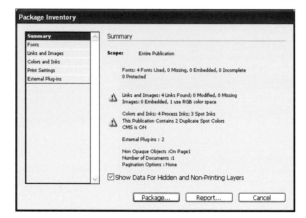

2 Click Package.

3 In the Printing Instructions dialog box, type a filename for the instructions file that accompanies the InDesign document (for example, "Info for Printer"), and also include your contact information. Click Continue.

Adobe InDesign CS4 uses this information to create an instructions text file that will accompany the InDesign file, links, and fonts in the package folder. The recipient of the package can use the instructions file to better understand what you want done and how to contact you if there are questions.

4 In the Package Publication dialog box, browse to locate the Lesson_13 folder. Notice that the folder created for the package is named 13_Brochure Folder. InDesign automatically names the folder based on the document name, which you assigned at the beginning of this lesson.

5   Confirm that the following options are selected:

- Copy Fonts (Except CJK)

- Copy Linked Graphics

- Update Graphic Links In Package

6   Click Package (Windows) or Save (Mac OS).

7   Read the warning message that informs you about the licensing restrictions that may affect your ability to copy fonts, and then click OK.

8   Switch to your operating system and navigate to the 13_Brochure Folder in the Lesson_13 folder (located inside the Lessons folder within the InDesignCIB folder on your hard disk). Open the folder.

Notice that Adobe InDesign CS4 created a duplicate version of your document and also copied all fonts, graphics, and other linked files necessary for high-resolution printing. Because you selected Update Graphics Links In Package, the duplicate InDesign file now links to the copied graphic files located in the package folder instead of the original linked files. This makes the document easier for a printer or service provider to manage, and also makes the package file ideal for archiving.

9   When you have finished viewing its contents, close the 13_Brochure Folder and return to InDesign CS4.

Creating an Adobe PDF proof

If your documents need to be reviewed by others, you can easily create Adobe PDF (Portable Document Format) files to transfer and share. There are several benefits to this convenient format: files are compressed to a smaller size, all fonts and links are self-contained in a single composite file, and cross-platform Mac/PC compatibility. Adobe InDesign CS4 exports directly to Adobe PDF.

Saving a composite of your artwork in Adobe PDF has many advantages: you create a compact, reliable file that you or your service provider can view, edit, organize, and proof. Then later, your service provider can either output the Adobe PDF file directly, or process it using tools from various sources for such post-processing tasks as preflight checks, trapping, imposition, and color separation.

1   Choose File > Export.

2   Choose Adobe PDF from the Save As Type (Windows) or Format (Mac OS) menu, and for the filename, type **Proof**. If necessary, navigate to the Lesson_13 folder, and then click Save. The Export Adobe PDF dialog box opens.

3   In the Adobe PDF Preset menu, choose [High Quality Print]. This setting creates PDF files suitable for output on an office laser printer.

4 In the Compatibility menu, choose Acrobat 6 (PDF 1.5). This is the earliest version that supports more advanced features in the PDF file, including layers.

5 In the Options section of the dialog box, select the following options:

- View PDF After Exporting
- Create Acrobat Layers

Automatically viewing the PDF file after exporting is an efficient way of checking the results of the file export process. The Create Acrobat Layers option converts the layers from the InDesign CS4 layout into layers that can be viewed in the resulting PDF file.

6 Choose Visible Layers from the Export Layers menu.

You have the option to choose the layers to be exported when creating the PDF. You can also choose All Layers or Visible & Printable Layers.

7 Click Export.

● **Note:** If you do not have Adobe Reader, you can download it for free from the Adobe Web site (www.adobe.com).

8 If a warning dialog box appears informing you that some of the objects in the layout are on hidden layers, click OK. An Adobe PDF file is generated and displays on your monitor in Adobe Acrobat or Adobe Reader.

9 Review the Adobe PDF in Adobe Acrobat or Adobe Reader, and then return to Adobe InDesign CS4.

Viewing a layered Adobe PDF file using Adobe Acrobat 9

Using layers in an InDesign document (Window > Layers) can help you organize the text and graphic elements in a publication. For example, you can place all text elements on one layer and all graphic elements on another. The ability to show/hide and lock/unlock layers gives you further control over the design elements. In addition to showing and hiding layers in Adobe InDesign CS4, you can also show and hide layers in InDesign documents that have been exported as Adobe PDF by opening the documents with Adobe Acrobat 9. Use the following steps to view a layered PDF file created with Adobe InDesign CS4.

1   Click the Layers icon along the left side of the document window, or choose View > Navigation Panels > Layers, to display the Layers panel.

2   Click the plus sign (+) located to the left of the document name in the Layers panel.

The layers in the document are displayed.

3   Click the eye icon (⊛) to the left of the Text layer. When the icon is hidden, so are all objects on this layer.

4   Click the empty box to the left of the Text layer to turn the visibility back on for the text.

5   Choose File > Close to close the document. Return to Adobe InDesign CS4.

Previewing separations

If your documents need to be color-separated for commercial printing, you can use the Separations Preview panel to gain a better understanding of how each portion of the document will print. You'll try out this feature now.

1   Choose Window > Output > Separations Preview.

2   Select Separations from the View menu in the Separations Preview panel. Move the panel so that you can see the page and adjust its height so that all of the listed colors are visible. If it's not already selected, choose View > Fit Page in Window.

● **Note:** The Pantone ink company uses the PMS (Pantone Matching System) to specify their inks. The number indicates the color hue, while the letter indicates the type of paper the ink is best suited for. The same PMS number with different letters means the inks are a similar color but intended to print on different paper stocks. U is for uncoated papers, C is for coated glossy papers, and M is for matte-finish papers.

3 Click the eye icon (👁) next to each of the three Pantone 1817 colors to disable the preview of these ink colors in the document.

Notice how certain objects, images, and text disappear each time you click to disable viewing of a Pantone color. This occurs because the Pantone colors have been applied to different objects. You may have noticed that the three Pantone colors share the same number. While these are similar colors, they represent three kinds of inks intended for different print uses. This may cause confusion at output, or incur the expense of unwanted printing plates. You will correct this later using the Ink Manager.

4 Choose Off from the View menu in the Separations Preview panel to enable viewing of all colors.

Previewing how transparency will be flattened

The images in this brochure have been adjusted using transparency features like opacity and blending modes. You use the transparency flattener to determine how the transparency impacts the final printed version.

1 Choose Window > Output > Flattener Preview.

2 Double-click the Hand tool (✋) to fit the document to the current window size, and position the Flattener Preview panel so that you can see the entire page.

3 In the Flattener Preview panel, choose Affected Graphics from the Highlight pop-up menu.

4 If it's not already selected, choose [High Resolution] from the Preset menu. You'll use this setting again later in this lesson when imaging this file.

Notice how a red highlight appears over some of the objects on the page. These objects are affected by the transparency that has been used in this document. You can use this highlight to help identify areas of your page that may be unintentionally affected by transparency, so that you can adjust your transparency settings accordingly.

Transparency can be applied in Photoshop CS4, Illustrator CS4, or directly in the InDesign CS4 layout. The Flattener Preview identifies transparent objects, regardless of whether the transparency was created using InDesign or imported from another application.

5 Choose None from the Highlight menu.

Previewing the page

Now that you've seen how the separations and transparency will look when printed, you'll preview the entire page.

1 If you need to change the display magnification to fit the page to the document window, double-click the Hand tool (✋).

2 Choose Edit > Deselect All.

3 At the bottom of the Tools panel, click the Preview Mode button (▣) and choose Preview from the displayed menu. All guides, frame edges, and other nonprinting items are hidden.

4 Click Preview Mode and choose Bleed Mode (▣). Additional space outside the perimeter of the final document size is displayed. This confirms that the color background extends beyond the edge of the document, ensuring complete coverage in the printed piece. After the job is printed, this excess area is trimmed to the final printed size.

5 Click the Bleed Mode button in the lower-right corner of the Tools panel, and choose Slug Mode (▣). The page now displays additional space beyond the edge of the bleed area. This additional area is often used to print production information about the job. You can see this slug area below the bottom of the document. If you want to set up the bleed or slug areas in an existing file, choose File > Document Setup and click More Options to reveal the bleed and slug setup options.

▶ **Tip:** It is common to set up bleed and slug areas when you create a new InDesign document. After you choose File > New, click More Options in the New Document dialog box to display bleed and slug controls.

After confirming that the file looks acceptable, you are ready to print it.

About flattening transparent artwork

If your document or artwork contains transparency, it usually needs to undergo a process called flattening to be output. Flattening divides transparent artwork into vector-based areas and rasterized areas. As artwork becomes more complex (mixing images, vectors, type, spot colors, overprinting, and so on), so does the flattening and its results.

Flattening may be necessary when you print or when you save or export to other formats that don't support transparency. To retain transparency without flattening when you create PDF files, save your file as Adobe PDF 1.4 (Acrobat 5.0) or later.

You can choose a flattener preset in the Advanced panel of the Print dialog box or of the format-specific dialog box that appears after the initial Export or Save As dialog box. You can create your own flattener presets or choose from the default options provided with the software. The settings of each of these defaults are designed to match the quality and speed of the flattening with an appropriate resolution for rasterized transparent areas, depending on the document's intended use:

[High Resolution] is for final press output and for high-quality proofs, such as separations-based color proofs.

[Medium Resolution] is for desktop proofs and print-on-demand documents that will be printed on PostScript color printers.

[Low Resolution] is for quick proofs that will be printed on black-and-white desktop printers and for documents that will be published on the web or exported to SVG.

—From InDesign Help

Printing a laser or inkjet proof

InDesign makes it easy to print documents to a variety of output devices. In this part of the lesson, you'll create a print preset to save settings—and save time in the future—without having to individually set each option for the same device.

1   Choose File > Print.

2   From the Printer pop-up menu, choose your inkjet or laser printer.

Notice how Adobe InDesign CS4 automatically selects the PPD (printer description) software that was associated with this device at the time you installed the equipment.

3   On the left side of the Print dialog box, click the General option, and then choose Print Layers: Visible Layers.

● **Note:** If you do not have a printer connected, choose PostScript File from the Printer list and choose Device Independent from the PPD list. This allows you to follow the steps in this lesson without being connected to a printer.

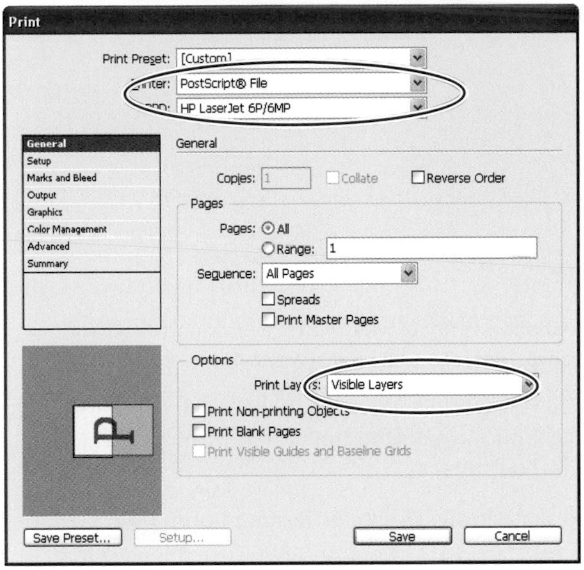

4   On the left side of the Print dialog box, click the Setup option, and then choose the following options:

- Paper Size: Letter
- Orientation: Portrait
- Scale to Fit

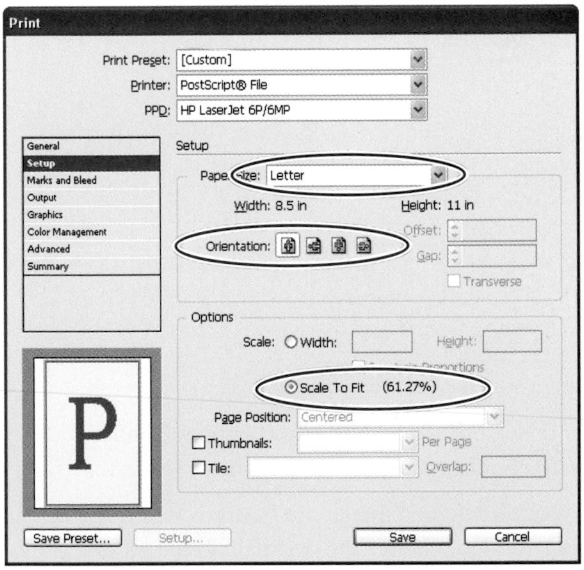

● Note: If you selected PostScript File along with the Device Independent PPD, as opposed to an actual printer, you cannot apply scaling or adjust the positioning of the file.

5 On the left side of the Print dialog box, click the Marks And Bleed option, and then choose these options:

- Crop Marks
- Page Information
- Use Document Bleed Settings
- Include Slug Area

6 Enter a Marks Offset value of .125 in. This value determines the distance beyond the page edges where the specified marks and page information appear.

The crop marks print outside of the page area and provide guides showing where the final document is trimmed after printing. The page information automatically adds the document name, along with the date and time it was printed, to the bottom of the printout.

Using the document bleed and slug settings causes InDesign to print objects that extend outside the edge of the page area. These options eliminate the need for entering the amount of extra area that should be imaged.

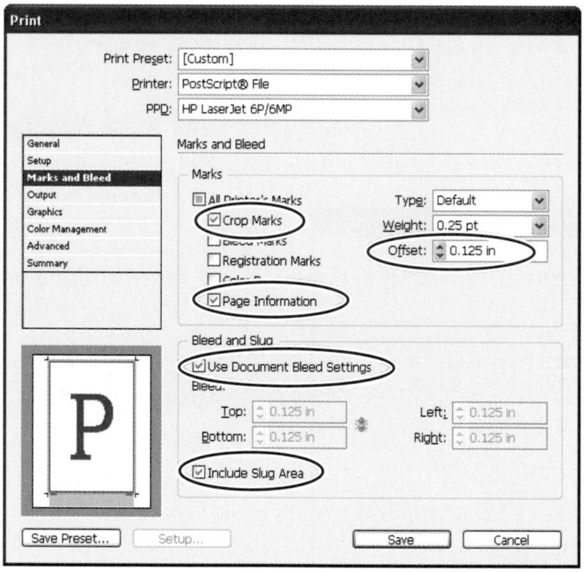

The blue-shaded box in the lower-left preview pane indicates the slug area.

Note: You can have InDesign maintain the existing colors used in a job by choosing Composite Leave Unchanged in the Color pop-up menu. Additionally, if you are a printer or service provider and need to print color separations from Adobe InDesign CS4, choose Separations or In-RIP-separations based upon the workflow that you use. Also, certain printers, such as an RGB proofer, may not let you choose Composite CMYK.

7 On the left side of the Print dialog box, click the Output option. Confirm that Color is set to Composite CMYK in the Color pop-up menu.

This setting causes any RGB objects, including images, to be converted to CMYK at the time of printing. This setting does not change the original, placed graphic. This option is not available if you are printing to a PostScript file.

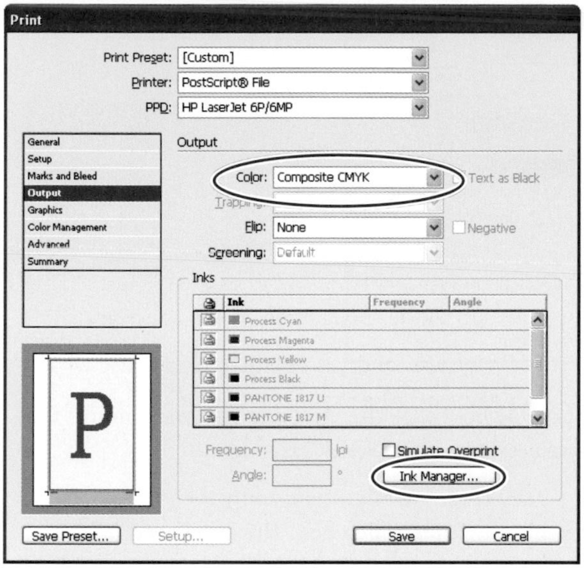

8 Click the Ink Manager button in the lower-right corner of the Print dialog box.

You can use the Ink Manager to convert spot colors, such as Pantone colors, to process (CMYK) colors, and to manage duplicate spot colors.

9 In the Ink Manager dialog box, click the spot icon (◉) to the left of the Pantone 1817 U color swatch. It changes to a CMYK icon (✖). The color now prints as a combination of CMYK colors instead of printing on its own, separate color plate.

This is a good solution to limit the printing to four-color process without having to change all spot colors in the source files.

10 Click the CMYK icon that now appears to the left of the Pantone 1817 U color swatch to convert it back to a spot color. Keep the Ink Manager dialog box open.

11 Again in the Ink Manager dialog box, click the Pantone 1817 M color swatch and then choose Pantone 1817 U from the Ink Alias pop-up menu. The Ink Alias tells Adobe InDesign CS4 to treat these two colors as if they were identical so that they will print as one color separation rather than as multiple separations.

Applying an Ink Alias means that all objects with this color now print on the same separation as its alias color. Rather than getting two separate color separations, you get one.

12 Repeat this process to select Pantone 1817 C and choose Pantone 1817 U from the Ink Alias menu. Now all three Pantone colors print on the same separation. Click OK.

Note: When printing to a PostScript file, the Send Data option is not available.

Note: The Optimized Subsampling option cannot be changed if you are using the Device Independent PPD, because this generic driver can't determine what information a specific printer chosen later may need.

13 On the left side of the Print dialog box, click the Graphics option. Confirm that Optimized Subsampling is selected from the Send Data menu.

When Optimized Subsampling is selected, InDesign sends only the image data necessary for the printer selected in the Print dialog box. This can speed up the time it takes to send the file to print. To have the complete high-resolution graphic information sent to the printer, which may take longer to image, select All from the Send Data pop-up menu.

14 If necessary, choose Subset from the Font Download menu. This causes only the fonts and characters that are actually used in the job to be sent to the output device.

15 Click the Advanced option and set the Transparency Flattener Preset to High Resolution from the Preset pop-up menu.

The flattener preset determines the print quality of placed artwork or images that include transparency. It also impacts the print quality of objects using transparency features and effects applied to them within InDesign, including objects with drop shadows or feathering. You can choose the appropriate transparency flattener preset for your output needs.

16 Click Save Preset, name the preset **Proof**, and click OK.

Creating a print preset saves these settings so you do not need to individually set every option each time you print to the same device. You can create multiple presets to meet various quality needs of individual printers you may use. When you want to use these settings in the future, you can choose them from the Print Preset pop-up menu at the top of the Print dialog box.

Options for printing graphics

When you are exporting or printing documents that contain complex graphics (for example, high-resolution images, EPS graphics, PDF pages, or transparent effects), it will often be necessary to change resolution and rasterization settings to obtain the best output results.

Send Data—Controls how much image data in placed bitmap images to send to the printer or file.

All—Sends full-resolution data, which is appropriate for any high-resolution printing, or for printing grayscale or color images with high contrast, as in black-and-white text with one spot color. This option requires the most disk space.

Optimized Subsampling—Sends just enough image data to print the graphic at the best possible resolution for the output device. (A high-resolution printer will use more data than a low-resolution desktop model.) Select this option when you're working with high-resolution images but printing proofs to a desktop printer.

Note: InDesign does not subsample EPS or PDF graphics, even when Optimized Subsampling is selected.

Proxy—Sends screen-resolution versions (72 dpi) of placed bitmap images, thereby reducing printing time.

None—Temporarily removes all graphics when you print and replaces them with graphics frames with crossbars, thereby reducing printing time. The graphics frames are the same dimensions as the imported graphics and clipping paths are maintained, so you can still check sizes and positioning. Suppressing the printing of imported graphics is useful when you want to distribute text proofs to editors or proofreaders. Printing without graphics is also helpful when you're trying to isolate the cause of a printing problem.

—From InDesign Help

Options for downloading fonts to a printer

Printer-resident fonts are stored in a printer's memory or on a hard drive connected to the printer. Type 1 and TrueType fonts can be stored either on the printer or on your computer; bitmap fonts are stored only on your computer. InDesign downloads fonts as needed, provided they are installed on your computer's hard disk.

Choose from the following options in the Graphics area of the Print dialog box to control how fonts are downloaded to the printer.

None—Includes a reference to the font in the PostScript file, which tells the RIP or a post-processor where the font should be included. This option is appropriate if the fonts reside in the printer. TrueType fonts are named according to the PostScript name in the font; however, not all applications can interpret these names. To ensure that TrueType fonts are interpreted correctly, use one of the other font downloading options.

Complete—Downloads all fonts required for the document at the beginning of the print job. All glyphs and characters in the font are included even if they're not used in the document. InDesign automatically subsets fonts that contain more than the maximum number of glyphs (characters) specified in the Preferences dialog box.

Subset—Downloads only the characters (glyphs) used in the document. Glyphs are downloaded once per page. This option typically results in faster and smaller PostScript files when used with single-page documents, or short documents without much text.

Download PPD Fonts—Downloads all fonts used in the document, even if those fonts reside in the printer. Use this option to ensure that InDesign uses the font outlines on your computer for printing common fonts, such as Helvetica and Times. Using this option can resolve problems with font versions, such as mismatched character sets between your computer and printer or outline variances in trapping. Unless you commonly use extended character sets, you don't need to use this option for desktop draft printing.

—From InDesign Help

► **Tip:** You can use absolute page numbering when working with multipage documents that are broken into sections. For example, to print the third page of a document, you can enter **+3** in the Page Range section of the Print dialog box. You can also use section names. For more information, see "Specifying pages to print" in InDesign Help.

17 Click Print. If you are creating a PostScript file, click Save and browse to the Lesson_13 folder. The PostScript file could be provided to your service provider or commercial printer, or converted to an Adobe PDF file using Adobe Acrobat Distiller.

18 Choose File > Save to save your work, and then close the file.

Congratulations! You've completed this lesson.

Exploring on your own

1   Create new print presets by choosing File > Print Presets > Define. Define presets to use for oversized formats, or for printing to various color or black-and-white output devices you may use.

2   Open the 13_Brochure.indd file and explore how each color separation can be enabled or disabled using the Separations Preview panel. Choose Ink Limit from the View menu in the same panel. See how the total ink settings used in creating CMYK colors affects how various images print.

3   With the 13_Brochure.indd file active, choose File > Print. Click Output on the left side of the Print dialog box, and examine the different options for printing color documents.

4   Choose Ink Manager from the Swatches panel menu and experiment with adding ink aliases for spot colors and converting spot colors to process.

Review questions

1 What problems does InDesign look for when using the Preflight command?

2 What elements does InDesign gather when it packages a file?

3 If you want to print the highest-quality version of a scanned image on a lower-resolution laser printer or proofer, what options can you select?

Review answers

1 You can confirm that all items necessary for high-resolution printing are available by choosing File > Preflight. By default, the Preflight panel confirms that all fonts used in the document or inside placed graphics are available. InDesign also looks for linked graphic files and linked text files to confirm that they have not been modified since they were initially imported and also warns you of overset text frames.

2 Adobe InDesign CS4 gathers a copy of the InDesign document along with copies of all the fonts and graphics used in the original document. The original items remain untouched.

3 InDesign sends only the image data necessary to an output device as its default setting. If you want to send the entire set of image data, even if it may take longer to print, in the Print dialog box under the Graphics options, you can choose All from the Send Data pop-up menu.

14 CREATING RICH INTERACTIVE DOCUMENTS

Lesson Overview

In this lesson, you'll learn how to do the following:

- Create a new document for online use.

- Switch to the RGB blend space.

- Switch to points (pixels) measurement system.

- Add buttons, page transitions, and a hyperlink.

- Export as Flash.

- Export as Adobe PDF.

- Convert a print document for online use.

 This lesson will take approximately 60 minutes.

The color palette includes a range of black, gray and muted hues, with a few bright colors for use as a contrast.

COLOR PALETTE

BLACK C	PMS 1788	PMS 504	PMS 429	PMS 450	PMS 576	PMS Process Cyan	PMS 2746	PMS 431	PMS 459
RGB	**RGB**	**RGB**	**RGB**	**RGB**	**RGB**	**RGB**	**RGB**	**RGB**	**RGB**
R: 0	R: 240	R: 90	R: 180	R: 105	R: 90	R: 0	R: 30	R: 105	R: 245
G: 0	G: 80	G: 30	G: 180	G: 105	G: 135	G: 175	G: 55	G: 115	G: 230
B: 0	B: 50	B: 30	B: 180	B: 50	B: 40	B: 240	B: 140	B: 120	B: 140
CMYK	**CMYK**	**CMYK**	**CMYK**	**CMYK**	**CMYK**	**CMYK**	**CMYK**	**CMYK**	**CMYK**
C: 40	C: 0	C: 65	C: 0	C: 60	C: 50	C: 100	C: 100	C: 10	C: 5
M: 30	M: 85	M: 100	M: 0	M: 50	M: 0	M: 0	M: 90	M: 0	M: 5
Y: 30	Y: 90	Y: 100	Y: 0	Y: 100	Y: 100	Y: 0	Y: 0	Y: 0	Y: 55
K: 100	K: 0	K: 35	K: 35	K: 20	K: 40	K: 10	K: 10	K: 65	K: 0

PMS 5415	PMS 1805	PMS 5463	PMS 7409	PMS 427	PMS 102	PMS Warm Red	PMS 549	PMS 4635	PMS 451
RGB	**RGB**	**RGB**	**RGB**	**RGB**	**RGB**	**RGB**	**RGB**	**RGB**	**RGB**
R: 100	R: 190	R: 0	R: 255	R: 230	R: 255	R: 240	R: 90	R: 155	R: 175
G: 135	G: 50	G: 50	G: 185	G: 230	G: 240	G: 100	G: 160	G: 90	G: 165
B: 160	B: 25	B: 65	B: 35	B: 230	B: 0	B: 50	B: 190	B: 15	B: 120
CMYK	**CMYK**	**CMYK**	**CMYK**	**CMYK**	**CMYK**	**CMYK**	**CMYK**	**CMYK**	**CMYK**
C: 40	C: 0	C: 100	C: 0	C: 0	C: 0	C: 0	C: 50	C: 0	C: 35
M: 10	M: 90	M: 0	M: 30	M: 0	M: 0	M: 75	M: 5	M: 50	M: 30
Y: 0	Y: 100	Y: 20	Y: 95	Y: 0	Y: 100	Y: 90	Y: 0	Y: 95	Y: 60
K: 40	K: 25	K: 85	K: 0	K: 10	K: 0	K: 0	K: 25	K: 45	K: 0

Color

◀ ▶

You can design Adobe InDesign CS4 documents that can be exported to Flash or Adobe PDF for online viewing. For Flash files, you can specify the page size according to monitor resolution, and then add buttons, page transitions, and hyperlinks before exporting in either SWF or XFL format. For Adobe PDF files, you can add bookmarks, hyperlinks, buttons, movies, and sound clips to create dynamic documents.

Getting started

● **Note:** If you have not already copied the resource files for this lesson onto your hard disk from the Adobe InDesign CS4 Classroom in a Book CD, do so now. See "Copying the Classroom in a Book files" on page 2.

In this lesson, you'll work on a layout that contains several design elements—logos, color palette, and fonts—for a fictional magazine. But instead of creating a layout that's intended for print output as you've done in other lessons, in this lesson you'll begin by creating a new layout from scratch that's intended for electronic distribution and online viewing. You'll then add the finishing touches—buttons, hyperlinks, and page transitions—to an almost-finished version of the layout and export it as a Flash (SWF) file.

You'll also export the layout—including the buttons, hyperlinks, and page transitions—as an Adobe PDF file that preserves all of the interactivity and provides another option for electronic distribution. Finally, you'll open a print version of the publication that's been converted for online use and export the layout as a SWF file that can be opened and viewed with Flash Reader or opened and edited with Adobe Flash.

1   To ensure that the preference and default settings of your Adobe InDesign CS4 program match those used in this lesson, move the InDesign Defaults file to a different folder following the procedure in "Saving and restoring the InDesign Defaults file" on page 2.

2   Start Adobe InDesign CS4. To ensure that the panels and menu commands match those used in this lesson, choose Window > Workspace > [Advanced], and then choose Window > Workspace > Reset Advanced.

3   To see what the finished document looks like, open the 14_End.indd file in the Lesson_14 folder, located inside the Lessons folder within the InDesignCIB folder on your hard disk.

Setting up an online document

Online publications differ in many ways from print publications. So the settings you select when you create online publications will also differ from traditional print settings. For example, the page size of online publications is related to the size of computer monitors, while many print publications use standard paper sizes. The color space also differs: where print documents typically use the CMYK color space, online documents use the RGB color space.

Creating a new document for online use

You'll begin by selecting a publication size suitable for online viewing, as you create a new document.

1 Choose File > New > Document.

2 In the New Document dialog box, set the following:

- In the Number of Pages box, type **5**.

- Uncheck Facing Pages.

- Choose 1024 x 768 from the Page Size menu. These are the dimensions of a standard 17-inch monitor.

- In the Columns section, type **3** in the Number box.

3 Click OK.

4 Choose File > Save As, name the file **14_DesignElements1.indd**, navigate to the Lesson_14 folder, and click Save.

Changing the transparency blend space and measurement system

Because you'll export the layout you'll create as a Flash (SWF) file for online viewing, you'll change the document to a compatible transparency blend space. To blend the colors of transparent objects on a page, InDesign converts the colors of all objects to a common color space using either the CMYK or RGB color profile for the document. Flash documents use the RGB color space, so you'll switch from the default CMYK blend space that's appropriate for print publications to RGB. And because you're working with a document whose dimensions are expressed in pixels, you'll switch to a different measurement system.

1 Choose Edit > Transparency Blend Space > Document RGB to switch to the RGB blend space.

2 Choose Edit > Preferences > Units & Increments (Windows) or InDesign > Preferences > Units & Increments (Mac OS) to open the Preferences dialog box.

3 In the Ruler Units section, choose Points from the Horizontal and Vertical menus. A point equals 1/72 inch.

4 Click OK to save the changes you made in the Preferences dialog box.

5 Choose File > Save to save the document, and then choose File > Close to close it. You'll continue this lesson by working on an almost-finished version of the document.

Adding buttons, page transitions, and hyperlinks

Once you begin designing an online publication, many of the tasks are identical to those you perform when working on print publications—formatting type; creating, modifying, and arranging text and graphic elements; adding and deleting pages; and so on. You learned how to perform all of these tasks in earlier lessons, so now you'll add some elements that aren't found in print publications—buttons, hyperlinks, and page transitions—to an otherwise-finished layout.

Adding navigation buttons

Navigation controls in an online document provide an easy way for viewers of the document to access the information. Next, you'll convert a pair of objects into Previous Page/Next Page buttons that will allow viewers of the exported SWF and Adobe PDF files to navigate from page to page.

1   Choose File > Open. Locate and open the 14_DesignElements2.indd file in the Lesson_14 folder, located inside the Lessons folder within the InDesignCIB folder on your hard disk.

2   Choose File > Save As, name the file **14_DesignElementsFinal.indd** in the Lesson_14 folder, and click Save. Saving the document using a different name preserves the original file for later use by other learners who use the sample files.

3   Choose Window > Pages to display the Pages panel, and then double-click the A-Master page icon to display the master page in the document window.

4   Use the Selection tool (▶) to select the left-pointing triangle at the bottom of the page. If you want, you can use the Zoom tool (🔍) to zoom in on the two arrows as you work on them. (The triangles were created with the Polygon tool.)

All pages of an online publication require navigation controls for displaying different pages. Placing these elements on a master page ensures that they'll appear and work the same on all pages.

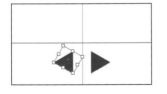

5   Choose Object > Interactive > Convert to Button to convert the object into a button and display the Buttons panel.

▶ **Tip:** You can also click Convert Object To A Button at the bottom of the Buttons panel to convert an object into a button.

6 In the Buttons panel, type **Previous Page** in the Name box to identify the button. In the Event menu, make sure that On Release is selected. This event triggers the Previous Page button when a viewer of the exported Flash and Adobe PDF files clicks it and releases the mouse button.

Now that you've named the button and set the trigger event, you need to select what action will occur.

7 Click Add New Action For Selected Event (⊞), and choose Go To Previous Page from the menu. You've configured the button so that when a viewer of the exported SWF file clicks it, the previous page will be displayed.

Now you'll repeat the procedure to create a button to move forward through the pages.

8 Use the Selection tool (▶) to select the right-pointing triangle, and then choose Object > Interactive > Convert To Button.

9 In the Buttons panel, type **Next Page** in the Name box. Click Add New Action For Selected Event (⊞), and choose Go To Next Page.

10 Close the Buttons panel, and then choose File > Save to save your changes.

You will be able to see the behavior of the buttons later in this lesson, after you export the file as Flash and Adobe PDF and then open the exported files.

Adding page transitions

New in InDesign CS4 is the ability to add animated page transitions that users will see as they change pages in the SWF and PDF files you export. You can preview page transitions in InDesign as Flash animations and experiment with different speeds and transition directions. Among the dozen page transition options are Curl, Wipe, Dissolve, and Split Window. When a viewer of the online file clicks the buttons you created earlier to navigate from page to page, the page transitions you specify in the following steps determine what happens visually when one page replaces another onscreen.

1 In the Pages panel, double-click Page 1 to display it in the document window. If necessary, choose View > Fit Page In Window to display the entire page.

2 Choose Window > Interactive > Page Transitions to display the Page Transitions panel.

3 In the Page Transitions panel, choose Dissolve from the Transition menu. Leave the Speed at Medium. If you move the pointer within the preview rectangle at the top of the Page Transitions panel, a preview of the selected transition is displayed.

4 Choose Apply To All Spreads from the Page Transitions panel menu to apply the Dissolve transition to all five pages in the document.

5 Close the Page Transitions panel, and then choose File > Save to save your changes.

Like the navigation buttons you added earlier, you can't see the page transitions you've applied until you view the exported Flash or Adobe PDF file.

Adding a hyperlink

You can add hyperlinks to a document so that after you export the document as Flash or Adobe PDF, a viewer of the file can click the link to jump to other locations in the same document, in another document, or on a Web site. Next, you'll add a hyperlink that lets viewers jump from the exported Flash and Adobe PDF files to a Web site.

To create a hyperlink, you will first create a hyperlink destination and then assign that destination to a hyperlinked text frame or a hyperlinked graphics frame. Here, you'll create a hyperlink destination and assign it to a hyperlinked text frame.

1 In the Pages panel, double-click the A-Master page icon to display the master page in the document window.

2 Choose Window > Interactive > Hyperlinks to display the Hyperlinks panel.

3 Choose New Hyperlink Destination from the Hyperlinks panel menu. In the New Hyperlink Destination dialog box, set the following options:

   • From the Type menu, choose URL.

   • In the Name box, type **checkmagazine online**.

   • In the URL box, type **http://www.checkmagazine.com**.

4 Click OK to close the dialog box. Then use the Type tool (**T**) to select the footer text "checkmagazine.com" in the lower-right corner of the page. You can triple-click the text to select all of it, or you can drag to select the text. If you want, use the Zoom tool (🔍) to zoom in on the text frame.

5 Choose New Hyperlink from the Hyperlinks panel menu.

6 In the New Hyperlink dialog box, make sure that the following settings are specified:

   • Link To menu: Shared Destination.

   • Document menu: DesignElements2.indd.

   • Name menu: checkmagazine online.

   • The URL is http://www.checkmagazine.com.

   • Appearance Type: Invisible Rectangle.

7 Click OK to save the new hyperlink and close the dialog box.

8 Close the Hyperlinks panel, and then choose File > Save to save your changes.

Like the navigation buttons and page transitions you added earlier, the hyperlink you just created won't work until you export the layout as a Flash or Adobe PDF file.

Exporting as Flash

Now that you've finished adding buttons, page transitions, and hyperlinks to your layout, you're ready to export it as a Flash file. After you export the layout, you'll open the file in your Web browser, use the navigation buttons and hyperlinked text you created earlier and view the page transitions. You would perform a similar check of the buttons and hyperlinks before you posted the layout for live viewing on a Web site.

1 Choose File > Export.

2 In the Export dialog box, choose SWF from the Save As Type menu (Windows) or the Format menu (Mac OS). Name the file **14_DesignElements.swf**, navigate to the Lesson_14 folder, and click Save.

3 Leave the settings in the Export SWF dialog box unchanged.

By default, Generate HTML File is selected under Pages in the Export SWF dialog box. This option creates an HTML version of the file automatically on exporting the SWF file, which allows you to view the file even if you don't have the free Adobe Flash Player application or Adobe Flash software. You'll open this HTML file after you export as SWF to view the SWF file.

Export SWF

Size (pixels): ⊙ Scale: `100%` ▾
  ○ Fit To: `1024 x 768 (Full Screen)` ▾
  ○ Width: `1024` ▾   🔗 Height: `768` ▾

Pages: ⊙ All
  ○ Range: `1-5`
  ☑ Spreads
  ☐ Rasterize Pages
  ☑ Generate HTML File
  ☑ View SWF after Exporting

Text: `InDesign Text To Flash Text` ▾

Interactivity: ☑ Include Buttons
  ☑ Include Hyperlinks
  ☑ Include Page Transitions
  ☑ Include Interactive Page Curl

Image Compression: `Auto` ▾
JPEG Quality: `Medium` ▾
Curve Quality: `Medium` ▾

[OK] [Cancel]

4 Click OK to close the Export SWF dialog box and generate an SWF file, as well as an HTML file.

The 14_DesignElements.html file opens automatically in your default Web browser. This file contains an embedded copy of the exported SWF file that was created when you clicked OK in the Export SWF dialog box.

● **Note:** If you have Adobe Flash, you can open SWF files exported from Adobe InDesign CS4 and edit them. You can also open SWF files with Adobe Flash Player, available for free from the Adobe Web site (www.adobe.com).

5 In your Web browser, click the navigation buttons you created earlier in this lesson to move from page to page. (If necessary, use your browser's scroll bars to display the navigation buttons.) The page transitions you specified earlier appear when you change pages.

When you export a SWF file, the Include Interactive Page Curl option in the Interactivity section is selected by default. This option provides another method for navigating within the exported file.

6 Move the pointer over the lower-right or lower-left corner of a page. Notice the animated page curl that's displayed. Clicking the animated curl at the lower-left corner of a page displays the previous page; clicking the curl at the bottom-right corner of a page displays the next page. (Note: An animated page curl is not displayed at the lower-left corner of the first page or the lower-right corner of the last page.)

7 Click the hyperlinked text in the lower-right corner of the page to go to the associated URL.

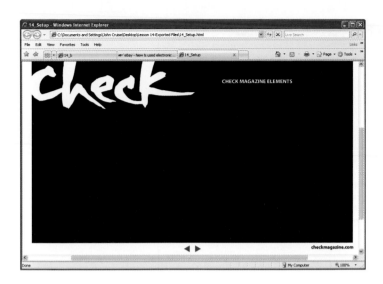

8 When you have finished exploring the online document, close your browser and return to Adobe InDesign CS4.

Exporting as Adobe PDF

Like exported Flash files, Adobe PDF files exported from Adobe InDesign CS4 can include buttons, page transitions, and hyperlinks. In addition, PDF files can contain SWF, QuickTime, and sound files to create an immersive reading experience.

Now you'll export the layout as an Adobe PDF file, open the file in Adobe Reader or Adobe Acrobat Professional and use the buttons and hyperlinked text you created earlier and view the page transitions.

1 Choose File > Export.

2 In the Export dialog box, choose Adobe PDF from the Save As Type menu (Windows) or the Format menu (Mac OS). Name the file **14_DesignElements.pdf**, navigate to the Lesson_14 folder, and click Save.

3 In the Export Adobe PDF dialog box, choose Smallest File Size from the Adobe PDF Preset menu. Choosing this option helps ensure the fastest possible display of the exported Adobe PDF file.

4 On the left side of the Export Adobe PDF dialog box, click General in the list. Then in the Options section to the right, make sure that View PDF After Exporting is selected. This option specifies that the Adobe PDF file opens automatically after it has been exported. In the Include section, select Hyperlinks and Interactive Elements; you're choosing which interactive elements will appear in the exported file.

5 Click Export to export the file and close the dialog box. An Adobe PDF file is generated and displayed on your monitor.

On Windows, Adobe PDF files are opened automatically in Adobe Reader if it's installed; on Mac OS, Adobe PDF files are automatically opened in Preview if Adobe Reader or Adobe Acrobat Professional aren't installed.

● **Note:** If you do not have Adobe Reader, you can download it for free from the Adobe Web site (www.adobe.com).

6 Try out the interactive elements in the exported Adobe PDF file:

- Click the navigation buttons you created earlier in the lesson to move from page to page.

- Click the hyperlinked text in the lower-right corner to open the associated URL in a browser.

- To see the page transitions, choose View > Full Screen Mode to switch to Full Screen mode in Adobe Acrobat Professional or Adobe Reader.

7 When you have finished exploring the interactive document, return to Adobe InDesign CS4 and choose File > Save to save your changes.

8 Choose File > Close to close the document.

Converting a print document for online use

In addition to creating online documents from scratch, it's easy to convert print publications for electronic distribution and online display. Next, you'll open a print version of the online layout you worked on earlier. Then you'll export a version of the print layout that has been converted for online use with the addition of buttons, page transitions, and hyperlinks.

1 Choose File > Open. Locate and open the sample document 14_DesignElementsPrint.indd in the Lesson_14 folder.

2 Use the Pages panel to view the document and master pages.

You'll find that the layout is very similar to the online layout you worked on earlier in the lesson. It's a print version (8.5 x 11 inches) that contains the same text and graphic elements as the online version. Because this layout was designed for print, it doesn't have any of the elements you added to the online version—buttons, page transitions, and hyperlinks. Rather than repeat the same steps you performed earlier to create these elements, you'll open an updated version of the document that includes them.

3 Choose File > Close to close the 14_DesignElementsPrint.indd document.

4 Choose File > Open. Locate and open the sample document 14_DesignElementsPrint2.indd in the Lesson_14 folder.

5 Use the Pages panel to view the document and master pages. It's the same as the print version you just viewed with the addition of the buttons, page transitions, and hyperlinks you added to the online layout.

6 Choose File > Export.

7 In the Export dialog box, choose SWF from the Save As Type menu (Windows) or the Format menu (Mac OS). Rename the file **14_DesignElementsPrint2.swf**, navigate to the Lesson_14 folder, and click Save.

8 Leave the settings in the Export SWF dialog box unchanged and click OK.

9 Choose File > Close to close the 14_DesignElementsPrint2.indd document.

The 14_DesignElementsPrint2.html file opens automatically in your default Web browser. This file contains an embedded copy of the exported SWF file that was created when you clicked OK in the Export SWF dialog box.

Congratulations. You have finished the lesson.

Exploring on your own

A good way to expand on the skills you've developed in this lesson is to revisit some of the key features and experiment with them by making different choices. Here are a couple of things to try:

1 For practice, open the 14_DesignElements2.indd file that you worked on earlier. Instead of using the Dissolve page transition, try some of the others—Fade, Wipe, Zoom In or Zoom Out, and so on. Instead of using one transition for all pages, try using different transitions for different pages. Each time you export a version with different transitions, open the exported file and see how it looks.

2 Create more buttons with different actions. Create another button at the bottom of the master page and assign a different action, such as Go To First Page (a handy navigation aid for any online layout).

Review Questions

1   What kinds of elements can you add to online publications that don't work with print publications?

2   How do you convert an object into a button?

3   How can you tell what a particular page transition looks like?

4   What must you do before you can create hyperlinked text?

5   When you export a layout that's been designed for electronic distribution and online display, what file formats preserve the functionality of the buttons, page transitions, and hyperlinks?

Review Answers

1   Online publications can include buttons, page transitions, and hyperlinks. PDF files can also include bookmarks, sounds, and movies.

2   Select an object with the Selection tool, and then choose Object > Interactive > Convert To Button. Use the controls in the Buttons panel to specify the behavior of the button.

3   In the Page Transitions panel, choose an option from the Transition menu, and then move the pointer within the preview rectangle at the top of the panel.

4   Before you can create hyperlinked text, you must create a hyperlink destination. Once you create a hyperlink destination, you can assign it to text or a graphic.

5   SWF, Adobe PDF, and Adobe Flash Pro CS4 Pro (XFL) files support buttons, page transitions, and hyperlinks.

INDEX

fills, 197
transparency and, 332–334
graphics, 48–52. *See also*
graphics frames; images
bitmap, 43, 263–264
centering, 110–111, 116,
118, 121
cropping, 52
importing. *See* importing
graphics/images
inline, 278–281
links to, 263, 377
moving, 52, 118–119
placeholder frames for,
71–72
placing in frames, 49–50,
107
placing on pages, 83–84
positioning in frames, 48,
49–50, 108–109
positioning on pages,
83–84
printing, 387
resizing, 43, 108–109
revised, 267–268
rotating, 119–120
scaling, 43
selection tools, 48
in table cells, 303–306
in tables, 302–306
text, 83–84
text wraps, 280–281
updating, 267–268
vector, 263–264
view quality, 269
working with, 48–52
wrapping text around, 73,
113–115
graphics frames, 105–115. *See
also* frames; graphics
changing shape of, 111–
113, 115–117
compound shapes,
115–116
creating, 105–106
image size, 108–109

placing/positioning images
in, 48, 49–50, 107–109
replacing contents of,
110–111
resizing, 107–109
graphics library, 284–286
grayscale images, 319–321
grids
adding, 62
baseline, 163–166, 171
hiding/showing, 34, 88
grouped items
applying effects to,
322–323
objects, 48, 122–124, 126
panels, 17
guides
adding text, 35–36
adding to master page, 62
bleed, 72
described, 62
dragging from rulers,
63–64, 71
fitting to margins, 62
hiding/showing, 34, 88
locking/unlocking, 74
pasteboard, 63
Smart Guides, 99, 113
snapping to, 71

H

Hand tool, 24, 32, 50,
108–109
hanging indents, 181–182
hanging punctuation, 172
header cells, 299–301
headers, running, 348–351
headlines, 35
Help feature, 3
HTML files, 401–403
hyperlinks, 400–401

I

ICC profiles, 208, 209, 274
Illustrator

color management, 221,
223–224
embedded profiles,
221–222
Illustrator files
adjusting transparency,
328–330
importing, 281–283,
328–330
placing into InDesign,
223–224
images. *See also* graphics
adjusting transparency,
327–328
cropping, 52
feathering, 332–334
grayscale, 319–321
importing. *See* importing
graphics/images
moving, 52
opening, 274
updating, 218–219
view quality, 269
importing graphics/images
with Adobe Bridge,
287–288
alpha channels and,
272–273
assigning profiles, 215–
216, 219–220
color management,
215–224
identified images already
imported, 264–265
importing/colorizing
grayscale images,
319–321
from other programs, 263
importing items
Illustrator files, 281–283,
328–330
managing links, 264–266
from other programs, 263
paragraph styles in tables,
306–308

Production Notes

The *Adobe InDesign CS4 Classroom in a Book* was created electronically using Adobe InDesign. Additional art was produced using Adobe Illustrator and Adobe Photoshop.

References to company names in the lessons are for demonstration purposes only and are not intended to refer to any actual organization or person.

Typefaces used

Set in Adobe Myriad Pro and Adobe Minion Pro OpenType families of typefaces. These along with European Pi, Lucida Sans Typewriter, and Warnock Pro Fonts are used throughout the lessons. For more information about OpenType and Adobe fonts, visit www.adobe.com/type/opentype/.

Team credits

The following individuals contributed to the development of new and updated lessons for this edition of the *Adobe InDesign CS4 Classroom in a Book*:

Writers: John Cruise and Kelly Kordes Anton
Project Editor: Susan Rimerman
Production Editor: Lisa Brazieal
Copy Editor: Judy Walthers von Alten
Technical Reviewers: Gabriel Powell and Cathy Palmer
Proofreader: Liz Welch
Compositor: Jan Martí
Indexer: Karin Arrigoni
Media Producer: Eric Geoffroy
Cover design: Eddie Yuen
Interior design: Mimi Heft